GRE
Power
Vocab

Anne Curtis and the Staff of The Princeton Review

PrincetonReview.com

The Princeton Review
24 Prime Parkway, Suite 201
Natick, MA 01760
E-mail: editorialsupport@review.com

Published in the United States by
Penguin Random House LLC, New York,
and in Canada by Random House of
Canada, a division of Penguin Random
House Ltd., Toronto.

ISBN: 978-1-101-88176-7
eBook ISBN: 978-1-101-88178-1
ISSN: 2376-7324

Some of the content in *GRE Power Vocab*
has previously appeared in *Word Smart
for the GRE*, published as a trade paper-
back by Random House in 2007.

Editor: Aaron Riccio
Production Editor: Emily Epstein White
Production Artist: Deborah A. Silvestrini

Printed in the United States of America
on partially recycled paper.

10 9 8 7 6 5 4 3 2 1

Editorial

Rob Franek, Senior VP, Publisher
Casey Cornelius, VP Content Development
Mary Beth Garrick, Director of Production
Selena Coppock, Managing Editor
Calvin Cato, Editor
Colleen Day, Editor
Aaron Riccio, Editor
Meave Shelton, Editor
Orion McBean, Editorial Assistant

Random House Publishing Team

Tom Russell, Publisher
Alison Stoltzfus, Publishing Manager
Melinda Ackell, Associate Managing Editor
Ellen Reed, Production Manager
Kristin Lindner, Production Supervisor
Andrea Lau, Designer

Acknowledgments

Thanks to Kyle Fox and Nicole Pirnie for their hard work and attention to detail on this project.

Special thanks to Adam Robinson, who conceived of and perfected the Joe Bloggs approach to standardized tests and many of the other successful techniques used by The Princeton Review.

Contents

Introduction

Welcome to GRE Power Vocab

This book is designed to help you learn commonly tested vocabulary words found on the GRE. The goal of Power Vocab is to familiarize you with some of the essential vocabulary on the GRE and teach you effective strategies to learn these, and other, words.

The GRE is full of interesting but tough vocabulary that some students may be unprepared for. To amend that, *GRE Power Vocab* contains terms and quizzes to help you learn and remember frequently tested words so you can optimize your score. You'll even get a chance to practice some of these words in the context of real GRE questions. Get ready to learn some vocabulary!

How This Book Is Organized

This book includes our GRE Hit Parade, comprised of the words most frequently tested on the exam, as well as other words that are likely to show up and that often give students problems. Some of these are words that seem familiar, but for which many people don't know the exact definition or proper usage. Others are words whose primary definitions are easy, but which have less common secondary definitions. Unsurprisingly, the folks who write the GRE like to try to trick you with those secondary definitions. (They wouldn't want to make it too easy, right?) For example, the word *pedestrian,* which most of us think of as the guy walking across the street, will mean "commonplace or trite" if it is used on the GRE. We've noted these secondary definitions in the master list in Chapter 4, so keep an eye out for them, paying particular attention to their parts of speech.

In Chapter 1, we'll talk about the role vocabulary plays on the Verbal Reasoning and Analytical Writing sections of the GRE, as well as how improving your vocabulary will help you more generally. Chapter 2 is devoted to successful strategies for learning new words. You'll find Warm-up Quizzes in Chapter 3 that will give you a sense of your starting point—how familiar you are with the level of vocabulary tested on the GRE.

The core of *GRE Power Vocab* is the list of words in Chapter 4. For each word you will find its part of speech, definition, common pronunciation, and a couple of sentences that illustrate the word's proper usage. Some of the entries also include important variations of a word. In addition, we'll point out any common misuses of words, or other words with which they are easily confused (e.g., foreword and forward). After every five to fifteen words, there is a Quick Quiz to help you test how well you've retained information from the preceding section. Some people like to start with the A's and work their way systematically through the book, using these quizzes to check their progress. Others like to browse, dipping into the book at random intervals to create flashcards, and then returning to catch any words missed along the way. Some prefer to start with the final exam in Chapter 6 and look up the words they missed. Pick the approach that works best for you.

Chapter 5 contains a list of roots, examples of words that contain each of them, and tips for incorporating roots into your vocabulary-learning regimen. Chapter 6, as we mentioned above, contains a comprehensive exam that tests all of the words in the main list. Both the Warm-Up Quizzes and the Final Exam contain question types that will help you build the skills you need to do well on the GRE. Answers for all of the quizzes in this book, as well as the Final Exam, can be found in Chapter 11.

Once you've got all of those GRE vocabulary words under your belt (or if you just want a break from studying them), check out Chapters 7 through 10. There, you'll find handy, subject-specific glossaries that will help you hold your own in conversation—no matter what the topic at hand might be!

GRE Power Vocab will help you build your vocabulary, which will in turn help you improve your performance on the GRE and amaze and impress your friends. That is, it will do all of these wonderful things if you use it. You shouldn't stop there, though. Once you've mastered the words in this book, keep going. Pay attention to the words you encounter around you. Get a good dictionary and use it. Read material that challenges your vocabulary. Language is an amazing tool. The more you learn about it, the better you'll be able to use it.

Our Pronunciation Key

Instead of using a pronunciation key like those found in most dictionaries, we've decided to use a simplified method. Our key is based on consistent phonetic sounds, so you don't have to memorize it. Still, it would be a good idea to take a few minutes now and familiarize yourself with the following table. (Pay close attention to how the *e* and the *i* are used.)

The letter(s)	is (are) pronunciated like the letter(s)	in the word(s)
a	a	bat, can
ah	o	con, on
aw	aw	paw, straw
ay	a	skate, rake
e	e	stem, hem, err
ee	ea	steam, clean
i	i	rim, chin, hint
ing	ing	sing, ring
oh	o	row, tow
oo	oo	room, boom
ow	ow	cow, brow
oy	oy	boy, toy
u, uh	u	run, bun

y (ye, eye)	i	climb, time
ch	ch	chair, chin
f	f, ph	film, phony
g	g	go, goon
j	j	join, jungle
k	c	cool, cat
s	s	solid, wisp
sh	sh	shoe, wish
z	z	zoo, razor
zh	s	measure
uh	a	abridge

All other consonants are pronounced as you would expect. Capitalized letters are accented.

The Princeton Review Approach

The philosophy behind The Princeton Review is simple: We teach exactly what students need to know, and we make our courses smart, efficient, and fun. We were founded in the early 1980s, and just a few years later, we grew to have the largest SAT course in the country. Our success is indisputable. We're proud to compare our results with those of any preparation course in the nation. In addition, our first book, *Cracking the SAT,* was the first of its kind to appear on the *New York Times* bestseller list.

Our innovative method of teaching vocabulary is responsible for much of our success. Some of the questions on standardized tests are really vocabulary questions, such as the Vocabulary in Context questions in Reading passages on the SAT or the ACT. To score high on these tests, students need to know the right words.

We've put a lot of thought into how people learn—and remember—new words. The methods we've developed are easy to use and, we believe, extremely effective. There's nothing particularly startling about them. But they do work. And they can be used advantageously by anyone who wants to build a stronger, smarter vocabulary.

Get More GRE Practice

If you want to practice your vocabulary on questions just like those found in the Verbal Reasoning section of the GRE, check out our book *Verbal Workout for the GRE.* To sharpen your skills and learn our techniques for mastering the entire test, try *Cracking the GRE* or *Crash Course for the GRE.*

Chapter 1

Vocabulary and the GRE

Using Language

Humans communicate through language, and although gestures and facial expressions are important means of communication, we most often rely on words to express ourselves. How many times have you been frustrated because you didn't have the right words to say what you meant? The broader your vocabulary, the more precisely you can communicate your ideas to others.

Think about playing Telephone, the game in which the first player whispers something to the second, and then the second player whispers what she heard to the third person, and so on. You find out how mangled the original sentence has become by the time it reaches the last person. The more carefully the first player articulates the sentence, the less extreme the alterations are along the way. Of course, playing Telephone is not much fun if the sentence doesn't change. The whole point of the game, after all, is to see how distorted the original sentence becomes. What is entertaining in Telephone, however, is frustrating when you are trying to make a point. When you use words that *sort of* mean what you want to say, the margin of error for your listener or reader is much greater than if you can choose the words that mean *exactly* what you intend them to. In effect, you have greater control over the message when you have a clear command of the words that convey it.

The way you express yourself may also have an impact on how people view you. How do you decide how "smart" you think someone is? These days it's probably not the fountain pen, or the monocle, or the stack of weighty tomes under someone's arm that gives you an impression of intelligence. For better or worse, people draw their sense of our abilities largely from the language we use. In the end, *how* you say something matters as much as *what* you are trying to say.

The same thing will be true in grad school: You will be evaluated not only by the ideas you have, but also by how well you convey those ideas. Words are the tools you will use to express yourself in your personal statement when you apply to grad school, and later in your coursework, seminar papers, and publications. The more precisely you can use language, the more seriously your ideas will be taken.

Before you can get to grad school, though, you've got to deal with the GRE.

Vocabulary and the GRE

For the most part, the GRE doesn't measure what you know. Instead, it tests how you work through certain kinds of problems. The most important exception to this is vocabulary. In this way, vocabulary is one of the few "content areas" tested on the exam. You'll be happy to know that the level of math tested on the GRE is not any higher than the level tested on the SAT. However, the trickiness of the vocabulary tested on the GRE can be harder than that on the SAT. The company that makes the test, the Educational Testing Service (ETS), figures that even if you haven't studied math since your first year in college, you should still have been building your vocabulary continuously since high school. Thus, the range of words ETS expects you to know on the GRE is that much wider.

There is some good news, though. Memorizing the dictionary is *not* the best way to improve your knowledge of the vocabulary that will be tested on the GRE. There is a particular range of words tested, and plenty of words in the dictionary will never show up on this test. The words that the GRE tests range from words you know well (*fruit, angry, write*), to words you recognize and may use on occasion (*cohesion, discrete, replicate*), to words you may never have encountered before (*taciturn, stentorian, palliate*). Because the GRE does not test your knowledge of specific subjects, you don't need to know the technical language, or jargon, particular to any discipline. Nor does the test include truly esoteric words that are very technical, or specific to a discipline, or just plain weird (words like *sesquipedalian*).

Not only does ETS stick to a range of vocabulary, but it also seems to go through phases in which certain words pass in and out of vogue. Some words show up frequently on the test, and then seem to fall out of favor, only to return to their former glory at some later point. The vocabulary in this book includes the GRE Hit Parade, the words most frequently tested on the GRE, along with a bunch of ETS's other perennial favorites. We keep the Hit Parade updated to reflect the words that currently appear with the greatest frequency. By memorizing these words, you are learning the words that tend to yield a higher score on the Verbal.

Of course, there's no guarantee that any individual word will show up on the test you take, but the ones in Chapter 4 of this book are the ones most likely to appear. As you learn these words, you will also get a sense of the vocabulary tested on the GRE. You will start to recognize words as "GRE words" and can augment your list accordingly. You will also be increasing your ability to communicate your ideas precisely in your daily life. Pretty cool, huh?

The Verbal Section of the GRE

Now that the kinds of words that are used on the GRE have been introduced, it's important to look at how they are used in the questions and how expanding your vocabulary can help you succeed. The Verbal portion of the GRE is comprised of 4 question types: Text Completions, Sentence Equivalence, Reading Comprehension, and Arguments. (ETS considers Argument questions to be a type of Reading Comprehension question.) These question types utilize vocabulary in different ways.

Text Completion questions provide a sentence or series of related sentences with one, two, or three blanks in place of words in the sentence. The answer choices will reflect these blanks and you will have to fill in the blank using the words in the answer choices. The words in the answer choices may be fairly familiar, but these can get tricky, as the second, less-common definition of the word is often the one being tested. The sentence itself tends to use vocabulary of a higher difficulty level, but tends to provide you with context clues that can be used to fill in the blanks. Use everything that you're given, as without understanding the context, it will be difficult to select the word that most accurately completes the sentence.

Much like Text Completions, Sentence Equivalence questions will present a sentence with a blank and ask you to fill in the blank with the answer choices. However, each Sentence Equivalence question presents you with six answer choice options and asks you to select the two words that best complete the sentence and create similar meanings. This question type typically tests the toughest vocabulary on the test and frequently features incorrect answer choice pairs that are related to each other, but do not complete the intended meaning of the sentence. A good grasp on GRE vocabulary helps to eliminate words that do not match the sentence's intended meaning, which aids in finding the correct answers.

Reading Comprehension questions test vocabulary in similar ways. They don't necessarily require you to know the definition of a tough word, but they may present an unfamiliar word in the context of the passage or argument that must be read or analyzed. Without knowledge of these pivotal words, you may not achieve a full under-standing of the passage.

This book contains many different kinds of methods for learning the words commonly tested on the GRE. Some of these tactics include analogies and antonyms, which are not included on the GRE. However, because this kind of word association work is very valuable in learning new vocabulary, we have decided to include these types of drills in this book. Note also that while the Complete the Sentence drills are very similar in structure to the One Blank Text Completions that you'll see on the GRE, their emphasis is on learning vocabulary. For more information and examples regarding the types of questions you'll see on the verbal sections of the GRE, check out our *Cracking the GRE* book.

Adaptive Tests and the Importance of Vocabulary

The GRE is adaptive by section, which means that your performance on the first scored verbal section will determine the difficulty level of the next scored verbal section. If you do well on the first section, you'll get vocabulary that the GRE considers to be tougher in the second section. While this increases the maximum score you can earn, an abysmal performance on these harder questions is actually less valuable than turning in solid work on the medium versions of both sections. To that end, it is useful to gain familiarity with as many vocabulary words as possible, as the greater the number of words that you know, the greater your chances are of fully under-standing passages, identifying common answer traps, and recog-nizing clues to questions. A good grasp of vocabulary will also help you to quickly identify words and eliminate incorrect answer choices, which will allow you to maximize time on the questions you may be more unsure of.

Analytical Writing

Although the Analytical Writing portion of the GRE does not directly test your vocabulary, the language you use will definitely play a role in the score you receive. As we discussed earlier, the more precisely you choose your words, the more certain you can be of accurately conveying your ideas. Also, using a variety of words properly will improve your score. Notice that we said properly! This is an impor-tant caveat for the GRE essays and the rest of your life. A big word improperly used can be more dangerous than a nice safe word used correctly.

Using a word properly doesn't just mean picking a word with a dictionary definition that matches your intended meaning. Context matters too. You have to know whether the word you want is only used in the plural, or if it always goes with a particular preposition. Is there a particular phrase it's usually seen in? Is it only used literally or can it be used metaphorically as well? Learning words in context will ensure that you can answer these questions. It will also allow you to use your new vocabulary on the two essays with confidence. That's why each of the definitions in this book is accompanied by one or more sentences illustrating how the word is used in context. We've also tried to point out the most common errors people make, along with any other useful clues to using these words in a truly erudite fashion.

Now that you know how these words will help you improve your score on the GRE and enable you to express yourself more effectively, we're ready to discuss strategies for learning them.

Chapter 2

Strategies for Learning New Words

Three Kinds of Words

Before we discuss specific strategies for learning vocabulary, we need to talk about how you know which words you already know. Sounds a little weird, doesn't it? You may think it's like a light switch with only two positions: You either know a word or you don't. However, your vocabulary is actually divided into three categories: words you know, words you sort of know, and words you've never heard of.

The best way to figure out which category a word belongs in is to imagine yourself walking down the street when a small spaceship lands in front of you. An alien emerges to greet you. Since we've already got you imagining a close encounter, it shouldn't be too much of a stretch to imagine that the alien starts asking you for help defining words. The first word it asks you to define is *apple*. You respond by saying, "An apple is a type of fruit that grows on a tree, has an edible skin and a core with seeds in it, and is usually green, red, or yellow." *Apple* is therefore a word you know, because it's one for which you can provide a dictionary definition. The next word the alien asks about is on the opposite end of the spectrum— *acarpous*, for instance. For all you know, this might be a word in Alienese; it falls into the "Huh?" category of words you don't know at all. Finally, the alien, whom you've grown somewhat fond of by now, asks you to define *integrity*. This is probably a word you've seen many times and used yourself, but how do you define it for your new friend? If you use examples or a story to explain integrity, it falls into the category of words you sort of know.

It is easy to see why you need to learn the words you don't know at all that are likely to appear on the GRE. It might be a little less obvious why the "sort of" words are important, but it is every bit as critical to recognize these and learn their dictionary definitions. Although it might seem fine to skip over these words since you already sort of know them, you must be able to define them clearly in order to deal with them effectively on the test. If you are ever unsure about whether a word is one that you "sort of" or "definitely" know, try defining it for your alien visitor. You can also use the warm-up tests in the next chapter to help you identify some of your "sort of" words and make sure they go onto flashcards. The good news is that those "sort of" words are typically easier to learn than the "Huh?" words, because you already have a head start!

There may also be words in this book you are sure you know, but that have secondary definitions ETS loves to try to trick you with. Always check your definition against the ones included here. Often these secondary definitions involve a change in a word's part of speech. For example, you probably know "color" as a noun, but do you know what it means as a verb? (It's in Chapter 4 if you don't.)

Techniques and Tools

There are many approaches to learning new vocabulary. The right way is the way that works for you. Generally, this is going to involve a combination of techniques and tools, a number of which we explain in this chapter. One of the advantages you have over that younger version of yourself that took the SAT or ACT is that now you know more about how you learn best. Are you a visual learner? Do you learn most effectively by doing? Do you have an easier time remembering things you hear or things you read? The key is to use the strategies that mesh best with your optimal learning style. When in doubt, try a variety of approaches to see what works.

Again, whichever tools you end up using, you will find they work best in combination. Our brains seem to develop different pathways for remembering things based on how we receive information. Writing a word and its definition is likely to reinforce the memory of reading it. Saying the definition out loud can augment the memorizing you did when you heard it said. The most effective program of study will be one that consistently uses reading, writing, listening, and speaking to memorize words.

One other key component to a successful program, which shouldn't come as much of a surprise, is being able to follow it. The best-laid plan that you promptly ignore won't do you any good at all. Make sure your program is realistic and then follow it.

Flashcards

They may not seem very "hi-tech" or glamorous, but using flash-cards is still one of your best techniques for learning vocabulary. Not all flashcards are equally effective, however. First, you want to ensure that your cards are portable. Did you notice the size of this book? We designed it to be compact so that you can slip it into your backpack or briefcase and carry it with you. Flashcards need to be even easier to carry around with you. Take 3×5 index cards and cut them in half. Write one vocab word on the front and its definition on the back. On the back of the card, you should include at least one of the mnemonic devices outlined in the next section. More than one device per card is even better.

You need to make your flashcards compact, because cramming doesn't work for studying vocabulary. Staring at a list of words for an hour at a time isn't at all efficient or effective, and it's certainly not much fun. Instead, the key is to work with a group of words for brief periods—ten minutes or so—several times a day. This does two things for you. First, it uses your brain's memorization processes most effectively. Second, it makes it possible to study vocabulary for a significant amount of time each day without requiring major schedule changes. Count up all the times in a day that you wait around for something for at least five minutes. Commit to reviewing your flashcards that many times per day. Here's a sample of what your flashcard review schedule might look like:

- On bus/train to work
- During morning coffee break
- At lunch

- On bus/train home

- Waiting for dinner to finish cooking

- Right before bed

If you muted the TV during commercials, you'd have at least 15 minutes to review your cards every hour, and all you'd be sacrificing is commercial watching. Doesn't sound too painful, does it? The trick with all this is to make sure you have your cards with you all the time. Unexpected wait at the doctor's office? Golden opportunity for learning some vocabulary, as long as you have your flashcards with you.

Make a specific plan for the number of new words you will learn each week and make new cards as you go. Be sure to periodically cycle earlier words back into the stack of cards you carry with you, so you don't forget the ones you've already learned.

Mnemonic Devices

Mnemonic devices are things that help you remember something. They work by creating a link in your memory between a word and its definition *through* another associated image, phrase, or sound (or smell for that matter, but we don't have any good examples for those). When you come up with a mnemonic tool, you are helping your brain by working with or creating associations that make it easier for you to remember a definition.

There are very few rules when it comes to good mnemonics. In fact, there's only one that really matters: If it works, it's good. Look at a word and its definition. Is there anything about either one that makes you think of something else? Reminds you of something or someone? If so, is there a way you can connect that association with the word and its definition? Let's take a simple example for the word *fallow*. If you looked at the definition for the word (*untilled, inactive, dormant*) and the first thing that popped into your head was a picture of your brother Fred, who's been out of work for the last six months and has spent that time lying on the couch, then you could use that image as a mnemonic device. The initial F in each word, Fred and *fallow*, links the two, and you associate Fred with inactivity, which reminds you that fallow means inactive and dormant. You do have to be careful here to distinguish between the association as a tool to remember the definition, and the definition itself, since idiomatic usage dictates that *fallow* is not usually used to describe people, though it can be used to describe parts of people (such as their minds).

While this example used an association from personal life, some mnemonics rely primarily on similar sounds and (often crazy) images to create associations. To come up with these, try to find a part or parts of the word that look or sound like other words that can lead you to the correct definition of the original. The connecting words should create specific, detailed images in your mind that have associations with the definition you are looking for. The sillier the images, the better they work! Here are some examples:

Vocabulary Word	**Mnemonic Tool**
Benevolent	Ben is never violent (picture Ben as a peace-loving hippy)
Conscientious	Conscience sent us (to do the right thing)
Repugnant	Repulsive pug
Solvent	Solves the rent problem
Prophetic	Prophet-like
Partisan	Party's man (as in political party)
Sonorous	A song for us

Mnemonics don't work unless you use them, so practice! Don't forget to write them down on your flashcards as well. It's not always easy to come up with good ones right away, but if you keep trying it gets easier. If nothing else, you will probably have memorized the word in the process of trying to come up with a mnemonic device for it. In the end, any association that gets you to the correct definition is good, so feel free to use anything that works: songs, your friends' less endearing qualities, characters in books, anything at all!

Use Them

All vocabulary stays abstract until you use it in real life. As we discussed with the writing sample portion of the GRE, context matters. It not only helps you remember words, but putting words in context also helps you become comfortable with their idiomatic usage. As you learn new words, try them out in conversation and writing. It is really no different from learning a foreign language; practice and immersion work best.

Test Yourself

Periodically testing how well you have learned new words will keep you on track and point out any gaps in what you know. Chapter 3 has a series of warm-up tests to use as a means of assessing your starting level. You can also use these warm-up tests, as well as the short quizzes that appear after every 10 or 15 words in Chapter 4, and the final exam at the end of the book to check your progress as you go. Get other people to quiz you as well. All you need to do is hand your flashcards over to friends and have them ask you a series of words as they flip through the stack. If at all possible, set up a regular schedule. Can you get your significant other to quiz you at dinner? What about your co-workers on your lunch break? If you treat it as fun, other people will want to join in. Remember how Tom Sawyer got everyone else to whitewash the fence for him by acting as if it were a treat instead of a chore? Use the same principle and make your flashcards the centerpiece while hanging out with your friends. Everyone will want to see how many words they know, and you get practice while dazzling everyone with how many *you* know.

Roots

Learning common word roots will help you remember the definitions of words that contain them, because they act like instant mnemonics. Some students find it very effective to simultaneously learn and memorize words that share common roots. In Chapter 5, we've included a list of the roots that most often show up in GRE words. This is a great place to start your detective work.

Games

We've saved the best for last. Playing vocab games combines many of the best techniques for learning words. Here are some examples of games, but you should also be creative and come up with some of your own. These games are designed so that you can play them by yourself, but getting others to play along will only increase the games' effectiveness.

Creative Writing

Choose ten words at random and write a brief story using all of them. Try to have the story make as much sense as possible, but silly is fine! Once you get the hang of it, give yourself a time limit (15 minutes or so).

The Name Game

Pick 40 or 50 adjectives at random from the list of words in Chapter 4. Now write down the names of 10 friends. Assign each adjective to one of your friends, based on their personalities. This is a great source of new mnemonics. Try the same thing with a list of 10 celebrities.

Concentration

Pick 20 words and write each one on a blank index card (one word per card). Take another set of cards and write the definitions for the same 20 words on the new cards (one definition per card). You should now have 40 cards: 20 with words and 20 with definitions. The other side of each card should be blank. Shuffle the cards and lay them down on a table, making a rectangle four cards wide and ten cards long. (Depending on space, you could also make one five cards wide and eight cards long.) Turn over two cards. If you get a word and a definition and they match, remove the two cards. If they don't match, or you get two words or two definitions, turn them both back over. Your goal is to remove all the cards in as few moves as possible by remembering where words and definitions are on the "board." Keep track of how many moves you make before clearing the board. Try to improve your record each time.

Simple Yet Effective

Pick one word each day. Use it at some point that same day, in conversation, in an e-mail, wherever. If you get ambitious, go for two or even three in the same day.

Chapter 3

Warm-Up Quizzes

Warm-up Quizzes

Use the following pre-tests to evaluate your starting point. Remember to pay particular attention to words you "sort of" know. Answers are in the back of the book.

Warm-Up Quiz #1

Definitions

Match each word on the left with its definition on the right. (Watch out for secondary definitions!)

1. austere h
2. plastic d
3. steep a
4. flag c
5. contentious g
6. rail i
7. beatify a
8. nice f
9. archaic b
10. brook e

a. completely soak
b. outdated
c. sag or droop
d. not rigid
e. tolerate
f. bless
g. argumentative
h. without adornment
i. complain bitterly
j. exacting

Warm-Up Quiz #2

Pair 'Em Up

In each of these lists, circle the two words that are most similar in meaning. The other word may be an opposite, or may not be related at all.

1. dogmatic · waver · intransigent
2. didactic · pedagogical · whimsical
3. synthesize · conjoin · analyze
4. canonical · iconoclastic · heretical
5. tenuous · inherent · inveterate
6. accolade · opprobrium · elegy
7. hackneyed · trite · piquant
8. emollient · sophomoric · puerile
9. inchoate · nascent · reticent
10. renege · regale · rescind

Warm-Up Quiz #3

Synonyms

Match the word in the first column with the word in the second column that is most nearly the SAME in meaning.

1.	auspice F	a.	loquacious
2.	inimical h	b.	exculpate
3.	neophyte i	c.	phlegmatic
4.	garrulous a	d.	inherent
5.	timorous g	e.	itinerant
6.	indolent c	f.	portent
7.	capricious j	g.	diffident
8.	exonerate b	h.	pernicious
9.	inveterate d	i.	tyro
10.	peripatetic e	j.	mercurial

Warm-Up Quiz #4

Complete the Sentence

Based on clues within each sentence, choose the answer choice that, when placed in the blank, best completes the meaning of the sentence.

1. The Masked Marauder's attempt to _____ with the money was foiled, since the police caught him before he left the building.

   a) laud

   b) censure

   c) abscond

   d) vacillate

   e) amalgamate

2. On Thanksgiving, _____ of turkey left us in desperate need of a nap.

   a) a surfeit

   b) an anomaly

   c) a torque

   d) an acumen

   e) a cacophony

3. The newspaper columnist strongly condemned the _____ used by the company to make a profit, pointing out that the only way it stayed in business was by cheating the public.

   a) bombast

   b) predilection

   c) shard

   d) plethora

   e) chicanery

4. We realized how _____ his plans were when he couldn't even tell us where he was going the next day.

   a) aberrant

   b) morose

   c) garrulous

   d) nebulous

   e) contiguous

5. The critic pointed out that the Model T the main character, Jones, drives around is _____, given that the novel is set in Victorian England.

   a) an anachronism

   b) a hyperbole

   c) a cynicism

   d) a neologism

   e) a diatribe

6. George was a frequent source of _____ for his colleagues, often frustrating them with his complete lack of tact.

   a) derision

   b) vexation

   c) quiescence

   d) convention

   e) hubris

7. Although Gretchen's delivery was _____, her words contained a wealth of meaning.

   a) prodigal

   b) martial

   c) profuse

   d) audacious

   e) terse

8. The town had to be evacuated when the _____ gas was accidentally released from the chemical plant.

   a) extemporaneous

   b) noxious

   c) heretical

   d) laconic

   e) urbane

9. His attempts to _____ the conflict were apparently successful, since now at least the two sides are talking.

   a) burgeon

   b) aver

   c) harangue

   d) ameliorate

   e) obfuscate

10. The _____ language Foucault uses can sometimes make it difficult to follow his ideas.

   a) glib

   b) convoluted

   c) solicitous

   d) voracious

   e) transient

Warm-Up Quiz #5

Definitions

Match each word on the left with its definition on the right. (Watch out for secondary definitions!)

1. fetid	a. entertain
2. denigrate	b. cautious
3. indolent	c. belittle
4. regale	d. stinking
5. adulterate	e. lazy
6. gossamer	f. punish
7. castigation	g. assistance
8. succor	h. reduce purity
9. pillory	i. delicate
10. chary	j. severe criticism

Warm-Up Quiz #6

Pair 'Em Up

In each of these lists, circle the two words that are most similar in meaning. The other word may be an opposite, or may not be related at all.

1. avaricious	penurious	garrulous
2. indolent	pious	phlegmatic
3. glib	pithy	fundamental
4. plaintive	melancholy	pristine
5. quaff	abstain	satiate
6. cacophony	din	mellifluous

GRE Power Vocab

7.	stymie	impute	filibuster
8.	laconic	loquacious	prolix
9.	inimical	malevolent	inimitable
10.	disabuse	beguile	dupe

Warm-Up Quiz #7

Antonyms

Match each word in the first column with the word in the second that is most nearly OPPOSITE in meaning.

1.	dearth	a.	rare
2.	assuage	b.	unhealthful
3.	volatile	c.	false
4.	torpid	d.	condemnation
5.	ubiquitous	e.	abundance
6.	adulation	f.	incite
7.	disinterested	g.	wither
8.	salubrious	h.	constant
9.	unfeigned	i.	energetic
10.	burgeon	j.	biased

Warm-Up Quiz #8

Complete the Sentence

Based on clues within each sentence, choose the answer choice that, when placed in the blank, best completes the meaning of the sentence.

1. Despite the loss to their crosstown rivals at the beginning of the season, the Garfield Geese were still highly _____ by their fans.

    a) dissembled

    b) relegated

    c) flouted

    d) touted

    e) disparaged

2. Cassandra's _____ about the upcoming battle were not quieted by the tendency of others to dismiss them.

    a) queries

    b) axioms

    c) hegemony

    d) parodies

    e) qualms

3. Everything was calm until the mysterious stranger came into town; he must have been the _____ for the gunfight.

    a) catalyst

    b) eulogy

    c) impunity

    d) connoisseur

    e) tirade

4. Bob's _____ observations revealed a number of flaws in the design plan that no one else had seen.

   a) discordant

   b) untenable

   c) capricious

   d) ephemeral

   e) trenchant

5. The _____ splendor of the Irish countryside was a source of constant amazement to Liza, who had lived in a city her whole life.

   a) eclectic

   b) irascible

   c) bucolic

   d) impetuous

   e) virulent

6. Although the _____ of Clyde's argument was sound, all his peripheral claims fell apart when he was questioned closely.

   a) effrontery

   b) approbation

   c) ennui

   d) pith

   e) iconoclast

7. The desert air will _____ anything that doesn't get regular access to water.

   a) desiccate

   b) refute

   c) bolster

   d) abate

   e) divulge

8. Sheila's attempt to _____ her previous controversial statement about the mayoral race didn't win her many supporters; voters seemed not to believe her apparent change of heart.

   a) exculpate

   b) inveigle

   c) recant

   d) vilify

   e) fulminate

9. Dennis's complete lack of _____ shocked his fellow diners, especially when he kicked off his shoes, stood on the table and danced a vigorous jig.

   a) fallacy

   b) alacrity

   c) grandiloquence

   d) decorum

   e) mendacity

10. The _____ family feud between the Capulets and the Montagues had begun long before Romeo and Juliet entered the picture.

   a) incipient
   b) facetious
   c) eloquent
   d) rancorous
   e) inert

Chapter 4
Word List

A

ABATE (a BAYT) *v* to lessen in intensity or degree

- We realized with great relief that the storm had *abated* before breaking through the sea well.

- Attempts by the administration to *abate* the intensity of the controversy were mostly unsuccessful; it continued to consume everyone's attention.

Abatement is a lessening in amount or degree.

- The city's new noise *abatement* plan targeted live music venues, but many people felt the focus should be on decreasing the number of low flying airplanes passing over the city.

ABERRANT (A bur unt) *adj* deviating from the norm

- Jim's *aberrant* behavior at the dance raised some eyebrows; he was certainly the only one who spent the night walking (and dancing) on his hands.

Someone or something *aberrant* is an *aberration*.

- The D Jenny received on the chemistry test was just an *aberration*, since she has received only A's the rest of the semester.

ABJURE (ab JUR) *v* to renounce or reject solemnly; to recant; to avoid

- The reformed socialite *abjured* her former lifestyle and all those with whom she had previously associated.

- Steve had to *abjure* all indulgence when he entered the training camp.

For a related word, see *recant*.

ABROGATE (AB roh gayt) *v* to abolish or annul by authority; put down

- The court ruling *abrogated* the defendant's rights to any profit from the sale of the house.
- Darren *abrogated* his responsibility to the paper when he went on vacation without submitting his article before the deadline.

ABSCISSION (ab SI zhun) *n* act of cutting off or removing

- Dr. Carter recommended an immediate *abscission* of the abscess in order to minimize any further infection.

Abscise means to cut off or remove.

- When she called for the resignation of key legislators, the congresswoman claimed that it was the only way to *abscise* the corruption before it spread.

Abscission can also mean the actual cut itself.

ABSCOND (ab SKAHND) *v* to depart clandestinely; to steal off and hide

- Doug was left penniless when the two con men *absconded* with his life savings.
- Raccoons are notorious for *absconding* and hiding shiny objects; no one knows why they need all those spoons and watches, though.

ABSTAIN (ab STAYN) *v* to refrain from an activity

- Sheryl chose to *abstain* from eating chocolate, her favorite treat, for the season of Lent.

The act of abstaining is called *abstinence.*

- The old health textbook recommended *abstinence* from sexual activity as the primary means of birth control.

Abstemious is a related word meaning *marked by moderation,* particularly where food and drink are concerned.

- Though some regard the diet as a fad, in fact it recommends some very traditional habits, such as consuming sugar and alcohol *abstemiously.*

ABSTRUSE (ab STROOS) *adj* hard to understand

- While the book received great praise in academic circles, it was too *abstruse* for the average person to comprehend.

- Her research paper contained a number of *abstruse* arguments that only those well-versed in her field would understand.

ACCOLADE (AK o layd) *n* an expression of praise; an award

- The diva received her *accolades* graciously, blowing kisses to her adoring fans.

- Doris so craved her coach's *accolades* that she showed up an hour early to every practice.

The word *accolade* comes from a French word meaning to embrace, which, logically enough, comes from the same root as *collar.* You can also associate *lade* with *laud* (meaning praise), though they probably don't have the same etymological backgrounds.

ACCRETION (uh KREE shun) *n* growth, increase by successive addition, build up

- Limestone is formed by the *accretion* of tiny particles from objects such as shells and coral over a very, very long time.

- The *accretion* of dirt has changed the color of the kitchen floor from white to brown, which is pretty disgusting.

ACERBIC (uh SUHR bik) *adj* having a sour or bitter taste or character

- Dorothy Parker was famous for her wit, which could be quite *acerbic*; Parker could be devastating when she wanted to be.

- I like my lemonade with very little sugar in it; the *acerbic* tang is refreshing when the weather's warm.

ACUMEN (AK u men) *n* quick, keen, or accurate knowledge or insight

- The media often comments on the CEO's business *acumen*, remarking on his company's financial successes, but I think his fashion sense is much more interesting.

- Her *acumen* in anticipating her opponent's strategy is legendary; it's what makes her so hard to beat.

If you think about it, you probably know several words with *acu* in them that mean "sharp." *Acute* is frequently used to describe sharp pain and sharp angles (less than 90 degrees). People with good *acumen* are often described as being sharp, too! That's because these words come from the Latin root *acus*, which means needle.

Quick Quiz #1

Match each word in the first column with its definition in the second column. Check your answers in the back of the book.

1.	abstain	a.	deviating
2.	accolade	b.	keen insight
3.	aberrant	c.	abolish
4.	abate	d.	lessen in intensity
5.	abscond	e.	sour or bitter
6.	acumen	f.	depart secretly
7.	acerbic	g.	building up
8.	abscission	h.	renounce
9.	accretion	i.	removal
10.	abjure	j.	praise
11.	abrogate	k.	refrain
12.	abstruse	l.	hard to understand

ADMONISH (ad MAH nish) *v* to reprove; to express warning or disapproval

- How many times has your roommate *admonished* you to put the toilet seat down?

An *admonition* is a warning or a scolding and *admonitory* means expressing warning or disapproval.

- He tried to *admonish* us not to open the secret passageway, but his *admonition* fell on deaf ears. Man, were we sorry we hadn't listened to him when all the monsters came rushing out!

- Dad's *admonitory* tone made us feel guilty about ruining our appetites with pre-dinner cookies.

ADROIT (uh DROYT) *adj* adept, dexterous

- Karl had always been an *adroit* manipulator; even when he was a kid he could get people to do what he wanted.

- Although her *adroit* handling of the situation minimized the damage, nothing could really save the conference after the room flooded.

- Since he is ambidextrous, he is equally *adroit* at shooting marbles with either hand.

Maladroit means clumsy or bungling.

- Adam Sandler was able to make a career out of playing *maladroit* characters.

ADULATION (a ju LAY shun) *n* excessive praise; intense adoration

- Taylor Swift is the object of much adolescent *adulation*.

- Samuel had taken his little brother's *adulation* for granted until his brother grew four inches taller and was no longer as easily impressed.

An *adulator* is someone who shows excessive admiration or devotion.

ADULTERATE (uh DUL tur ayt) *v* to reduce purity by combining with inferior ingredients

- There was a huge scandal when customers discovered that the health food store had been *adulterating* the wheat grass juice with clippings from the front lawn.

- In an effort to determine why the house's foundation was crumbling, the inspectors tested the concrete to see if it had been improperly *adulterated* when it was mixed.

Adulteration is the process or effect of adulterating. *Unadulterated*, appropriately enough, means pure.

- I could tell that what her used car salesman was saying was one hundred percent pure, *unadulterated* hogwash.

ADUMBRATE (a DUM brayt) *v* to foreshadow vaguely, intimate, suggest, or outline sketchily

- The possibilities for further cooperation between the two parties were *adumbrated* at the first, private meeting, but nothing was finalized until much later.

- The first volume of the trilogy only *adumbrates* the basics of the story that will be developed in the next two books.

ADVOCATE (AD vuh cayt) *v* to argue for or support a cause

- Though the senator did not openly *advocate* for the bill, he voted for it because he thought it would save him some face among his critics.

A person who *advocates* for something is called an *advocate*, but be careful; the noun form is pronounced differently.

AESTHETIC (es THET ik) *adj* dealing with, appreciative of, or responsive to art or the beautiful

- Many people say they see no *aesthetic* value in some modern artwork, claiming the pieces look like a kindergartner's finger painting.

- Her finely tuned *aesthetic* sensibilities made it very painful for her to be around so much baby blue polyester.

AGGRANDIZE (uh GRAND yz) *v* to increase in intensity, power, or prestige; to make appear greater

- Michael's attempts to *aggrandize* his achievements produced the exact opposite effect; everyone ended up thinking he had accomplished less than he really had. In other words, he would have been better off without the *self-aggrandizing*.

- The multi-million dollar advertising campaign was part of a plan to *aggrandize* the company's stock before it went public.

ALACRITY (uh LAK ruh tee) *n* eager and enthusiastic willingness

- Amy responded to the invitation to join the planning committee with *alacrity*, and even volunteered to take on additional responsibilities.

- The *alacrity* with which Calvin offered to do the dishes made his mother suspicious; usually he would only do chores kicking and screaming.

ALCHEMY (AL kuh mee) *n* a magical or wonderful transformation

Alchemy was originally a medieval science aimed at changing metals, particularly into gold and silver, and the creation of a remedy that could cure all diseases. Though *alchemy* wouldn't be considered science today, *alchemists* did make some important strides in understanding chemistry.

- The remarkable *alchemy* among the cast members made watching the familiar and sometimes boring play into a completely new experience.

An *alchemist* practices or studies *alchemy*.

Quick Quiz #2

Match each word in the first column with its definition in the second column. Check your answers in the back of the book.

1. adroit
2. advocate
3. adumbrate
4. adulation
5. admonish
6. alchemy
7. alacrity
8. adulterate
9. aggrandize
10. aesthetic

a. foreshadow
b. adept
c. warn or express disapproval
d. increase in power
e. relating to or appreciating art or beauty
f. excessive praise
g. enthusiastic willingness
h. reduce purity of something
i. magical transformation
j. argue for

ALLOY (uh LOY) *v* to commingle; to debase by mixing with something inferior

- *Alloying* the punch with prune juice turned out not to be such a good idea after all.

Alloy can also be a noun, in which case it is the mixture itself, as in an *alloy* between sitcom and game show.

Unalloyed means pure.

- The reviewer described the movie as an *unalloyed* pleasure, saying it was the first film in years in which every single minute was worth watching.

AMALGAMATE (uh MAL guh mayt) *v* to combine several elements into a whole

- A griffin, theoretically at least, is an *amalgamation* of an eagle and a lion into one mean-looking mythical creature.

- It makes sense that the metal used in fillings is called an *amalgam* since it is a combination of mercury and silver.

AMBIGUITY (am big YOO uh tee) *n* uncertainty in meaning

- The *ambiguity* of the poem's title allows scholars to interpret it many different ways.

The adjective form of the word is *ambiguous.*

- Samir left the note purposefully *ambiguous*, figuring that Sonya would give him the benefit of the doubt if she wished to.

Be careful; *ambiguity* is frequently confused with *ambivalence.*

AMBIVALENCE (am BIV uh lunts) *n* the quality of having opposing ideas or feelings

- Nikki's *ambivalence* about the job offer was apparent; on one hand, the money and benefits would be better than at her current job, but on the other, she didn't want to risk losing the wonderful work environment she already had.

Ambivalent is the adjective form of *ambivalence.*

Be careful; *ambivalence* is often confused with *ambiguity,* probably because *ambivalence* can also mean uncertainty (particularly about what course one should follow).

AMELIORATE (uh MEE lee or ayt) *v* to make better or more tolerable

- Jonas was sure that nothing could *ameliorate* the taste of beets; brussels sprouts, on the other hand, could be made quite palatable with the introduction of plenty of butter.

- All attempts to *ameliorate* the relationship between the long-standing adversaries seemed futile; they were as hostile toward one another as ever.

AMENABLE (uh MEE nuh bul) *adj* agreeable; responsive to suggestion

- If you're *amenable*, let's go for a walk before lunch.

- The actress was known for being *amenable* to direction, which made her a favorite of directors.

If you think you see the word *amen* in *amenable*, you're right. *Amen* is an expression of agreement or approval, which is why it often follows a prayer. *Amenable*, of course, comes from the same root.

ANACHRONISM (uh NA krah ni zum) *n* something or someone out of place in terms of historical or chronological context

- The wristwatch worn by one of the characters in the period movie set in Rome in 25 B.C. was just one of the many *anachronisms* that spoiled the movie's credibility.

- Mr. Jones' students felt his insistence on strict classroom discipline was an *anachronism* and that he should "get with the times."

ANATHEMA (uh NA thuh muh) *n* a solemn or ecclesiastical (religious) curse; accursed or thoroughly loathed person or thing

- He was an *anathema* to his entire town once it was revealed that he had been a secret police informant.

- The percepts of eugenics became almost universally *anathema* around the world once the horrors of World War II began to be revealed.

- Hearing the *anathema* pronounced against her filled her with foreboding.

ANODYNE (AN uh dyn) *adj* soothing

- Don't you agree that nothing is quite so *anodyne* as a long soak in a bubble bath?
- I've also found that its *anodyne* effect can be enhanced by some good music and a glass of wine.

Anodyne can also be a noun, spelled the same way, and meaning something that assuages or allays pains, or comforts.

- After such a hectic week, Casey very much looked forward to the *anodyne* of a relaxing weekend of camping at the lake.

For words with similar meanings, see *emollient* and *mollify*.

ANOMALY (uh NAH muh lee) *n* deviation from the normal order, form, or rule; abnormality

- Pickles for sale in a tire store would be an *anomaly*; tires for sale in a pickle store would be equally weird.
- The *anomalous* results the scientist received the third time she ran the experiment made her question her initial hypothesis, since she couldn't find any other reason for the deviation from her prior results.

ANTAGONIZE (an TAG uh nyz) *v* to irritate or cause hostility

- Alonzo constantly *antagonized* his younger sister by stealing her lunch money and refusing to give it back.

Antagonize has the greek root *agon*, which means contest. *Agony* has the same root. The hero's primary rival or adversary in a play is called the *antagonist*. The hero, on the other hand, is called the *protagonist*.

ANTIPATHY (an TI puh thee) *n* aversion, dislike

- Sam very clearly expresses his *antipathy* toward certain breakfast foods in the Dr. Seuss classic, *Green Eggs and Ham.*

- Her longstanding *antipathy* toward her boss was tempered with at least a little gratitude after she received her big raise and promotion.

Antipathetic means showing a strong aversion.

- He was completely *antipathetic* to any new ideas, especially any that might suggest that his way wasn't the best way. I've never met such a closed-minded person.

Quick Quiz #3

Match each word in the first column with its definition in the second column. Check your answers in the back of the book.

1. ameliorate
2. amenable
3. ambiguity
4. ambivalence
5. amalgamate
6. antipathy
7. anathema
8. anomaly
9. anachronism
10. alloy
11. anodyne
12. antagonize

a. soothing
b. combine into a whole
c. agreeable
d. make better
e. strong dislike
f. make less pure
g. curse
h. something out of place historically
i. abnormality
j. feeling two opposing things
k. to irritate
l. uncertainty

ANTITHETICAL (an tuh THET i cul) *adj* diametrically opposed, as in antithesis

- I couldn't help but feel that he always deliberately expressed a position *antithetical* to mine, as if he enjoyed playing devil's advocate even more than he cared about expressing what he really thought.

- Nothing could be more *antithetical* to the spirit of sportsmanship than point shaving.

The *antithesis* is the opposite of something.

- The *antithesis* of poverty is wealth.

APATHY (A puh thee) *n* lack of interest or feeling

- There was such a pervading air of *apathy* in the high school that most clubs were shut down due to lack of interest.

The adjective form is *apathetic*.

- Though my pipes have been leaking for days, my landlord is so *apathetic* that he hasn't answered any of my phone calls or come by to fix anything.

Apathy shares a root with the word *pathos*, which means feeling. The prefix *a-* means without.

APOCRYPHAL (uh PAH cri ful) *adj* of dubious authenticity or origin; spurious

You may have heard this word before—or something close to it—in a religious context. The Apocrypha were religious writings that were not included in the Bible because they weren't considered canonical (see canon) by the Protestant church of the day, or their authenticity was in question. If you see the word *Apocryphal* with a capital A, the writer is referring to those writings specifically.

- Most people believe that stories of alien abduction are *apocryphal*, but what if there really is a big government conspiracy and all those stories are true?

- My favorite urban myth is the one about the fate of Little Mikey swallowing pop rocks and then drinking soda. I know it's *apocryphal*, but I still think it pays to be careful.

APOGEE (A poh jee) *n* farthest or highest point; culmination; zenith

- No one could have foreseen that receiving the Pulitzer Prize at the age of eighteen would be the *apogee* of his career, and that nothing he produced afterward would achieve any kind of critical success.

Perigee is the lowest or closest point, or the nadir.

- The moon is at *apogee* when it is at its farthest point away from the earth in its orbit; it is at *perigee* is when it is closest to earth.

For a related word, see *nadir* in this book.

APOSTATE (uh PAH stayt) *n* one who abandons long-held religious or political convictions, a betrayer of a cause

- Jordan was an *apostate* of modern culture; he renounced all the trappings of modern life that he used to love, and went to live in a cave.

- His fellow party members were shocked when Fred became an *apostate*, running for office on his former opponent's ticket.

APOTHEOSIS (uh pah thee O sis) *n* deification, glorification to godliness, the perfect example

- The *apotheosis* of technology in modern society seems to be reaching new highs; computers and gadgets are practically worshipped by consumers.

- She is the *apotheosis* of nurturing motherhood; she makes soup for sick friends, nurses wounded birds, and listens to everyone's problems.

APPOSITE (A pah zit) *adj* appropriate, pertinent, relevant, apropos

- His choice of songs for the opening ceremony was entirely *apposite*; everyone agreed that it was perfectly suited to the event.

- The fact that she hasn't called for two weeks is hardly *apposite* to whether she's going to call me today, since she hadn't read my amazing love poem before.

APPRISE (uh PRIZ) *v* give notice to, inform

- The officer *apprised* Chris of his rights before questioning him.

- The shipping department left a message to *apprise* me of the status of the shipment, letting me know it was scheduled to arrive the following day.

APPROBATION (a pruh BAY shun) *n* an expression of approval or praise

- Providing *approbation* for good behavior is the best way to train puppies; the praise is particularly effective when accompanied by treats.

- The judges expressed their *approbation* of Stephen's performance by awarding him the gold medal.

To *approbate* is to approve something officially. *Disapprobation* is an expression of disapproval.

APPROPRIATE (uh PRO pree ayt) *v* to take for one's own use, confiscate

- As they passed through the town, both armies *appropriated* housing, food, and ammunition from the town's residents. Whatever hadn't been taken by the first was taken by the second, leaving the inhabitants with insufficient resources to survive the coming winter.

- My friend Oscar is a natural mimic; he unintentionally *appropriates* the mannerisms of others until it's impossible to tell which ones are his own.

Even though this word looks like one you may use and hear every day, be careful! The meaning and pronunciation are different when it is used as a verb.

Quick Quiz #4

Match each word in the first column with its definition in the second column. Check your answers in the back of the book.

1. appropriate	a. spurious
2. apostate	b. zenith
3. apotheosis	c. perfect example
4. apathy	d. diametrically opposed
5. apogee	e. inform
6. antithetical	f. relevant
7. approbation	g. one who abandons faith
8. apposite	h. confiscate
9. apprise	i. expression of praise
10. apocryphal	j. lack of interest

ARABESQUE (ar uh BESK) *n* complex, ornate design

- A beautiful *arabesque* of fruits and flowers surrounded the central pattern of the print.

An *arabesque* is also a position in ballet, and is sometimes used metaphorically in this sense.

- Her assistants performed an *arabesque* of practiced efficiency around her as she prepared for the press conference.

ARCANE (ar KAYN) *adj* mysterious, abstruse, esoteric, knowable only to initiates

- Elizabeth was a font of *arcane* knowledge; she could tell you not only the names of the pets of every cabinet member of every administration, but also know many gumballs are produced annually.

- Knowledge of the *arcane* secrets of any bureaucracy is always restricted to those who work within it. They're the only ones who know how to fill out the forms, too.

Arcana are deep secrets. The singular is *arcanum*, but it's almost always used in the plural.

ARCHAIC (ar KAY ik) *adj* outdated; associated with an earlier, perhaps more primitive time

- Geoff's *archaic* leisure suit looked like it had been in storage for thirty years, and it probably should have stayed there.

- The *archaic* instruments used in the village clinic shocked the visiting physicians.

ARDUOUS (AR juh wus) *adj* strenuous, taxing, requiring significant effort

- This is the third time since she got here that Grandpa's told us the story of his *arduous* trips to and from school when he was a kid—uphill in the snow both ways.

- Learning all these vocab words may seem like an *arduous* task, but if you just learn a few a day, it will be a piece of cake, I promise.

ARRANT (AR unt) *adj* impudent; in every way, being completely such, bare-faced, utter

- Don Juan's *arrant* philandering made him a legend. He seemed to have had the ability to turn many of his admirers into *arrant* fools.

Don't confuse this with errant, which means itinerant.

ARREST (uh REST) *v* to suspend; to engage

- Sometime I think my brother's emotional development was *arrested* at a young age; he often acts like a five year old.
- My attention was immediately *arrested* by the view, a breath-taking panorama of mountains and lakes that had me completely mesmerized.

Arresting means holding one's attention.

- It was a most *arresting* portrait; there was a crowd of people starting at it for hours.

ARTICULATE (ar TIK yoo layt) *v* to enunciate or pronounce clearly; to express oneself clearly

- The new radio announcer could not be understood because he had not yet learned to *articulate* his words clearly.

As an adjective, *articulate* is used to describe someone who can *articulate* ideas clearly. But be careful; the pronunciation changes even though the spelling doesn't.

- Though she was just six years old, Misha presented a cogent and *articulate* argument for why she should receive an allowance.

ARTLESS (ART luhs) *adj* completely without guile; natural, without artificiality

- Her *artless* portrayal of the young ingénue charmed the critics, who all commented on her fresh, unaffected performance.

The opposite of artless is *artful*.

- The *Artful* Dodger was a cunning pickpocket in Dickens's *Oliver Twist*.

Artful can also mean showing art or skill, and *artless* can mean without skill, but the definitions above are the ones more likely to be tested on the GRE.

ASCETIC (uh SET ik) *n* one who practices rigid self-denial, especially as an act of religious devotion

- A true *ascetic* would be able to resist eating these chocolate éclairs, which is why I know I'm not an *ascetic*.

Ascetic can also be an adjective, meaning austere or stark.

- His *ascetic* lifestyle was indistinguishable from that of a monk.

- In keeping with Larry's *ascetic* taste in home furnishings, the only place to sit was the floor, which didn't even have a rug.

Asceticism is the adherence to or belief in *ascetic* practices. To learn about practices an *ascetic* would not espouse, see *hedonism*.

ASPERITY (uh SPER uh tee) *n* severity, rigor; roughness, harshness; acrimony, irritability

- The *asperity* of her response to his pleas for leniency suggested that there was no chance she would be ending his detention any time in the next three months.

- The *asperity* of a northern winter can lead to serious depression.

Quick Quiz #5

Match each word in the first column with its definition in the second column. Check your answers in the back of the book.

1.	arcane	a.	outdated
2.	arduous	b.	mysterious
3.	arabesque	c.	hold one's attention
4.	asperity	d.	impudent
5.	ascetic	e.	strenuous
6.	arrant	f.	complex design
7.	artless	g.	austere
8.	articulate	h.	harshness
9.	archaic	i.	natural
10.	arrest	j.	to express clearly

ASPERSION (uh SPER zhun) *n* an act of defamation or maligning

- Pete resented the *aspersions* cast by his opponent, who called Pete a low-down, no good snake who didn't eat his vegetables.

- She had to resort to *aspersions* when she realized her argument wouldn't hold up against close scrutiny.

ASSIDUOUS (uh SID yoo us) *adj* diligent, hardworking

- Pedro's *assiduous* preservation of every fragment of the document that had survived eventually allowed him to reconstruct whole stanzas of the poem.

- Carla was an *assiduous* note-taker. She wrote down almost every word of each of her professor's lectures.

ASSUAGE (uh SWAYJ) *v* to ease or lessen; to appease or pacify

- Convincing her that it was all the rage in Paris helped *assuage* Christine's fears about painting her walls chartreuse.

- Ken was able to *assuage* the pain of his headache by lying in a dark room with a damp cloth over his eyes.

Assuage is used to describe the lessening or easing of things that cause pain or distress, so you don't *assuage* happiness or good humor (unless they're causing you pain in some way).

ASTRINGENT (uh STRIN junt) *adj* having a tightening effect on living tissue; harsh; severe

- Although she hadn't intended to be quite so harsh, Kayla's *astringent* remarks apparently made the board drop the proposal altogether.

- Witch hazel is a mild *astringent* that is sometimes applied to the face.

ATTENUATE (uh TEN yoo ayt) *v* to rarefy, weaken or make thinner, lessen

- Copper's highly ductile nature allows it to be *attenuated* to a thin filament without breaking, and makes it a useful material for wiring.

- The atmosphere at the top of Mt. Everest is so *attenuated* that climbers must carry oxygen with them in order to breathe for any length of time.

- The endless discussion *attenuated* the point until everyone lost interest in it.

For a related word, see *rarefy*.

AUDACIOUS (aw DAY shus) *adj* daring and fearless; recklessly bold

- Liz is an *audacious* mountain climber who goes where few of her competitors dare to follow.

- No matter how *audacious* a cartoon villain's plan for world domination may be, there always seems to be hero waiting to foil it.

Audacity is the quality of being *audacious*.

- His friends were surprised by Lewis's *audacity*; he just went up to the podium and started speaking, even though he wasn't on the program for the evening.

AUGURY (aw GYUH ree) *n* omen, portent, the reading of omens

- *Augury* in ancient Rome and other societies was performed largely by interpreting the flight of birds.
- His first attempts at glassblowing gave little *augury* of the skill he would later develop with practice.

Augur means to predict if it is used as a verb, and the person or thing doing the foretelling if it's used as a noun.

- The flowers my girlfriend sent *augur* well for the weekend.

AUGUST (aw GUST) *adj* majestic, venerable

- The *august* presence of the pharaohs endures through the millennia, embodied in their massive tombs.
- Despite his simple dress and advanced years, the *august* politician managed to convey a sense of dignity and subtle power.

AUSPICE (AW spis) *n* protection or support, patronage

- As long as we were working under the *auspices* of the local authorities, the villagers were extremely cooperative; once we headed out on our way, however, we found that no one wanted to talk to us.

Auspice can also mean sign or portent.

- Since the *auspices* seemed good, we decided to go ahead and buy thirty lottery tickets.

Match each word in the first column with its definition in the second column. Check your answers in the back of the book.

1. auspice
2. audacious
3. augury
4. assuage
5. astringent
6. august
7. aspersion
8. attenuate
9. assiduous

a. harsh
b. diligent
c. daring
d. omen
e. ease
f. defamation
g. patronage
h. make thinner
i. majestic

AUSPICIOUS (aw SPI shus) *adj* favorable, propitious, successful, prosperous

- The sold-out opening night and standing ovation from the audience provided an *auspicious* beginning for the play's run on Broadway.

- Weddings are generally considered *auspicious* occasions; you can tell by all the toasting and well-wishing that goes on.

AUSTERE (aw STEER) *adj* without adornment; bare; severely simple; ascetic

- The building's *austere* façade gave no indication of the rich ornamentation inside.

- Lincoln's often *austere* appearance reflected the somber, grave side of his personality, but not his sense of humor.

- The *austerity* of her writing style can make it seem as if her meaning is similarly simple, but she is actually known for the subtle complexity of her ideas.

Austerity can also mean rigid economy. If used in this sense, it is often followed by *measures.*

- The prime minister imposed *austerity* measures in an attempt to stop the country's downward economic spiral.

AVARICE (A vuh rus) *n* greed, especially for wealth

- Her *avarice* for power was matched only by her lust for money; even when she had more money than she could ever spend in a lifetime, she schemed to get still more.

- King Midas' *avarice* led him to wish for the power to turn everything he touched to gold; we know how well that worked out for him.

Avaricious means greedy.

- Even though the jury decided in favor of the plaintiff, it awarded very little in the way of punitive damages; the jurors apparently felt the request for 40 million dollars was *avaricious.*

AVER (uh VUR) *v* to state as a fact; to confirm or support

- When the suspect solemnly *averred* that he had been on another planet when the burglary occurred, the investigators didn't know whether he meant it literally or figuratively, but they could tell he meant it.

- Although Michele *averred* that she would never be late again, her friends remained understandably skeptical.

AXIOM (AK see um) *n* a universally recognized principle; a generally accepted or common saying

- It is an *axiom* of the American legal system that one is innocent until proven guilty.

- .It is hardly surprising that every field has its *axioms*, which are universally held within the discipline; what can be surprising is how often they are mutually incompatible when compared across fields.

The adjective form of this word is *axiomatic*, which means generally accepted or taken as a given.

- In this society, we take it as *axiomatic* that individual merit rather than family name should be the basis for success in life.

- Nowadays it is *axiomatic* that most contagious diseases are caused by microscopic organisms, but it wasn't long ago that most people thought these diseases were caused by every-thing from harmful vapors to personality traits.

B

BALEFUL (BAYL ful) *adj* sinister, pernicious, ominous

- The basilisk is a notoriously cranky, albeit mythical, creature whose *baleful* glare is fatal.

Looks, glances, and glares are more often *baleful* than anything else is, but other things can be *baleful* too.

- A sort of *baleful* miasma lingered in the room after the infamous Sir Evildoer departed in a swirl of black and red cape.

BANE (bayn) *adj* cause of injury, source of harm; source of persistent frustration

- Even for those who recognize that smoking is far more of a *bane* than a benefit, quitting can be a struggle.

- Paolo's little sister was the *bane* of his existence; she followed him everywhere and told their mom whenever he did anything he wasn't supposed to.

Baneful means causing harm or ruin, pernicious, destructive.

- The *baneful* effect of the curfew on my social life cannot be overestimated.

BEATIFY (bee AT uh fy) *v* to bless, make happy, or ascribe a virtue to; to regard as saintly

- She was described in such a glowing way; every single quality she possessed was *beatified*.

Beatitude is a state of bliss, and beatific means having a blissful appearance.

- His *beatific* smile could only mean that he had just eaten some exceptionally good sushi.

Be careful not to confuse this with *beautify*, which means to make beautiful.

Quick Quiz #7

Match each word in the first column with its definition in the second column. Check your answers in the back of the book.

1.	baleful	a.	greed
2.	aver	b.	source of harm
3.	auspicious	c.	bare
4.	beatify	d.	universally recognized
5.	axiom		principle
6.	austere	e.	favorable
7.	avarice	f.	sinister
8.	bane	g.	regard as saintly
		h.	state as fact

BEDIZEN (bi DY zun) *v* to adorn, especially in a cheap, showy manner; festoon, caparison

- The speakeasy was *bedizened* with every manner of tawdry decoration.

- Sophie the cow came wandering home after the festival, *bedizened* with a wreath of flowers over each horn and somewhat the worse for wear.

BEGUILE (bih GAHYL) *v* to influence by trickery, flattery, etc.; to mislead

- He used a fake identity to *beguile* the investigators.
- In 2000, mortgage lenders *beguiled* a number of individuals into buying houses they could ill afford by offering misleading lending terms.

BELIE (bih LYE) *v* to give a false impression of, to misrepresent

- Carlos's disapproving countenance was *belied* by the twinkle in his eye, making it hard to believe that he was angry at all.
- Gabriela's seeming clumsiness *belied* her true grace as a dancer.

BELLICOSE (BEL i kohs) *adj* belligerent, pugnacious, warlike

- The bully's *bellicose* demeanor hid a tender side, but he was too busy getting into fights to reveal it.
- Ted's *bellicose* expression warned me that he had discovered I had eaten the last of the ice cream.

Bellicose shares a root with *belligerent*. Both come from the Latin *belliger*, which means warlike.

BENIGN (buh NYN) *adj* favorable, harmless

In medicine, we often hear *benign* describe a tumor that is not cancerous, though it certainly has other uses.

- Though we were afraid the tumor would be fatal, a biopsy showed that it was, in fact, *benign*.
- The pictures taken of the millionaire in the years before his death show a curmudgeonly scowl, but the ones taken of him as a young man show him beaming with a gentle and *benign* expression.

Many words that start with *ben-* have a positive connotation, such as *benefit*, *benefactor*, and *benediction*. Words that start with *mal-*, on the other hand, usually have a negative connotation. See *malevolent* for some more examples.

BENT (bent) *n* leaning, inclination, proclivity, tendency

- Puck was notorious for his mischievous *bent*; wherever there was trouble to be stirred up, he was certain to be found.

- Mike's *bent* for self-destructive behavior worried his friends.

BLANDISH (BLAND ish) *v* to coax with flattery, toady or fawn

- The minister was famous for his ability to *blandish* his way from obscurity to vicarious power; it seemed as if every ruler was receptive to bootlicking.

Blandishment is flattery intended to cajole or coax.

- *Blandishment* plus a really big present might convince me to forgive you.

Be careful not to confuse this with *brandish*, which means to shake or wave menacingly.

BLITHE (blithe) *adj* carefree, merry

- Stephanie's *blithe* disregard for what her peers might think made her the perfect hero for a clever yet moving coming-of-age teen movie.

- Paul's *blithe* attitude toward his housecleaning led to a comfortable, if sometimes dusty, clutter.

BOISTEROUS (BOY stur us) *adj* loud, noisy, rough, lacking restraint

- After a while, our neighbors became reconciled to our *boisterous* weekend gatherings, even joining us on occasion; the rest of the time they were probably wearing earplugs.

- A popular image of the Wild West is the *boisterous* saloon where the piano player pounds out songs while the burlesque dancers perform the cancan.

BOLSTER (BOL stur) *v* to provide support or reinforcement

- He hoped his frequent references to legal theory would *bolster* his argument, but all they did was make him seem pompous.

- I tried to *bolster* my confidence with some slow deep breaths, but I just ended up hyperventilating. I would have been better off picturing the audience in their underwear or having a stiff shot of whisky.

BOMBASTIC (bahm BAS tik) *adj* pompous; grandiloquent

- The self-important leader's speech was so *bombastic* that even his most loyal followers were rolling their eyes, and no one else could even figure out what he was talking about.

Bombast is self-important or pompous writing or speech.

- His books were always so filled with *bombast* that they were almost impossible to read; it sounded as if he had swallowed a thesaurus whole.

Quick Quiz #8

Match each word in the first column with its definition in the second column. Check your answers in the back of the book.

1.	bellicose	a.	inclination
2.	bent	b.	misrepresent
3.	blandish	c.	carefree
4.	bolster	d.	belligerent
5.	boisterous	e.	pompous
6.	blithe	f.	support
7.	belie	g.	fawn
8.	benign	h.	loud
9.	bedizen	i.	adorn
10.	bombastic	j.	favorable
11.	beguile	k.	trick

BOOR (boor) *n* a rude or insensitive person; lout; yokel

- I have learned never to take a *boor* to dine with royalty; last time we had tea with the Queen of England, my *boorish* boyfriend put his feet on the table!

- Although she was usually very sweet and considerate, she became downright *boorish* when she was drunk.

BRIDLING (BRAHYD ling) *v* to control or hold back, restrain

- Upon her 18th birthday she moved out of her parents' house and away from their *bridling* control.

BROACH (brohch) *v* bring up, announce, begin to talk about

- To *broach* the subject of her truly hideous brooch would have been impolitic. There's no way I could have managed to say anything nice about it.

BROOK (bruk) *v* to tolerate, endure, countenance

- Our drill sergeant made it very clear she would *brook* no insubordination; even any quiet grumbling would be grounds for endless push-ups.

- The conductor refused to *brook* any more delay and ordered those without tickets off the train immediately.

BUCOLIC (byoo KAH lĭk) *adj* rustic and pastoral; characteristics of rural areas and their inhabitants

- Pastoral poetry tends to depict *bucolic* wonderlands of shepherds tending their flocks in verdant meadows, but poets always leave out the part about getting up at five o'clock in the morning to take those flocks out to graze.

- Their plans for a life of *bucolic* tranquility were rudely shattered when they discovered the rolling fields pictured in the brochure for their new house were really part of a busy golf course.

BURGEON (BUR jun) *v* to grow rapidly or flourish

- When the wildflowers *burgeon* in April and May we know that spring has truly arrived.

- The *burgeoning* population transformed the town into a bustling metropolis.

BURNISH (BUR nish) *v* to polish, rub to a shine

- Be careful about *burnishing* certain old lamps; you never know which one is going to have a genie in it, and history shows that those three wishes lead to no good.

- Attempts to *burnish* the former council member's image were useless; he would forever be remembered as the one whose toupee was stolen by a bird during the Fourth of July parade.

BYZANTINE (BI zan teen) *adj* labrynthine, complex

- Tom's *byzantine* explanation of why he missed curfew was confusing even to his parents who were used to his convoluted punishment-avoidance strategies.

- I can't stand playing cards with Max because he makes up such *byzantine* rules that even he can't keep track of them.

You may occasionally see this word with a capital B, in which case it is referring to the city of Byzantium or the Byzantine Empire.

C

CACOPHONY (ca CAH fo nee) *n* harsh, jarring, discordant sound; dissonance

- The *cacophony* coming from the construction site next door made it impossible to concentrate on the test.

- It was a testament to unconditional love that the parents of the kindergartners could call the *cacophony* of the band recital "music." Some of them even seemed to enjoy the screeching racket.

For a related word see *dissonance*.

CADGE (kaj) *v* to sponge, beg, or mooch

- He was always *cadging* change from me, which added up to a lot of money over time, so eventually I presented him with a loan statement and started charging interest.

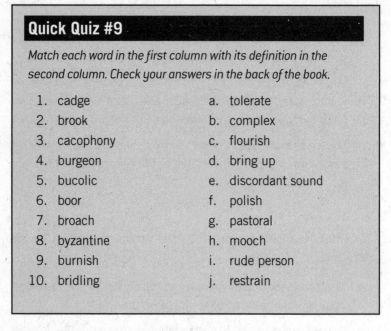

Quick Quiz #9

Match each word in the first column with its definition in the second column. Check your answers in the back of the book.

1.	cadge	a.	tolerate
2.	brook	b.	complex
3.	cacophony	c.	flourish
4.	burgeon	d.	bring up
5.	bucolic	e.	discordant sound
6.	boor	f.	polish
7.	broach	g.	pastoral
8.	byzantine	h.	mooch
9.	burnish	i.	rude person
10.	bridling	j.	restrain

CAJOLE (kuh JOL) *v* to inveigle, coax, wheedle, sweet talk

- Even though I resolve not to give in, my dog is always able to *cajole* an extra dog biscuit out of me just by looking at me with his big brown eyes.

- I can't believe Wendy *cajoled* her way out of another mess; all she has to do is smile sweetly and everyone agrees to her every demand.

CALUMNIATE (kuh LUM nee ayt) *v* to slander, make a false accusation

- Tom *calumniated* his rival by accusing him of having been unfaithful, but it backfired because when the truth came out, Tom ended up looking petty and deceitful.

Calumny means slander, aspersion.

- Whenever she was afraid someone would discover her own incompetence, she would resort to *calumnies* and claim everyone else was doing a bad job.

CANNY (KAN ee) *adj* careful, cautious, knowing

- Knowing all aspects of how to run her business, Emily has a *canny* eye for making a deal.

- In times of market uncertainty, *canny* investors may prefer to keep their money in gold rather than stock.

CANON (KA nun) *n* an established set of principles or code of laws, often religious in nature

- She was forever violating the *canons* of polite conversation by asking questions that were far too personal for the circumstances.

- Adhering to the dictates of his religion's *canon* meant that he couldn't eat pork.

Canonical means following or in agreement with accepted, traditional standards.

- The *canonical* status of the standard literary classics has been challenged by the emergence of the work of feminist and third-world scholars, among others.

CAPRICIOUS (kuh PRI shus) *adj* inclined to change one's mind impulsively; erratic; unpredictable

- Lee's *capricious* behavior this weekend shouldn't have come as much of a shock; its not as if he's usually all that stable and predictable.

Having *caprices* (sudden changes of mind or actions) makes you *capricious*, which then means that you can be described as tending toward *capriciousness*.

CARDINAL (KAHRD nul) *adj* of basic importance or consequence; primary

- His *cardinal* error was in failing to bribe his sister; otherwise his parents might never have found out about the party and grounded him.

- According to classical definition, the *cardinal* virtues are: prudence, justice, temperance and fortitude.

CARNALITY (kahr NAL uh tee) *n* something relating to the body or flesh

- Though the book was primarily concerned with spiritual matters, its descriptions of earthly pleasures were sometimes shocking in their sheer *carnality*.

Carnal desires are those that relate to bodily or sexual appetite.

- Mac intended the carnival ride as an aphrodisiac, but the effects of the spinning actually dampened any *carnal* desires that were already there.

It may seem a little odd, but the word *carnage* is related—it means physical remains.

CASTIGATION (KAS tuh GAY shun) *n* severe criticism or punishment

- Harriet's expression as she slunk out of the room indicated that the *castigation* she had received was even worse than expected, and that we were probably in for a similar tongue-lashing.

- The rack was one of the many gruesome tools of *castigation* available to the medieval torturer.

CATALYST (KAT uh list) *n* a substance that accelerates the rate of a chemical reaction without itself changing; a person or thing that causes change

- Enzymes are common biological *catalysts* which regulate the speed of many critical processes in the human body.

- Steve was hoping the romantic music would be all the *catalyst* the evening needed.

To *catalyze* is to act as a *catalyst*, to bring about.

- Some argue that while the assassination of Archduke Ferdinand *catalyzed* World War I, the war would still have happened in the absence of his death, even if it might have begun some months or years later.

CAUSALITY (kaw ZAL uh tee) *n* the relationship between cause and effect

- The fact that Caroline saw a stork the week before she became pregnant is merely a coincidence; it should not imply any *causality* whatsoever.

- Because the experiment tested so many factors at the same time, it is difficult to prove the *causality* of one agent over another.

CAUSTIC (KAW stik) *adj* burning or stinging; causing corrosion

- Even washing her hands repeatedly couldn't stop the stinging of the *caustic* bleach she had used on her clothes.

- Her *caustic* wit was legendary—everyone enjoyed reading Sandra's articles as long as he or she was not the target of her humor.

CENSURE (SEN shur) *v* to criticize severely; to officially rebuke

- Though the board *censured* the gallery for holding the exhibition, the event continued as planned, and even drew larger crowds than expected before the board's outspoken disapproval.

n a judgment involving condemnation; the act of blaming or condemning

- The chairman's misdeeds were only made public and held up to *censure* once it became certain that the board members could not be implicated.

Censorious (note the spelling) is an adjective that means tending to or expressing *censure*.

CHAOS (KAY ahs) *n* a condition of confusion or unpredictability

- Some seem to thrive on *chaos* in the workplace, but Lucy relishes a clean desk and predictable schedule.

Chaotic is an adjective that describes a state of *chaos*.

- When Shigeru arrived home after being robbed, he found his apartment in a *chaotic* state.

Originally, the Greek word for *chaos* meant space, or emptiness (think *chasm*), but now it has more to do with disorder.

Quick Quiz #10

Match each word in the first column with its definition in the second column. Check your answers in the back of the book.

1.	carnality	a.	slander
2.	canon	b.	criticize severely
3.	calumniate	c.	cautious
4.	censure	d.	unpredictable
5.	causality	e.	harsh criticism
6.	castigation	f.	primary
7.	capricious	g.	set of principles
8.	caustic	h.	substance that causes change
9.	cajole	i.	burning
10.	cardinal	j.	coax
11.	catalyst	k.	confusion
12.	canny	l.	bodily
13.	chaos	m.	relationship of cause and effect

CHARY (CHAR ee) *adj* wary; cautious; sparing

- Claudette was *chary* with her praise lest it go to Fredrick's head.

- *Chary* of revealing his hiding place, Fido only reluctantly led us to the spot behind the sofa where we discovered a stash of fifty dog bones.

CHASTEN (CHAY sun) *v* to chastise or correct; subdue

- The "time out" seems to have become a common parental means of *chastening* younger children, somewhat similar to being forced to sit in the corner wearing a dunce cap, but without the element of public humiliation.

- The piano teacher knew it would be difficult to *chasten* the student's rebellious spirit without breaking it. The trick was to get her to sit still long enough to learn something without destroying her spontaneous creativity.

Chastened as an adjective means corrected, punished, or humbled.

- Rita was *chastened* by the effect her thoughtlessness had on those around her, and she resolved to consider her actions more carefully in the future.

CHAUVINIST (SHOH vuh nist) *n* one blindly devoted to a group of which one is a member

- She was such a party *chauvinist*; her blind devotion made her refuse to acknowledge the changes underway that would lead to the party's downfall.

- His *chauvinism* for Dutch soccer led him to paint everything he owned, including his car, orange.

A male *chauvinist* believes in the inferiority of women to men. This term is often followed by the word *pig*.

CHIC (sheek) *adj* stylish and fashionable; sophistication in dress

- As a true native New Yorker, Kenya remained a *chic* dresser long after she moved to Kansas; it's too bad there was no one there to appreciate her sense of style.

- Jorge opened a *chic* boutique near the affluent suburb to cater to shoppers with fashionable tastes and expendable incomes.

CHICANERY (shi KAYN uh ree) *n* trickery or subterfuge

- Bernard's reputation for legal *chicanery* made judges and prosecutors distrust him, but his clients had a hard time seeing past his successes.

- I refuse to let such *chicanery* go unpunished!

CHIMERA (kye MEER uh) *n* an illusion

The *chimera* was originally an imaginary fire-breathing she-monster in Greek mythology. Its body was an amalgam of different animals, and sighting it was a bad omen. In today's speech, though, none of these bad connotations remain.

- Walter Mitty's life was a series of *chimeras*; the fantastic daydreams in which he starred were completely real to him.

Chimerical means illusory or improbable.

- The fantastic successes of some internet start-ups turned out to be *chimerical* once the tech boom ended.

CHOLERIC (KAHL er ik) *adj* tending toward anger

- *Choleric* by nature, the boxer had no trouble mentally preparing to face his opponent.

According to Aristotle, *choleric* personalities were supposed to be caused by too much stomach bile. This book contains vocabulary words based on three other personality types that he identified based on bodily fluids...can you find the rest?

CHURLISH (CHUR lish) *adj* boorish, vulgar, loutish; difficult and intractable

- Underneath Mr. Oleander's *churlish* exterior, there's a nice guy hiding somewhere; it's just hard to tell because he is so rude most of the time.

A *churl* is someone who is *churlish*.

- Since everyone knew that Brad became a *churl* whenever he'd had too much to drink, they were just waiting for him to start saying inappropriate things and getting into fights at the party.

CIRCUMSCRIBE (sur kuhm SKRAHYB) *v* enclose within bounds; limit or confine, especially narrowly

- The legislative and judicial branches of government serve to *circumscribe* the power of the president.

CLANGOROUS (KLANG er us) *adj* making a loud, resonant sound

- She thought that living in the country would be peaceful, and was therefore surprised by constant noise stemming from the *clangorous* cowbells tied around the cow's necks.

COALESCE (ko uh LES) *v* to come together; to fuse or unite

- It took a major internal crisis for the rival factions to *coalesce* around a single goal.
- Cosmologists theorize that matter began to *coalesce* into stars and galaxies about one billion years after the Big Bang.

CODA (KO duh) *n* concluding section to a musical or literary piece, something that concludes or completes

- The presentation of the lifetime achievement award was a fitting *coda* both to the evening and to his years of work with the organization.

COGENT (KO junt) *adj* appealing forcibly to the mind or reason; convincing

- I'll only let you borrow the Ferrari if you can give me a *cogent* reason for why you need to drive more than one hundred miles per hour.

- He may have gotten the day off because his argument for why he deserved it was so *cogent*, or it could just have been that it was Saturday and he wasn't scheduled to work anyway.

Quick Quiz #11

Match each word in the first column with its definition in the second column. Check your answers in the back of the book.

1.	chicanery	a.	boorish
2.	cogent	b.	come together
3.	coda	c.	illusion
4.	chary	d.	chastise
5.	chic	e.	convincing
6.	chauvinist	f.	trickery
7.	chasten	g.	blindly devoted member
8.	churlish	h.	concluding piece
9.	chimera	i.	wary
10.	choleric	j.	angry
11.	coalesce	k.	fashionable
12.	circumscribe	l.	loud
13.	clangorous	m.	limit

COLOR (KUH lur) *v* to change as if by dyeing, influence, distort, or gloss over

Though *color* is a simple enough word in everyday speech, its secondary definition is often tested on the GRE.

- Knowing that he had lied about his previous experience *colored* our evaluation of his application.

- He may have *colored* the truth a little bit when he said he had jogged 20 miles, because he probably hadn't run more than two.

COMMENSURATE (kuh MEN sur it) *adj* matching, corresponding, or proportionate in degree, size, amount, or other property

- Although Allen's salary at the Department of Social Work was hardly *commensurate* with his work experience and previous salary history, the challenge of the job and the feeling that he was giving back to the community made it worth his while.

- Only if the team won the national championship would the fans feel the team's performance was *commensurate* with its potential.

COMPLAISANCE (kum PLAY sunts) *n* the willingness to comply with the wishes of others

- A "yes man" is characterized by his *complaisance*.

Complaisant means showing a willingness to please.

- The patriarch was most likely to be *complaisant* after he had eaten a sumptuous meal, so everyone saved his or her requests for such a time.

Don't confuse this with *complacent*, which means self-satisfied.

CONFOUND (kun FOWND) *v* to cause to be confused; to frustrate

- By the time my roommate and I parted ways, our things were such a *confounded* mess that it was hard to remember what belonged to whom.

You probably already recognize the prefix *con-* (or *com-*), which often means joining or bringing things together. *Confound* means to mix together or *confuse* things. To be confused is to be *confounded*.

CONNOISSEUR (kah nuh SOOR) *n* an informed and astute judge in matters of taste; expert

- An internationally recognized *connoisseur* of wines, Natasha was often hired as a consultant for private collectors.

- Did you know that some people call themselves *connoisseurs* of water?

CONSEQUENTIAL (kahn suh KWEN shul) *adj* pompous, self-important

---

Be careful; this is one of those words with multiple definitions. The primary definitions are: *logically following; important*, but on the GRE it is more likely to be used as we've defined it here.

- Although he thought himself a respected and well-liked man, his *consequential* air was intensely annoying to those around him. He seemed to think he was the best thing since sliced bread.

CONTEMN (kun TEM) *v* to scorn or despise

- I *contemn* their attempts to curry favor; nothing is more contemptible than a sycophant.

Be careful not to confuse this with *condemn*, which seems very similar, but means to pronounce judgment against.

CONTENTIOUS (kun TEN shus) *adj* argumentative; quarrelsome; causing controversy or disagreement

- Sometimes Lydia's *contentious* nature really drove me crazy; it seemed as if she argued with everything I said simply out of habit or some sort of strange pleasure.

- The judges' *contentious* decision of the title bout led some to claim that undue influence had been exerted in deciding the outcome of the fight.

CONTIGUOUS (kun TIG yoo us) *adj* sharing a border; touching; adjacent

- The *contiguous* United States include all the states except Hawaii and Alaska, since they are the only ones that don't share at least one border with another state.

- The kitchen and dining room in our house are *contiguous*, making it easier to carry food and plates from one to the other.

CONTRITE (kun TRYT) *adj* regretful; penitent; seeking forgiveness

- Wayne was hardly *contrite* for the practical joke he pulled; even though he said he was sorry, the twinkle in his eye and barely suppressed grin seemed to indicate otherwise.

- David's *contrite* words were long overdue; if he had made his apologies last week, his sister would have been a lot more willing to accept them.

Contrition is regret or remorse.

- Once she expressed genuine *contrition* for wrecking my car I was willing to forgive her, though she would still have to pay for the damages.

CONVENTION (kun VEN shun) *n* a generally agreed-upon practice or attitude

- The *convention* of wearing a bridal veil was apparently begun by the Romans, who thought the veil would protect the bride from evil spirits.

- The *conventions* of modern poetry are much less rigid than those of classical poetry; in fact, it is difficult to find any two poets or critics who could even agree on definitions, much less rules.

Quick Quiz #12

Match each word in the first column with its definition in the second column. Check your answers in the back of the book.

1. contiguous
2. contemn
3. color
4. convention
5. consequential
6. contrite
7. commensurate
8. contentious
9. complaisance
10. confound
11. connoisseur

a. corresponding
b. willingness to comply
c. self-important
d. argumentative
e. penitent
f. expert
g. distort
h. scorn
i. touching
j. agreed-upon principle
k. confuse

CONVOLUTED (KAHN vuh loo ted) *adj* complex or complicated

- Cynthia's *convoluted* response to the question made her listeners think she was concealing something; it was as if she hoped they would forget the question as they tried to follow her answer.

- I do not know by what *convoluted* reasoning you arrived at the idea that you should have three weeks extra vacation, but I can't argue with the conclusion!

CORRIGIBLE (KOR uh juh bul) *adj* capable of being set right, correctable, reparable

- Stuttering is often a highly *corrigible* speech impediment, which can be corrected through speech therapy.

- The trend away from rehabilitative programming in prisons may indicate a decrease in the public's belief that inmates are *corrigible*.

Corrigibility, a noun, is the capacity to be set right.

- The *corrigibility* of the damage to the train could only be determined after extensive inspection and testing.

The opposite of *corrigible* is *incorrigible*, meaning not reformable, uncontrollable, recalcitrant.

- Julius was an *incorrigible* daydreamer; no matter how much his teachers scolded him, he would much rather be hanging out in his own imaginary world than paying attention to his lesson.

COUNTENANCE (KOWN tuh nunts) *v* to approve of or tolerate

- Her refusal to *countenance* any of what she called "back talk" made her an unpopular babysitter, but even the children had to admit that things were less chaotic when she was around.

- The dean fully *countenanced* the addition of the new athletic complex, saying that a healthy body would only aid in the development of a healthy mind.

Countenance can also be a noun, in which case it means mien, face, composure.

- The *countenance* of the woman in Dorothea Lange's famous photograph, "Migrant Mother, Nipomo, California" is one of the most powerful and enduring images of the Great Depression; the woman's face communicates such fear and despair, and yet also strength, that it has become iconic.

COZEN (KUH zun) *v* to deceive, beguile, hoodwink

- The corrupt televangelist *cozened* millions of dollars out of his viewers by convincing them that he would perform miracles to make them all win the lottery.

For a related word, see *guile*.

CRAVEN (KRAY vun) *adj* contemptibly fainthearted, pusillanimous, lacking any courage

- His *craven* cowardice in refusing to admit his mistake meant that a completely innocent person was punished.

- Steve lived in *craven* fear of being found out as a fraud.

CREDULOUS (KRE juh lus) *adj* tending to believe too readily; gullible

- That sculpture in the lobby was so obviously a fake that it would convince only the most *credulous* person; after all, the "gold" left something that looked suspiciously like paint on our fingers when we touched the sculpture.

- Nathan was so *credulous* that he believed us when we told him that naugahyde comes from horse-like creatures called naugas, who eat plastic grass.

CRESCENDO (kruh SHEN doh) *n* a gradual increase in intensity, particularly in music

Usually, *crescendo* is used to describe music or sound, but it can be used in more figurative ways, as well.

- The audience's attention was held rapt as the orchestra worked its way to a *crescendo*, filling every nook in the hall with thunderous sound.

- The *crescendo* of RSVPs seems to have passed, as we now are receiving only one or two replies per day.

CULPABLE (KUL puh bul) *adj* deserving blame

- Pat could hardly be thought *culpable* for spilling the cranberry juice on the floor, since he wasn't even in the room at the time.
- If she is judged *culpable* of improper conduct, the governing board will decide her punishment.

Culpability is blameworthiness.

- His *culpability* was never in doubt once the auditors traced the embezzlement back to his department.

For a related word, see *exculpate*.

CYNICISM (SIN uh si zum) *n* an attitude or quality of belief that all people are motivated by selfishness

- Tricia's *cynicism* was matched only by her own selfishness; she believed no one else was altruistic because she never was herself.

Someone who displays *cynicism* is called a *cynic*.

- The *cynics* say that these donations were made to receive public praise, but if that's true, why were they made anonymously?

D

DAMP (damp) *v* to diminish the intensity or check something, such as a sound or feeling

- Her hopes were *damped* when she checked the mailbox and there was still no letter for the fourth day in a row.
- Her mattresses and foam placed around the room *damped* the noise to a sufficient degree that the band could play without disturbing the neighbors.

DAUNT (dawnt) *v* to intimidate or dismay

- At first, the protagonist of the fairy tale was *daunted* by the task given to him; he didn't know how he would ever sort the gains of wheat and barley until the ants arrived to help him.

The adjective *daunting* means dismaying, disheartening.

- The *daunting* prospect of getting all our laundry done by Sunday afternoon was so overwhelming that we decided to put it off yet again.

There's another related adjective, *dauntless*, which means fearless, undaunted, intrepid.

- Robin Hood and his *dauntless* henchmen defeated the bad guy, Sheriff Nottingham.

Quick Quiz #13

Match each word in the first column with its definition in the second column. Check your answers in the back of the book.

1. countenance	a.	deserving blame
2. corrigible	b.	approve of; mien
3. culpable	c.	gullible
4. craven	d.	belief that everyone is
5. daunt		motivated by selfishness
6. convoluted	e.	deceive
7. crescendo	f.	complex
8. credulous	g.	lacking any courage
9. cozen	h.	correctable
10. damp	i.	discourage
11. cynicism	j.	diminish intensity
	k.	increase in intensity

DEARTH (durth) *n* smallness of quantity or number; scarcity; lack

- The *dearth* of snow this winter increases the likelihood of a drought next summer.

- Since there is a *dearth* of talented singers who auditioned for the part, I may actually end up singing, which isn't good at all!

DEBACLE (di BAH cul) *n* rout, fiasco, complete failure

- The performance was a complete *debacle*; not only did I end up singing, but the cloud props we were using also fell down midway through the play, prompting the audience to shout "the sky is falling, the sky is falling."

- Trying to avoid a *debacle*, the candidate decided to withdraw from the race shortly before election day.

DEBUNK (di BUHNGK) *v* to expose as being pretentious, false, or exaggerated

- The notion that the earth is flat has been completely *debunked*.

DECORUM (di COR um) *n* politeness or appropriateness of conduct or behavior

- In Shaw's *Pygmalion*, Henry Higgins attempts to train Eliza Doolittle in proper *decorum* for high society, with often very funny results.

- Where did we ever get the notion that extending one's pinky finger while drinking tea was the height of *decorum*?

Something marked by *decorum* is *decorous*.

- Olivia's *decorous* decline of our invitation was so politely and perfectly said that we could hardly take offense.

DELETERIOUS (del uh TEER ee us) *adj* injurious; harmful

- The symptoms originally seemed to indicate something as innocuous as the common cold, but eventually the disease's *deleterious* effects were better understood.

- Though it originally seemed like a good idea to cut the quality of the product, the overall effect on customer relationships has been *deleterious*.

Do you see *delete* inside of this word? It's no accident...something that is *deleted* is erased, and something *deleterious* is likely to have a similar harmful effect.

DEMUR (di MUR) *v* to question or oppose

- I hesitated to *demur* from the professor, until he said something factually inaccurate, at which point I felt I had to speak up.

- Bob *demurred* at the suggestion that he clean the house while we swim.

DENIGRATE (DEN i grayt) *v* blacken, belittle, sully, defame, disparage

- Though some might have *denigrated* our efforts at cooking breakfast, which consisted of cold eggs, bitter coffee and burnt toast, our mother was very appreciative of our attempt and bravely ate all of it.

- Edna was notorious for *denigrating* everyone else's work, but never being willing to hear the slightest criticism of her own.

- *Denigration* is the act of *denigrating*, or the act of making *denigrating* comments.

- William's confidence was so shaken by the months of *denigration* at the hands of his former boss, that he almost didn't believe the praise he was getting now.

DENOUEMENT (day noo MA) *n* an outcome or solution; the unraveling of a plot

- Receiving the Nobel Prize was a fitting *denouement* to his brilliant research.

- The *denouement* seemed completely contrived; the happy ending didn't fit with the tone of the entire rest of the movie.

DEPRECATE (DE pri kayt) *v* to disparage or belittle

- You can *deprecate* his work all you want but it won't affect my opinion; I don't care if his writing is sometimes amateurish, I still like it.

To be *self-deprecating* is to belittle yourself or your accomplishments.

- We worried that his *self-deprecating* humor wasn't as light-hearted as it seemed, but was instead a sign of deeper insecurity.

DEPREDATE (DE pruh dayt) *v* to plunder, pillage, ravage or destroy; to exploit in a predatory manner

- The pirates *depredated* every ship that came through the straits for two years, until no captain was willing to risk that route and the port town became deserted.

Depredations are attacks, or ravages.

- Ten years of the dictator's *depredations* had left the country a wasteland.

- The *depredations* of time and hard living have left his one handsome face a mass of wrinkles and broken blood vessels.

Quick Quiz #14

Match each word in the first column with its definition in the second column. Check your answers in the back of the book.

1.	denouement	a.	fiasco
2.	denigrate	b.	question or oppose
3.	dearth	c.	belittle
4.	deprecate	d.	plunder
5.	debacle	e.	scarcity
6.	decorum	f.	outcome
7.	deleterious	g.	disparage
8.	depredate	h.	polite conduct
9.	demur	i.	harmful
10.	debunk	j.	expose as false

DERISION (di RI zhun) *n* scorn, ridicule, contemptuous treatment

- Her *derision* was all the more painful because I suspected that her review of my performance was accurate.

To *deride* is to express contempt.

- The media *derided* her attempted comeback, calling her a "has been," even though she had been their darling only a few months before.

DERIVATIVE (di RI vuh tiv) *adj* unoriginal, obtained from another source

- Some people claim that there is nothing new under the sun, and that all contemporary art is therefore *derivative* of work that came before it.

DESICCATE (DES u kayt) *v* to dry out or dehydrate; to make dry or dull

- Pemmican, a food developed by Native Americans, is made by *desiccating* meat so that it can be preserved for long trips, then pounding it and combining it with other ingredients.

- His skin was so *desiccated* by sun exposure that it looked like parchment.

- The *desiccated* prose of the old volume of stories I found in the attic was as dull in style as its actual pages were dry and brittle.

DESUETUDE (DES wi tood) *n* disuse

- After sitting abandoned for years, the house's *desuetude* came to an end when the county bought it and turned it into a teen center.

DESULTORY (DES ul tor ee) *adj* random; thoughtless; marked by a lack of plan or purpose

- His *desultory* efforts in studying for the test were immediately obvious to his teacher as soon as she began to score his exam.

- We abandoned our *desultory* attempts to form a book club once our primary instigator gave up on us and joined another group.

DETRACTION (di TRAK shun) *n* slandering, verbal attack, aspersion

- Apparently the mayor's campaign of *detraction* backfired, since a record number of people voted for his opponent, many of them citing the vitriol of the mayor's attacks as the reason they voted against him.

- Terrence's *detraction* of Raul's performance only served to reveal how jealous he was of Raul's success.

DIAPHANOUS (dy AF uh nus) *adj* transparent, gauzy

- Her *diaphanous* gown left little to the imagination.

- As we stood behind the waterfall, the cascade of water formed a sort of *diaphanous* veil in front of us.

Quick Quiz #15

Match each word in the first column with its definition in the second column. Check your answers in the back of the book.

1.	desiccate	a.	disuse
2.	desultory	b.	scorn
3.	derivative	c.	verbal attack
4.	derision	d.	gauzy
5.	detraction	e.	dehydrate
6.	diaphanous	f.	thoughtless, unplanned
7.	desuetude	g.	unoriginal

DIATRIBE (DY uh tryb) *n* a harsh denunciation

- What started out as seemingly normal discussion about what to have for lunch, rapidly and somewhat bizarrely turned into a *diatribe* about the difficulty of finding a decent pickle.

- His anti-development *diatribe* was well-received by local residents who wanted to see the field preserved as an open space rather than turned into a shopping center.

DIDACTIC (dy DAK tik) *adj* intended to teach or instruct

- Rachel's attempt to hide the activity's *didactic* intent by wrapping it in the guise of a fun game didn't fool the third graders for a minute; they could always smell something educational a mile off.

- His *didactic* tone grated on me; whom did he think he was to try to teach me something while we were on a date?

DIFFIDENT (DIF uh dint) *adj* reserved, shy, unassuming; lacking in self-confidence

- He was a *diffident* reader of his own poetry, and which sometimes kept his audience from recognizing the real power of his writing.

The noun, *diffidence*, means a lack of confidence.

- I began to suspect that her *diffidence* was merely an act, and that this seemingly meek woman was really plotting to take over not only the department, but also the entire world.

DIGRESS (dy GRES) *v* to stray from the point; to go off on a tangent

- My aunt's tendency to *digress* is legendary; she can get so far off topic that no one can remember the starting point, but the journey is always fascinating.

A *digression* is something that has digressed.

- The speaker asked our indulgence while we made a short *digression*, the point of which would become clear eventually.

DILATE (DYE layt) *v* to become wider or more open

- Until Khoa's eyes *dilated* to let in more light, he couldn't find an empty seat in the darkened theater.

To *dilate* can also mean to speak or write about something at length.

DILATORY (DIL uh tor ee) *adj* causing delay, procrastinating

- The legislator was able to create the *dilatory* effect he sought by means of a twenty-three-hour filibuster.

- His *dilatory* habits were a source of exasperation for his boss, who never knew whether something would be finished on time or not.

DILETTANTE (DIL uh tahnt) *n* one with an amateurish or superficial interest in the arts or a branch of knowledge

- The negative connotation of a *dilettante* as one whose interest in a subject is trivial is relatively recent; it hasn't always been a bad thing to be a *dilettante*.

- *Dilettantes* did much of the scientific work in early America; professional positions for scientists are largely a phenomenon of the twentieth century.

A *dilettantish* effort or interest is one that is frivolous or superficial.

- Even though she didn't take it very seriously at the time, her *dilettantish* interest in the arts while in college laid the framework for a satisfying career as curator of a major art museum years later.

DIN (din) *n* loud sustained noise

- Because we couldn't hear each other over the *din* coming from the kitchen, I thought she said she had met Sasquatch, when she had really asked whether I was wearing my watch.

- The *din* of the faulty muffler drowned out all the other noises that would have confirmed the very poor odds of my car making it another five miles.

For a related word, see *cacophony*.

DIRGE (durj) *n* a mournful song or poem for the dead

- Because Grandma wanted no *dirges* sung at her funeral, we hired a singer to reinterpret some of her favorite popular music from her teen years.

Dirge can also be used figuratively, to describe something that sounds like a funeral lament.

- The only sound on the dark prairie was the *dirge* sung by the wolves.

DISABUSE (dis uh BYOOZ) *v* to undeceive; to set right

- The screws left over after he had assembled the bookcase, along with its tendency to tip over, *disabused* Joe of the idea that reading the instructions was optional.

- I hate to *disabuse* you of the notion of your own genius, but you just got a D on that midterm that you said you were going to ace.

DISCOMFIT (dis KUM fit) *v* to defeat, put down

Nowadays, *discomfit* also means to embarrass or make uncomfortable, but its original meaning is to thwart one's plans.

- The enemy's superior planning and resources *discomfited* us. They defeated us easily, despite our hopes of *discomfiting* their attack.

DISCORDANT (dis KORD int) *adj* conflicting; dissonant or harsh in sound

- Because the group had been fractured by *discord* for so long, it was surprising, to say the least, to watch them put aside their *discordant* views and begin to get along as if they had never disagreed.

- As one *discordant* note followed another, I started to get a headache from the noise.

Quick Quiz #16

Match each word in the first column with its definition in the second column. Check your answers in the back of the book.

1.	discordant	a.	harsh denunciation
2.	discomfit	b.	intended to teach
3.	disabuse	c.	shy
4.	din	d.	stray from the point
5.	dilettante	e.	causing delay
6.	dilatory	f.	amateur
7.	digress	g.	loud noise
8.	dilate	h.	undeceive
9.	diffident	i.	frustrate
10.	didactic	j.	conflicting
11.	dirge	k.	mournful song
12.	diatribe	l.	open

DISCRETION (dis KRE shun) *n* cautious reserve in speech; ability to make responsible decisions

- The matchmaker's *discretion* was the key to her remarkable success; her clients knew she would not reveal their identities inappropriately.

- The *discretion* required of the agent should not be underestimated; he will need to make critical decisions under severe time constraints and often at considerable risk to himself.

DISINTERESTED (dis IN ter est ed) adj free from self-interest; unbiased

This one gets a little complicated. *Disinterested* and uninterested have a pretty convoluted history. *Uninterested*, when it first showed up in the seventeenth century, meant "impartial." At some point, though, that meaning was replaced in popular usage with its current meaning: "not caring or having an interest in," as in the sentence, "I am completely *uninterested* in attending the concert." At about the same time, the original use of *disinterested* to mean "not caring or having an interest in" was changing in favor of "free from bias."

Confused yet? It gets worse. To recap: *disinterested* means "unbiased" and *uninterested* means "uncaring," right? However, increasingly writers are switching them back around. The people who police the proper usage of words in English say this isn't allowable, but the writers do it anyway. Usually you can tell from context which definition someone intends.

- We need a *disinterested* party to arbitrate the property dispute, since each of the participants has too much at stake to remain unbiased.

- Her *disinterested* assessment was that the food was terrible, which we had to believe since she had no reason to lie.

DISPARAGE (dis PAR aj) v to slight or belittle

- I don't think you have any right to *disparage* his attempts until you have tried riding the mechanical bull yourself.

Disparaging remarks are those that express a negative, usually dismissive, opinion of something or someone.

DISPARATE (DIS puh rut) *adj* fundamentally distinct or dissimilar

- I found it amazing that two people with such *disparate* tastes could decorate a house together.

- The *disparate* results of the two experiments confused the scientists who had conducted both in exactly the same manner; the only explanation seemed to be that the samples used were fundamentally different in a way the scientists had not previously realized.

DISSEMBLE (di SEM bul) *v* to disguise or conceal; to mislead

- Her coy attempts to *dissemble* her plagiarism were completely transparent; no one believed her.

- *Dissembling* on your grad school application is an absolute no-no.

DISSOLUTION (dis uh LOO shun) *n* disintegration, looseness in morals

- The *dissolution* of the warlord's power left a power vacuum in its wake that many minor chieftains competed to fill.

- The company would be threatened with *dissolution* if it were judged to be operating as a monopoly.

- Wilde's novel, *The Picture of Dorian Gray*, shows all the consequences of the protagonist's *dissolution* as a result of his excessive vanity.

The adjective *dissolute* means licentious, libertine.

- His *dissolute* indulgence in every form of hedonism horrified his morally conservative colleagues.

For related words see *libertine* and *hedonism*.

DISSONANCE (DIS uh nunts) *n* lack of harmony; conflict

Literally, *dissonance* refers to sounds, such as musical notes, that lack harmony. However, it can also refer to any conflict in a figurative sense.

- The *dissonance* in the grunge album suited Kumiko's foul mood perfectly.

- There is so much *dissonance* among the team members that it is difficult to reach consensus on even the smallest points of the proposal.

Something with *dissonance* can be described as *dissonant*.

DISTRAIT (dis TRAY) *v* distracted; absentminded, especially due to anxiety

- When he kept forgetting what he was talking about during dinner, it became clear that he was *distrait*, and was no doubt preoccupied with the meeting planned for the next day.

Be careful not to confuse this with the somewhat similar *distraught*, which means extremely agitated with emotion.

DIVULGE (di VULJ) *v* to disclose something secret

- She believed she had been fired because she had threatened to *divulge* information about the company's mismanagement.

- It is a basic tenet of most secret societies that members are not allowed to *divulge* anything about the initiation rites to outsiders.

- His journal *divulged* a side of his personality that no one had ever seen.

DOCTRINAIRE (DOK truh NAIR) *adj* fanatical; merely theoretical; impractical

- Mary was an idealist; she held *doctrinaire* beliefs that the country could be united under one political party.

DOGGEREL (DAW guh rul) *n* trivial, poorly constructed verse

- For some reason, I could always remember the bit of *doggerel* I read on the bathroom wall, though I had long since forgotten all the exquisite poetry I read in my classes in college.

DOGMATIC (dawg MA tik) *adj* authoritatively and or arrogantly assertive of principles, which often cannot be proved; stubbornly opinionated

- Evelyn's *dogmatic* insistence on the importance of following procedure to the letter frustrated her coworkers who were willing to cut a few corners in the interest of saving time.
- Percy always became *dogmatic* when it came to any discussion of music; he absolutely insisted that jazz was the only music worth listening to and that all other kinds were completely devoid of merit.

Dogma is a related word that you may be familiar with, and it means a statement of ideas that is considered to be absolutely true. Though these ideas can be set forth by a religious order; they don't have to be; the definition here is purely secular.

DROSS (drahs) *n* slag, waste or foreign matter, impurity, surface scum

- We discarded the *dross* that had formed at the top of the cider during the fermentation process.
- Howard has convinced himself that his poor memory is a consequence of all the unnecessary information his brain has accumulated over the years; that's why he is busy cataloguing

all the *dross*, especially the obsolete telephone numbers and advertising jingles, that he plans to forget systematically in order to create space for more important information.

DULCET (DUL sut) *adj* melodious, harmonious, mellifluous

- The *dulcet* tones of the dulcimer were exquisite and made the performance particularly memorable.

- The fact that I thought her voice a *dulcet* wonder shows you how infatuated I was; most people thought she sounded like a sick moose.

DUPE (doop) *n* one who is deceived

- What do I look like—a *dupe*? No one with any sense could possibly believe the story you're trying to sell.

Dupe can also be a verb.

- No one will ever be able to *dupe* Sara into giving out her social security number again; that one case of identity theft was enough.

DYNAMO (DY nuh moh) *n* generator; forceful, energetic person

The technical definition of a *dynamo* is a generator of current, which gives rise to the metaphorical use for describing a person as forceful or energetic.

- Courtney was truly the *dynamo* of the group; without her we'd probably still be sitting on the couch instead of being three days into our road trip.

It's no accident if this word reminds you of *dynamite* or *dynamic*; all three words have roots in the Greek word for power.

Quick Quiz #17

Match each word in the first column with its definition in the second column. Check your answers in the back of the book.

1.	dogmatic	a.	disintegration
2.	dulcet	b.	trivial poetry
3.	dissolution	c.	disclose a secret
4.	dissemble	d.	energetic person
5.	dross	e.	belittle
6.	discretion	f.	stubbornly opinionated
7.	disparate	g.	free from bias
8.	divulge	h.	fundamentally different
9.	doggerel	i.	cautious reserve
10.	dupe	j.	melodious
11.	dynamo	k.	mislead
12.	disparage	l.	waste or impurity
13.	disinterested	m.	absentminded
14.	dissonance	n.	one who is fooled
15.	distrait	o.	conflict
16.	doctrinaire	p.	impractical

E

EBULLIENCE (ih BOOL yunts) *adj* the quality of lively or enthusiastic expression of thoughts and feelings

- Vivian's *ebullience* was contagious, which is what made her such a great tour guide; her infectious enthusiasm for her subject always communicated itself to her listeners.

- Allen's love of birds was clear from the *ebullience* with which he described them.

ECCENTRIC (ek SEN trik) *adj* departing from norms or conventions

- Although he was often described by colleagues as a bit *eccentric*, it was precisely the unconventionality of his bedside manner that made the doctor so beloved by his young patients.

Something or someone *eccentric* demonstrates *eccentricity*.

- The big purple flower tied to the antenna of Felicia's car is hardly a mark of *eccentricity*; it's there so she can easily find her car in a parking lot.

ECLECTIC (ek LEK tik) *adj* composed of elements drawn from various sources

- It was easy to get a sense of Alison's *eclectic* taste from looking at her music collection, which contained everything from Mahler to Metallica.

- The house's *eclectic* architectural style somehow managed to combine elements of seemingly incongruous periods into one cohesive design.

EDIFYING (ED i fy ing) *adj* enlightening, informative

- The lecture we attended on the consequences of globalization was highly *edifying*, but what I learned only made me want to know more.

Edification is the process of *edifying*.

- Upon his promotion, Krishna attended a seminar on being a first-time manager that his boss recommended for professional development and *edification*.

Some people incorrectly use *edifying* to mean satisfying, and while being enlightened can be satisfying, the two are not the exactly the same.

EFFICACY (EF ih kuh see) *n* the ability to produce an intended result

- Though anecdotal stories abound regarding the *efficacy* of the herb, its effectiveness has not been studied scientifically in any major way.

- The *efficacy* of the ad campaign cannot be definitely measured at this stage in the game, but already the public response seems positive.

Efficacy shares a root with *effectiveness*, and means pretty much the same thing.

EFFLORESCENCE (ef luh RES uns) *n* the state or a period of flowering; an example or result of growth and development

- The scholarly works she created early on in her academic career showed the *efflorescence* of her genius.

EFFRONTERY (i FRUNT uh ree) *n* extreme boldness; presumptuousness

- The *effrontery* of her demand astonished everyone; no one had ever dared ask the head of the department to explain his reasoning before.

- Gary's *effrontery* in inviting himself to the party said a lot about his inflated sense of himself as well as his lack of sense about how others saw him.

- Teresa couldn't believe her boss's *effrontery* in asking her to start a new project at eight o'clock on a Friday night.

EFFUSIVE (i FYOO siv) *adj* gushing; excessively demonstrative

- Her *effusive* good wishes seemed a bit forced; it was hard to believe she was no longer bitter about having had her own grant proposal turned down.

- The *effusiveness* of the review from a critic known for his stinginess with praise might have had something to do with the VIP treatment from the entire restaurant staff.

EGRESS (EE gres) *n* exit

Egress can either be a noun, meaning an exit or going out, or a verb, meaning to exit or emerge. *Ingress* is the opposite of *egress*.

- The dancer's final *egress* from the stage brought the audience to its feet in a standing ovation.

- Although the *egress* was clearly marked with a big green sign saying "EXIT," I still had trouble locating it because I had lost my glasses by the time I was ready to leave.

ELEGY (EL uh jee) *n* a mournful poem, especially one lamenting the dead; any mournful writing or piece of music

- His *elegy* for the long-lost carefree days of his youth was moving, if somewhat clichéd.

- It seemed a little silly for him to compose an *elegy* for his pet tadpole, especially since it hadn't died, even if now it was a frog instead of the tadpole he once loved.

It's very easy to confuse *elegy* with *eulogy*, which is also in this book, but the two aren't exactly the same.

ELOQUENT (EL uh kwent) *adj* well-spoken; expressive; articulate

- It was hard to believe English wasn't her native language given her *eloquent* use of it.

- Admittedly, it's hard to be *eloquent* with peas in your mouth and mashed potatoes on your nose, but I think you communicated your ideas quite clearly nonetheless.

- The *eloquence* of his prose is even more incredible given its simplicity; he conveys his meaning clearly and beautifully without any frills at all.

EMOLLIENT (i MAHL yint) *adj* soothing, especially to the skin; making less harsh; mollifying

- Oatmeal's *emollient* qualities when added to bath water make it an effective aid in soothing the discomfort of poison oak.

- Her kind words had an *emollient* effect on us, soothing our bruised egos.

EMPIRICAL (im PIR i kul) *adj* based on observation or experiment

- Skeptics demanded *empirical* evidence before accepting the psychic's claims that he was communicating with representatives from beyond the grave.

- The *empirical* data produced by the study was surprising to many; it contradicted the assumptions researchers had been operating under for decades.

ENCOMIUM (en KOH mee um) *n* glowing and enthusiastic praise; panegyric, tribute, eulogy

- The recently released tribute album was created as an *encomium* to the singer many considered the grandfather of soul music.

- The *encomiums* swelled to a torrent as details of the philanthropist's billion-dollar donation became known; each newspaper tried to outdo the others in praising her.

ENDEMIC (en DEM ik) *adj* characteristic of or often found in a particular locality, region, or people; restricted to or peculiar to that region; indigenous

- Some pundits argue that the corruption *endemic* to politics today is responsible for the public apathy evident in record low voter turnouts.

- The species of badger *endemic* to the region has recently been placed on the endangered species list; its territory is being encroached upon by housing developments and that specific habitat is the only one in which it can survive.

For a related word, see *pandemic*.

ENERVATE (EN ur vayt) *v* to weaken; to reduce in vitality

- We were so *enervated* by the heat and humidity that we didn't even have the energy to turn on the fan.

- Having braved the malls on the day after Thanksgiving, we were so *enervated* by the time we got home that we didn't even make it all the way into the house; we had to take a nap on the front steps first.

- *Enervation* is a common symptom of anemia.

Be careful! *Enervate* is extremely easy to confuse with *innervate*, which is also in this book. Although their spellings are similar, their meanings and pronunciations are very different. See *innervate* for more information.

ENGENDER (en JEN dur) *v* to cause, produce, give rise to

- Clyde's announcement that he plans to retire at the end of the year *engendered* intense speculation about whom he will appoint as his successor.

- Technical manuals, ostensibly designed to make things easier, can sometimes *engender* even more confusion than they prevent.

ENIGMATIC (en ig MAT ik) *adj* mysterious, obscure, difficult to understand

- The only clue to the famous economist's disappearance was an *enigmatic* message left on his desk that said "gone home"; it took hours for anyone to realize that it meant nothing more mysterious than that he had gone home to feed the dog.

- Some archaeologists speculate that the *enigmatic* markings on the cave wall may be the earliest known human representations of religious worship.

Enigma is the noun form of *enigmatic* and means a mystery or puzzle.

ENNUI (ahn WEE) *n* dissatisfaction and restlessness resulting from boredom or apathy

- The end-of-summer *ennui* had set in, making Hannah and Jeremy almost look forward to the distraction of going back to school…almost.

- Serena's claim that a rousing game of Go Fish would cure us of our *ennui* left us somewhat skeptical.

ENORMITY (i NOR mi tee) *n* excessive wickedness, evilness

Be very careful not to confuse this with *enormousness*. Enormousness means huge size; enormity does not. Thus, if we talk about the enormity of a crime we are never talking about its size; we're talking about its wickedness.

• The *enormity* of the terrorist act stunned and outraged the world.

Quick Quiz #19

Match each word in the first column with its definition in the second column. Check your answers in the back of the book.

1.	empirical	a.	glowing praise
2.	enervate	b.	give rise to
3.	endemic	c.	soothing
4.	ennui	d.	evilness
5.	emollient	e.	based on observation
6.	enigmatic	f.	weaken the vitality of
7.	engender	g.	restlessness
8.	enormity	h.	mysterious
9.	encomium	i.	found in a particular location

EPHEMERAL (i FEM uh rul) *adj* brief; fleeting, short-lived

• My *ephemeral* first romance lasted precisely as long as summer camp did.

• The effects of the treatment were powerful but *ephemeral*, so that patients had to return to the hospital to repeat the procedure as often as once a day.

- Oh, how *ephemeral* is fame! It lasts but fifteen minutes, it seems!

EPICURE (EP i kyur) *n* one devoted to sensual pleasure, particularly in food and drink; gourmand, sybarite

- After watching too many cooking shows, Larry became such an *epicure* that he lost his ability to appreciate the gustatory pleasures of a frozen pizza.

Epicurean means appropriate to an epicure's taste.

- The exotic *epicurean* pleasures provided at the five star restaurant made it very popular despite its exorbitant prices.

EPISODIC (ep uh SAH dik) *adj* loosely connected, not flowing logically, occurring at intervals

- The *episodic* structure of the novel mirrored the main character's fragmented experience of events during the war.

- Malaria is an *episodic* illness; symptoms can disappear for years at a time, only to recur later.

EPITHET (EP uh thet) *n* disparaging word or phrase

- The *epithets* he flung in drunken anger came back to haunt him the next morning when everyone refused to talk to him.

- As word got out about the racial *epithets* spray-painted on the front steps of the courthouse, an angry crowd gathered to demand that immediate steps be taken to identify the perpetrators.

EPITOME (i PIT uh mee) *n* embodiment; quintessence

- To me, Lauren Bacall was the *epitome* of sophistication.

- A long afternoon by the pool with a good book and a frosty beverage is the *epitome* of relaxation.

EQUANIMITY (ee kwuh NIM uh tee) *n* composure, self-possession

- Theo's ability to maintain his *equanimity* was sorely tested by the end of two hours at the zoo; his composure was most threatened when his nephew reached into the cage to pull the monkey's tail.

- Liam strove unsuccessfully for *equanimity* in the face of the massive and unprovoked tickle attack.

EQUABLE (EK wuh bul) *adj* level; not able to be easily disturbed

- Emiko's *equable* temper allows her to deal with everyone calmly and graciously; it's too bad she's not in customer service.

- Because of the high levels of humidity in the region, *equable* temperatures are maintained almost year-round.

EQUIVOCATE (ee KWI vuh kayt) *v* to use ambiguous language with a deceptive intent

- She argued that the company was guilty of *equivocating* when it claimed it could "teach you to type in one hour or less" because it was unclear whether that meant they guaranteed you would be able to hit a single key or type fifty words a minute at the end of that hour.

- The *equivocal* language of the contract was designed to deceive gullible buyers—*caveat emptor* indeed!

ERRANT (ER unt) *adj* traveling, itinerant, peripatetic

- A knight-*errant* was a guy in armor who wandered around looking for adventures to prove his general studliness.

- *Travels with Charley* is Steinbeck's account of his *errant* journey across America with his French poodle, Charley.

Be careful! *Errant* doesn't have anything to do with errors, despite its appearance and even though *inerrant* means infallible.

ERRATIC (ur RAT ik) *adj* without consistency

- Chau's capability to regulate her movements seems to evaporate when she hits the dance floor, and she flails around to an *erratic* rhythm only she can hear.

- Though Lorne's boss always came up with wonderful ideas, Lorne sometimes found it difficult to follow her *erratic* trains of thought.

Erratic comes from a root meaning to wander, and that's just how you can think of this word: wandering off the steady course. *Eccentric* is a close synonym.

ERUDITE (ER yuh dyt) *adj* very learned; scholarly

- All six volumes of Gibbon's *erudite Decline and Fall of the Roman Empire* have long been required reading in Professor Smith's course on the history of classical scholarship.

Erudition is profound learning or extensive knowledge, learned primarily through books.

- Although his dissertation was generally hailed as a masterpiece of *erudition*, some critics who acknowledged the virtuosity of its scholarship nonetheless took issue with its lack of reference to the lived experience of actual people.

Match each word in the first column with its definition in the second column. Check your answers in the back of the book.

1.	episodic	a.	one devoted to sensual pleasure
2.	epithet	b.	embodiment
3.	ephemeral	c.	traveling
4.	errant	d.	disparaging word
5.	epitome	e.	scholarly
6.	erudite	f.	fleeting
7.	equivocate	g.	self-possession
8.	equable	h.	loosely connected
9.	epicure	i.	use ambiguous language to deceive
10.	equanimity	j.	without consistency
11.	erratic	k.	level

ESCHEW (e SHEW) *v* to shun or avoid

- Daniel was unwilling to *eschew* her company even though I reminded him of how many times she had stood him up in the past.

- Some vegans *eschew* all forms of animal products, refusing to wear leather or use lotions containing lanolin in addition to not eating anything that comes from animals.

ESOTERIC (e soh TER ik) *adj* intended for or understood by a small, specific group

- Even though most of the sect's practices were well-documented by anthropologists, some of its most *esoteric* rites had never been witnessed by outsiders.

- The most *esoteric* course offering this spring seems to be Advanced Pig Latin.

ESSAY (e SAY) *v* to test or try; attempt, experiment

- It was incredible to watch Valerie *essay* her first steps after her long convalescence; we were so proud of how hard she had worked at her rehabilitation.

Essay can also be a noun, meaning the attempt itself.

- My frequent *essays* at organization were always successful for a few weeks but fell apart shortly thereafter.

ESTIMABLE (EST uh muh bul) *adj* worthy, formidable

- Despite his *estimable* efforts, Alvin was unable to finish his spinach; it really was an impressive attempt, though.

- Garry Kasparov's *estimable* opponent in the famous man versus machine chess game was a computer named Deep Blue.

EULOGY (YOO luh jee) *n* a speech honoring the dead

- It was impossible for Sonya to conceal her grief at the funeral; she started weeping during the delivery of the *eulogy*.

- The *eulogy* briefly mentioned his many public accomplishments, but focused far more on how much he had meant to his friends and family.

You may have already seen the word *elegy* in this book. It is easy to confuse *elegy* with *eulogy*, but they're not entirely the same.

EVANESCENT (e vahn E sunt) *adj* tending to disappear like vapor; vanishing

- All trace of the *evanescent* first snow vanished as soon as the midday sun appeared.

- Thankfully, the pain of my first heartbreak was as *evanescent* as the romance itself; we fell in love on the way to school one morning, broke up on the monkey bars during lunch, and I was sufficiently recovered to fall in love with someone else on the way home.

EVINCE (i VINTS) *v* to show clearly, to indicate

- The expression on Jane's face *evinced* what she thought of the proposal; it's amazing how clearly "you must be kidding" can be communicated without speaking a word.

- Although Victor's work *evinced* great potential, he had significantly more to do before his article would be ready for publication.

- Yolanda *evinced* great heroism during the fire, reentering the house twice to save the children trapped inside.

EXACERBATE (ig ZA sur bayt) *v* to make worse or more severe

- My mother insisted that going outside with wet hair would only *exacerbate* my cold, and she was probably right since now I have pneumonia.

- The government's refusal to recognize the new ambassador *exacerbated* an already tense situation; many feared it could lead to war.

EXACT (ig ZAKT) *v* to demand, call for, require, take

- Celebrities often complain that fame *exacts* a heavy price in loss of privacy, but their fans don't seem to care much, perhaps thinking that this is a reasonable exchange for the money and glory.

- In the *Merchant of Venice*, a pound of flesh is *exacted* in exchange for money.

EXCORIATE (ex KOR ee ayt) *v* to censure scathingly, to upbraid

- The editorial *excoriated* those artists who attended the event instead of observing the boycott called for by human rights groups.

- Even though the mayor was *excoriated* by many for his role in the scandal, he nonetheless chose to run for reelection and seemed to have a reasonable chance of winning, which many found appalling.

EXCULPATE (EX cul payt) *v* exonerate; to clear of blame

- Far from *exculpating* him as he had hoped, the new evidence only served to convince the jury of his guilt.

- I was able to *exculpate* myself from the charges of cheating by taking another exam and receiving the same grade on it as I had on the first one.

For some examples of words with the same root, see *culpable*.

Quick Quiz #21

Match each word in the first column with its definition in the second column. Check your answers in the back of the book.

1.	esoteric	a.	attempt
2.	estimable	b.	censure scathingly
3.	exact	c.	worthy
4.	eulogy	d.	vanishing
5.	eschew	e.	show clearly
6.	exculpate	f.	avoid
7.	essay	g.	speech honoring the dead
8.	evanescent		
9.	evince	h.	exonerate
10.	exacerbate	i.	understood by only a small group
11.	excoriate		
		j.	demand
		k.	make worse

EXEMPLAR (ig ZEM plar) *n* typical or standard specimen; paradigm, model

- We were excited to find the perfect *exemplar* of the species of beetle we had studied in school; it conformed to the description in the guidebook in every way.

- He was the *exemplar* of success; if you looked up "successful" in the dictionary, you would probably find his picture next to the definition.

Exemplary means worthy of imitation, so an *exemplar* can be *exemplary*, but doesn't have to be.

EXHORT (ig ZORT) *v* to incite, to make urgent appeals

- At the last second I realized that he was waving his arms frantically to *exhort* me to look down before I fell off the cliff.

- Our coach *exhorted* us to greater and greater efforts, urging us not to give up even in the face of a twenty-point deficit.

- His *exhortations* failed to motivate us; we were just too tired from moving boxes all day.

EXIGENT (EX i junt) *adj* urgent; pressing; requiring immediate action or attention

- *Exigent* circumstances require extreme action; if we didn't act soon we would lose the scavenger hunt, so we just went to the store and bought the rest of the items. It may have been cheating, but we felt the situation required it.

Exigencies are urgent or pressing situations.

- The *exigencies* of the food shortage brought out a level of altruism and compassion in the townspeople that they didn't demonstrate under ordinary circumstances.

EXONERATE (ig ZAHN ur ayt) *v* to remove blame

- The number of death row inmates *exonerated* by DNA tests in the last few years has caused some to call for a moratorium on executions.

- Kim was *exonerated* of having taken her sister's shoes when the missing boots were discovered under a pile of dirty laundry.

Exculpate is similar in meaning to *exonerate*.

EXPATIATE (ex PAY shee ayt) *v* discuss or write about at length; to range freely

- My aunt and uncle *expatiated* on the subject of their Florida vacation for three hours, accompanied by slides, until we were all crazy with boredom.

- His ability to *expatiate* on such a variety of subjects without notes made watching him speak something like taking a trip without a map; the journey set its own course.

EXPIATE (EX pee ayt) *v* to atone or make amends for

- He feared that nothing could *expiate* the insensitivity of his comments.
- Elvira tried to *expiate* her lateness by bringing flowers.
- In the Middle Ages, it became a common practice to *expiate* one's sins by buying indulgences.

EXPURGATE (EX pur gayt) *v* to remove obscenity, purify, censor

- The *expurgated* version of the novel was incredibly boring; it turned out that the parts the censors removed had been the only interesting ones.
- The editorial committee removed some sections of the essay that it found morally objectionable, and it also *expurgated* a significant number of factual errors.

Expurgate shares a root with *purge*, which means to cleanse or make pure.

EXTANT (EK stunt) *adj* existing, not destroyed or lost

- There are 48 copies of the Gutenberg Bible *extant* today.
- Since there are no portraits *extant* of the famous general, we have only written descriptions to tell us how he looked.

EXTEMPORANEOUS (ek stem por AY nee us) *adj* improvised; done without preparation

- Her *extemporaneous* remarks at the reception demonstrated that her speechwriter must largely be responsible for her reputation for eloquence.

- Their skit was pure comic genius; I couldn't believe it was *extemporaneous*.

EXTIRPATE (EK stur payt) *v* to destroy, exterminate, cut out, pull out by the roots

- The dodo bird was *extirpated* by a combination of hunting by humans and predation by non-native animals.

- She set out on a self-improvement plan to *extirpate* every single one of her bad habits, but quickly realized she would have nothing left to do if she cut them all out.

- My worst summer job ever involved *extirpating* an entire acre of weeds.

Quick Quiz #22

Match each word in the first column with its definition in the second column. Check your answers in the back of the book.

1.	extemporaneous	a.	incite
2.	exonerate	b.	atone for
3.	expiate	c.	remove obscenity
4.	extant	d.	remove blame
5.	exemplar	e.	not destroyed
6.	extirpate	f.	destroy
7.	exhort	g.	model
8.	exigent	h.	improvised
9.	expatiate	i.	urgent
10.	expurgate	j.	discuss at length

F

FACETIOUS (fuh SEE shus) *adj* playful; humorous; not serious

- It took me a while to figure out that his offer to pay me a million dollars for doing the dishes was *facetious*; it wasn't all that funny since I didn't get the joke until after I had spent an hour cleaning up.

- I hope this comment about the thirty page paper due tomorrow was *facetious*, or I'm going to be up all night writing.

FALLACY (FAL uh see) *n* an invalid or incorrect notion; a mistaken belief

- Penny refused to listen to any attempts to explain the Easter Bunny *fallacy*; every spring she went looking for a big pink fuzzy rabbit carrying baskets of chocolate eggs.

- Unfortunately, the *fallacies* of diet programs promising effortless weight loss continue to find plenty of people willing to be fooled.

FALLOW (FAL oh) *adj* untilled, inactive, dormant

- The farmer hoped that leaving the field *fallow* for a season would mean that next year he could grow a bumper crop of Brussels sprouts.

- Joe's experiment in applying agricultural principles to self-help was unsuccessful; it turns out that a mind left *fallow* for two months is not rejuvenated the way soil is.

FANATICAL (fuh NAT ik ul) *adj* zealous; single-mindedly obsessed with one thing

- The protagonist of Nick Hornby's *Fever Pitch* is *fanatical*: he is a man so obsessed with his favorite team that major life events have to be scheduled around its games.

Fanatic originated from the Latin word for temple, because possession by a god or demon could cause someone to behave *fanatically*. *Fanatic* is also the source of a very common word in today's speech: *fan*.

FASTIDIOUS (fa STID ee us) *adj* excessively particular, critical, or demanding; hard to please

- She was so extremely *fastidious* about how her house should look that rather than hire a maid she did all of the cleaning herself.

FATUOUS (FAT yoo us) *adj* silly, inanely foolish

- We suspected that the *fatuous* grin on Amy's face was evidence of a chocolate chip cookie overdose; she had eaten so many that she had become completely goofy.

- Despite the sitcom's *fatuous* dialogue, it continued to be number one in the ratings.

Fatuous often has a connotation of smugness to go along with the foolishness.

- The politician's *fatuous* remarks revealed that he was not only pompous, but also not very bright.

FAWN (fawn) *v* to flatter or praise excessively

- Hector used to think it would be great to be a rock star and have groupies *fawning* all over him; he changed his mind the first time the fans tore all his clothes off.

- Even though the press *fawned* over him incessantly, Brian was able to see though the flattery and realize that only his close friends really respected him.

FECKLESS (FEK lus) *adj* ineffectual; irresponsible

- My *feckless* brother managed to get himself grounded again, proving one more time that I am the more responsible sibling.

FELICITOUS (fi LI suh tus) *adj* apt; suitably expressed, well chosen, apropos; delightful.

- She can always be counted on for the most *felicitous* remark; she has something appropriate for every occasion.

- We found our favorite restaurant by a *felicitous* accident; we misread the directions to our planned destination and ended up someplace much better.

Felicity is the state of or something that causes happiness. *Infelicitous*, on the other hand, means unfortunate or inappropriate.

- It was an *infelicitous* mix-up when the clown and the exotic dancer got the addresses mixed up for the birthday parties at which they were supposed to perform.

FERVENT (FUR vunt) *adj* greatly emotional or zealous

- It looks as if it is going to be a long night of polka, since the band rejected our *fervent* pleas for a change in musical selection.

- Her *fervent* support of environmental protection policies led her to write over a thousand letters to Congress last year alone.

Fervor is a related word that means passion or intense emotion.

FETID (FE tud) *adj* stinking, having a heavy bad smell

- We were never able to determine exactly what the *fetid* green substance we found in the refrigerator was; no one was willing to get close enough to that horrible smell to investigate.

- The *fetid* swamp that lay between the beach and us led us to reconsider our plans for the day; staying inside with all the doors closed started sounding—and smelling—pretty good.

Quick Quiz #23

Match each word in the first column with its definition in the second column. Check your answers in the back of the book.

1.	fawn	a.	playful, humorous
2.	fallow	b.	mistaken belief
3.	fetid	c.	dormant
4.	fervent	d.	silly
5.	facetious	e.	flatter excessively
6.	felicitous	f.	irresponsible
7.	fallacy	g.	apropos
8.	feckless	h.	extremely particular
9.	fanatical	i.	zealous
10.	fatuous	j.	stinking
11.	fastidious	k.	obsessed

FETTER (FE tur) *v* to shackle, put in chains, restrain

- Fran was *fettered* in her attempts to find the hotel by her inability to speak French.

Fetters are literally shackles that are used to bind someone's feet or ankles together, but the word can also be used figuratively to mean anything that restrains.

- The image of the freedom fighter tearing off the *fetters* that bound her became a worldwide symbol of liberation.

- Responsibilities to her family and caring for her younger brothers and sisters were the *fetters* that kept Connie from pursuing her dream of acting.

Unfettered means free or unhampered.

FICKLE (FIK ul) *adj* a likeliness to casually change one's mind

- Because of his *fickle* heart he never stayed in any one relationship for too long.

- The weather in Seattle can be quite *fickle*; one day it is sunny, the next it rains.

FILIBUSTER (FIL uh bus tur) *n* intentional obstruction, usually using prolonged speechmaking to delay legislative action

- Strom Thurmond holds the record for the longest *filibuster* in the history of the U.S. Senate, speaking for more than twenty-four hours to block a bill.

Filibuster can also be used as a verb.

- The senator threatened to *filibuster* in order to stop the bill from reaching a vote.

FILIGREE (FIL uh gree) *n* an ornamental work, especially of delicate lacelike patterns; resembling such a pattern

- The decorative *filigree* of its design disguised the wrought iron fence's practical purpose.

As a verb, to *filigree* means to adorn.

- The brooch was *filigreed* with a delicate pattern of vines and grapes.

FLAG (flag) *v* to sag or droop, to become spiritless, to decline

- The fan's spirits *flagged* when the opposing team intercepted the ball in the last few minutes of the game and scored.

- Our *unflagging* efforts, aided by a few pots of coffee, were rewarded when we finished the project in time for the competition.

FLIP (flip) *adj* sarcastic, impertinent

- His *flip* remarks were intended to keep anyone from realizing how much he actually cared.

- One more *flip* answer out of you, young man, and you're going to your room without supper.

Flippant and *flippancy* probably come from this word and have related meanings.

- Her *flippant* attitude made her beloved by her classmates and distrusted by her teachers.

FLORID (FLOR id) *adj* flushed with color, ruddy, ornate

- Glen always became a little *florid* when he drank; his face became bright red.

- His *florid* prose style was perfect for romance novels, but not very well suited to his current job writing for a business magazine.

FLOUT (flowt) *v* to demonstrate contempt for

- Gertrude's reputation for *flouting* the rules was so well known that she was no longer able to get away with anything at all.

- Alice *flouted* convention by showing up for the wedding in a bathing suit and the picnic in a tuxedo.

FOMENT (FOH ment) v to stir up, incite, rouse

- Although they accused Kayla of *fomenting* the protest, she had actually been the one trying to calm everyone down.

- When Eris, the goddess of discord, threw the golden apple into the wedding to which she had not been invited, she *fomented* the conflict that would result in the Trojan War.

Be careful not to confuse this with *ferment*. Both can mean to agitate, but *ferment* usually means to cause to undergo the chemical change of *fermentation*.

FORBEARANCE (for BAYR unts) *n* patience, willingness to wait

- Lacy hoped that her professor's reputation for *forbearance* was well founded and that she would get an extension on her paper.

- You have tested my *forbearance* as far as it can go; if you don't stop drinking my milk I'm going to pour it over your head.

Forbearance can also be a legal term describing a creditor's agreement not to demand payment of a debt when it is due. For instance, if a *forbearance* is granted, you might be able to pay your student loans over a longer period of time than originally allowed.

Forbear means to refrain from and the past tense is *forbore*. The noun *forbear* is a variation of *forebear*, which is an ancestor.

FORD (ford) *v* to wade across the shallow part of a river or stream

- I may have lost my shirt and my pants while trying to *ford* the river, but at least I still had my hat when I got to the other side.

Match each word in the first column with its definition in the second column. Check your answers in the back of the book.

1.	florid	a.	shackle
2.	ford	b.	prolonged speechmaking
3.	foment	c.	delicate ornamental work
4.	flip		
5.	filibuster	d.	sag or droop
6.	filigree	e.	sarcastic
7.	forbearance	f.	ruddy
8.	fetter	g.	demonstrate contempt
9.	flag	h.	incite
10.	flout	i.	patience
11.	fickle	j.	wade across
		k.	changeable

FORESTALL (for STAHL) *v* to act in a way to hinder, exclude or prevent an action; to circumvent or thwart

- Thank goodness Louise *forestalled* any further discussion of what we were going to eat for dinner by ordering a pizza; otherwise we'd still be hungry and talking five hours later.

- The famous actress was trying to *forestall* aging by undergoing ever more bizarre therapies and cosmetic surgeries.

FORSWEAR (for SWAYR) *v* to renounce, disallow, repudiate

- *Forswearing* all previous alliances, the paranoid dictator vowed to allow no one to share his power.

- Even though she *forswore* all other vices, Gina knew she wouldn't be able to give up smoking cigars.

FORTUITOUS (for TOO uh tus) *adj* happening by fortunate accident or chance

- The movie's reliance on the heroine's *fortuitous* meeting with her long lost brother in order to provide a happy ending displeased many critics.

- How *fortuitous* that I happened to be home when the sweepstakes people stopped by to give me a million dollars!

FRACAS (FRAY kus) *n* noisy fight or quarrel, brawl

- Every good honky tonk needs a *fracas* now and again in order to maintain its reputation.

- The *fracas* that started between the two cab drivers gradually grew until it included most of the bystanders as well and turned into a small riot.

FRACTIOUS (FRAK shus) *adj* quarrelsome, rebellious, unruly, cranky

- Vince's *fractious* response to my suggestion was completely uncharacteristic, given his usually easygoing and agreeable attitude.

- The party's *fractious* internal politics made it difficult for it to gain influence, since all its members' time was spent quarreling.

- Nothing makes me more *fractious* in the morning than not being able to find a parking space when it's raining.

FROWARD (FROH urd) *adj* intractable; not willing to yield or comply; stubbornly disobedient

- Two year olds have a reputation for being *froward*; they've discovered the pleasure of saying no.

- No matter how much I pleaded and prodded, my *froward* mule refused to take a single step.

Don't confuse this with *forward*!

FRUGAL (FROO gul) *adj* prudent in saving; not wasteful

- The television program *Extreme Cheapskates* shows people at their most *frugal*.

- Because she was very *frugal* with her money, she made most of her own clothes.

FULMINATE (FUL muh nayt) *v* to attack loudly or denounce

- Since he had been *fulminating* against corporate misconduct for years, his enemies were gleeful to uncover evidence of the million-dollar payoff he received from the state's largest company.

- Grandpa Joe's favorite activity was *fulminating* against the decline of modern civilization, as evidenced by heavy metal bands and game show hosts.

FURTIVE (FUR tiv) *adj* marked by stealth; covert; surreptitious

- The dog's *furtive* attempts to steal food from the table while no one was looking were thwarted when a whole turkey came crashing to the floor.

- His *furtive* glances around the room made him look guilty, even if he wasn't really trying to hide anything.

G

GAINSAY (gayn SAY) *v* to deny, dispute, contradict, oppose

- It is difficult to *gainsay* the critics when every new movie the director makes is a flop.

- Joel refused to be *gainsaid*, insisting all along that he was right despite the evidence to the contrary.

GALVANIZE (GAL vuh nahyz) *v* to startle into sudden action, stimulate

- Her powerful speeches *galvanized* people into action.

- The team's unexpected awful performance at last week's game *galvanized* the players into working out a lot harder.

GAMBOL (GAM bul) *v* to skip about playfully, frolic

- Every March, the students performed the rites of spring by *gamboling* about half naked.

- *Gamboling* in the meadow, the lambs were the very embodiment of playful innocence.

Quick Quiz #25

Match each word in the first column with its definition in the second column. Check your answers in the back of the book.

1.	furtive	a.	avert an action
2.	fortuitous	b.	renounce
3.	forestall	c.	happening by chance
4.	gainsay	d.	noisy quarrel
5.	forswear	e.	unruly
6.	gambol	f.	unwilling to yield
7.	froward	g.	attack loudly
8.	fulminate	h.	stealthy
9.	fractious	i.	contradict
10.	fracas	j.	frolic
11.	frugal	k.	stimulate
12.	galvanize	l.	not wasteful

GARNER (GAHR nur) *v* to gather and save, store up, acquire

- The ants *garnered* food for the winter while the cricket spent the whole summer playing.

- Lester was the class clown, always playing practical jokes in an obvious attempt to *garner* attention.

GARRULOUS (GAR uh lus) *adj* pointlessly talkative, talking too much

- It was easy to see how nervous Gary was by how much he was talking; he always gets *garrulous* when he is anxious.

- My *garrulous* neighbor is very sweet, so I try not to act too impatient when she tells me yet another long meandering story.

GAUCHE (gohsh) *adj* crude, awkward, tasteless

- In some cultures it is considered *gauche* to belch loudly at the end of dinner; in others it is the height of courtesy.

This word comes from a French word meaning left, because left-handedness used to be synonyms with clumsiness and awkwardness. These days it would be *gauche* to make fun of someone for being left-handed!

GERMANE (jur MAYN) *adj* relevant to the subject at hand; appropriate in subject matter

- I love reading her column because her remarks are always *germane* and central to the most important issues of the day.

- Although his stories were seldom *germane* to the topic at hand, it was impossible not to enjoy his entertaining tangents.

GLIB (glib) *adj* marked by ease for informality; nonchalant; lacking in depth; superficial

- Although everyone had thought he was virtually guaranteed the position, his *glib* attitude during the interview made the director think he didn't care and cost him the job.

- Laurence *glibly* dismissed his critics' attacks, refusing to take them at all seriously.

GOSSAMER (GAH suh mur) *adj* delicate, insubstantial or tenuous; insincere

- The kite was made out of a *gossamer* substance that seemed hardly substantial enough to let it survive even the lightest of breezes.

- His *gossamer* promises of justice turned out just to be a way to fool everyone into thinking he planned to be true to his word.

GRANDILOQUENCE (gran DI luh kwunts) *n* pompous speech or expression

- His *grandiloquence* made him an easy target for ridicule once we all figured out he didn't even know most of the big words he used.

- The author's *grandiloquent* style gave me a headache; it was so hard to wade through all the flowery language to get to the real meaning that I gave up after an hour.

For a related word, see *bombastic*.

GREGARIOUS (gri GAYR y us) *adj* sociable; outgoing; enjoying the company of other people

- Cherie's *gregarious* nature always made her the life of the party.

- Although they are not usually known as *gregarious* creatures, some cats love to be the center of attention and want to hang out with everyone who comes to visit.

GROUSE (grows) *v* to complain or grumble

- Although I always *grouse* about my roommates and their tendency to eat all the food and leave dirty dishes and laundry lying around, I still wouldn't trade them for anything in the world.

- Ferdinand's constant *grousing* about my violin playing has finally convinced me I might need lessons.

GUILE (GYE uhl) *n* trickery, duplicity, cunning

- The wily con man used *guile* to part us from our monkey, but at least we ended up with this lovely snake oil.

- I always admired his preference for *guile* over hard work; if I'd been able to get away with it I might have tried to accomplish things by trickery instead of effort as well.

Guileless, as you might expect, means naïve or free from guile.

- His *guileless* answers convinced everyone of his complete innocence and he was acquitted of any wrongdoing.

Beguile means to deceive by guile, or to charm.

- She beguiled us all by batting her lashes, right before she picked our pockets.

Another related word is *gullible*, which means able to be *beguiled*. A person who believes anything he or she is told would be known as a *gullible* person.

H

HACKNEYED (HAK need) *adj* rendered trite or commonplace by frequent usage

- Every *hackneyed* phrase began as something other than a cliché; it only ended up on the greeting card circuit because enough people repeated it over and over.

- Despite the often *hackneyed* writing, some pulp fiction can still be fun to read.

Want to insult a writer? Then call her a *hack*, which is a writer for hire (and often carries the connotation of being worn out). The word comes from horses that were hired out to drive hackney carriages, or taxicabs.

HALCYON (HAL see un) *adj* calm and peaceful, prosperous

- I always hated it when the *halcyon* days of summer were interrupted by the start of school in the fall.

The *halcyon* was a legendary bird that was thought to be able to calm the waves so that it could nest on the sea.

HALLOW (HAL oh) *v* to set apart as holy

- The site for the new church was set aside and *hallowed* in a special ceremony.

As an adjective, *hallowed* means consecrated, or highly venerated.

- Abraham Lincoln remains one of the nation's most *hallowed* heroes.
- Graceland is *hallowed* ground for Elvis's legions of fans.

HAPPENSTANCE (HAP uhn stans) *n* a chance happening or event

- They ran into each other at the grocery aisle of the supermarket by sheer *happenstance*; neither had planned on it.

HARANGUE (huh RANG) *v* to deliver a loud, pompous speech or tirade.

- After having been *harangued* for hours about the superiority of his methods, we should be forgiven for laughing when his demonstration failed.

A *harangue* is what you deliver when you are *haranguing* someone.

HARBINGER (HAR bin jer) *n* anything that foreshadows a future event; an omen; a sign

- Many scientists note that the growing number of hurricanes and tornadoes are *harbingers* of global climate change.

HARROW (HAR oh) *v* to distress, create stress or torment

- The sadistic professor loved to *harrow* his students with *harrowing* tales of the upcoming final exam that no student in the school's history had ever passed.

HEDONISM (HEE dun izm) *n* devotion to pleasurable pursuits, especially to the pleasures of the senses

- Spring break is popularly known as a festival of *hedonism* when thousands of college students gather for a week of debauchery in the sun.
- He had to give up his *hedonistic* lifestyle once he had a full-time job; it was just too hard to get up in the morning after a long night of partying.

Someone who embraces *hedonism* is called a *hedonist*. For an antonym to *hedonist*, see the entry for *ascetic*.

HEGEMONY (hi JEM uh nee) *n* the consistent dominance or influence of one group, state, or ideology over others

- It has been argued that the United States has achieved global *hegemony* in the post-Cold War era.
- Many people point to the growing power of multinational corporations as evidence of the *hegemony* of globalization and capitalism.
- The company's *hegemonic* control over the market was threatened by the gains its competitors were making as well as by the changing economy.

HERETICAL (huh RET i kul) *adj* violating accepted dogma or convention, unorthodox

- Galileo was brought before the Inquisition because of his *heretical* agreement with Copernicus that the earth moved around the sun.

- The once *heretical* notion that computers would become more than calculating machines or toys is now so obvious that it's hard to remember when we ever thought differently.

A *heresy* is an idea that is *heretical*.

HERMETIC (hur MET ik) *adj* airtight, impervious to outside influence

- The tomb's *hermetic* seal allowed its contents to be perfectly preserved for thousands of years.

- The hermit's *hermetic* existence in a cave kept him from hearing any news of the outside world.

- We discovered that the jar had not been *hermetically* sealed when we finally identified it as the source of the nasty smell in the cupboard.

Don't confuse this with *hermeneutic*, which means explanatory or interpretive.

Match each word in the first column with its definition in the second column. Check your answers in the back of the book.

1.	hedonism	a.	chance event
2.	heretical	b.	trite from overuse
3.	hallow	c.	calm
4.	hegemony	d.	consecrate
5.	harangue	e.	deliver a tirade
6.	happenstance	f.	distress
7.	harrow	g.	devotion to pleasure
8.	halcyon	h.	dominance of one
9.	hermetic		ideology over another
10.	hackneyed	i.	unorthodox
11.	harbinger	j.	airtight
		k.	omen

HETERODOX (HET ur uh dahks) *adj* unorthodox, heretical, iconoclastic

- Einstein's *heterodox* theories changed our fundamental understanding of time and space forever.

- The designer's *heterodox* assertion that it is perfectly fine to wear white after Labor Day shocked the fashion world.

A *heterodoxy* is an idea that departs from what is accepted.

HIDEBOUND (HAYD bound) *adj* narrow or rigid in opinion, inflexible; oriented toward or confined to the past; extremely conservative

- He was *hidebound* by outdated notions of chivalry.

HIRSUTE (HUR soot) *adj* hairy, shaggy

- If he hadn't been so *hirsute*, the werewolf might have escaped detection forever and settled down into a nice, quiet life in the suburbs.

- My *hirsute* dog sheds life-size replicas of himself and still has more hair left over.

HOMILY (HAH muh lee) *n* a sermon or morally instructive lecture, a platitude

- The subject of the minister's *homilies* ranged from the importance of compassion to the virtues of brushing one's teeth three times a day.

- Spare me the *homilies*; I already know why I should do the right thing.

Homiletics is the art of preaching.

- She was famous for her *homiletic* skill; people came from all of the surrounding counties to hear her preach.

HOMOGENOUS (hu MAHJ un us) *adj* same throughout

- The town had so little influx of new people and ideas that its population seemed *homogenous* to outsiders.

- What seemed like a *homogenous* coating from a distance was really a swirl of different colors and textures when you examined it up close.

Homogenous is a less common way of expressing the same idea; the current usage of *homogenous* probably came from the word *homogenize*, which is to process a liquid so that its particles do not separate.

HORTATORY (HAWR tuh tawr ee) *adj* Urging to some course of conduct or action; encouraging

- The dean's *hortatory* commencement speech encouraged all graduates to seek their own true path.

HUBRIS (HYOO brus) *n* arrogant presumption or pride

- Icarus was destroyed by the sun god, who melted the wax in Icarus's wings as punishment for his *hubris* in daring to fly so close to the sun.

- The company president's *hubris* turned out to be his downfall when he ignored all of the warnings of the coming depression, thinking that he could predict the future on his own.

Hubris is frequently used in describing classical and epic characters, such as humans who wish to be gods and kings who think they are infallible, but the word has just as many applications in the modern world.

HYPERBOLE (hy PUR buh lee) *n* an exaggerated statement, often used as a figure of speech

- I should have realized she was using *hyperbole* when she promised me the moon and stars; that way I wouldn't have been disappointed when I only got the moon.

Something or someone that uses *hyperbole* is *hyperbolic*.

- His *hyperbolic* claims for what the company could produce next quarter made him seem unreliable, since everyone knew he was wildly exaggerating.

I

ICONOCLAST (y KAHN uh klast) *n* one who attacks or undermines traditional conventions or institutions

- Frank always insisted on being the *iconoclast*; whenever everyone else agreed to "up," he would argue for "down."

- In a sense, all great innovators are *iconoclasts* who challenge the prevailing assumptions of the day.

Iconoclastic means attacking cherished beliefs, heretical.

- Jill's *iconoclastic* attitude shocked everyone when she made an impassioned argument to the class in support of the restoration of the British monarchy's rule over America.

IDOLATRIOUS (y DAHL uh trus) *adj* given to intense or excessive devotion to something

- Jim's family realized his love of football was truly *idolatrous* when they discovered the Raiders shrine in his closet.

Idolatry is the worship of idols and images or blind devotion to something.

IDYLL (Y dul) *n* a carefree, lighthearted pastoral or romantic episode or experience, a literary or musical piece describing such

- The smell of the ocean always made me nostalgic for our summer *idyll* on the coast two years ago.

- Theocritus is generally credited with originating the poetic form of the *idyll*, although it is not entirely clear whether he wrote all the bucolic poems we currently associate with him.

Idyllic means simple or carefree.

- Our once-*idyllic* house became a nightmare when the family of kazoo players moved in next door.

IGNOMINIOUS (ig nuh MIN ee us) *adj* shameful, dishonorable, ignoble, undignified, disgraceful

- It was an *ignominious*, though deserved, end to all his boasting when the wheels fell off his car halfway through the race.

- The company president made a hasty and *ignominious* retreat from public life when it was discovered that she had been embezzling money for years.

Ignominy is dishonor or humiliation.

ILLIBERALITY (ih LIB er al ih tee) *n* quality of being narrow-minded, bigoted

- Her *illiberality* against all those poorer than her became apparent when she berated the cleaning staff.

IMBROGLIO (im BROHL yo) *n* difficult or embarrassing situation

- We could see a public relations *imbroglio* developing before our eyes when the food fight started in the senior citizens' home right as the mayor began his speech.

- Clare tried to extricate herself from the *imbroglio* she started at the party by sneaking out the back door.

IMMINENT (IM uh nunt) *adj* about to happen; impending

- Alfred had a hunch that his luck was going to improve shortly and that good fortune was *imminent*; little did he know, though, that it would show up in the form of a pink poodle.

- They say that a sound like a freight train can be a sign of a tornado's *imminent* approach.

Don't confuse this with *eminent*, which means prominent or distinguished.

IMMUTABLE (im YOO tuh bul) *adj* not capable of change

- Her position on the matter was *immutable*; no reasoning could convince her that Elvis was not alive and well and working at the car wash down the street.

- Gravity is an *immutable* force—what goes up must come down.

IMPASSIVE (im PAS iv) *adj* revealing no emotion or sensibility

- The guards at Buckingham Palace are required to be completely *impassive*; they can't show any emotion whatsoever.

- The principal remained *impassive* in the face of our most impassioned pleas; even our tears didn't move him to leniency.

Quick Quiz #28

Match each word in the first column with its definition in the second column. Check your answers in the back of the book.

1.	hubris	a.	unorthodox
2.	idyll	b.	shaggy
3.	idolatrous	c.	sermon
4.	iconoclast	d.	arrogant pride
5.	immutable	e.	exaggeration
6.	hirsute	f.	one who attacks
7.	heterodox		conventions
8.	impassive	g.	excessively devoted
9.	hyperbole	h.	carefree episode
10.	homogenous	i.	shameful
11.	imbroglio	j.	embarrassing situation
12.	ignominious	k.	about to happen
13.	homily	l.	incapable of change
14.	imminent	m.	showing no emotion
15.	hidebound	n.	same throughout
16.	hortatory	o.	narrow-minded
17.	illiberality	p.	encouraging
		q.	inflexible

IMPECUNIOUS (im pek YOON ee us) *adj* lacking funds; without money

- The *impecunious* actor was so desperate for money that he had to sacrifice his artistic principles and work as a mime for a few months.

- The worst thing about the *impecunious* life of a grad student might be the endless diet of ramen noodles.

IMPERIOUS (imm PEER ee us) *adj* commanding, masterful, arrogant, domineering, haughty

- Her *imperious* manner was extremely annoying to her employees, who thought her arrogance was unfounded since she wasn't even that bright.
- The diva dismissed us from her presence with an *imperious* wave of her hand.

IMPERTURBABLE (im pur TUR buh bul) *adj* marked by extreme calm, impassivity and steadiness

- We were in awe of the teacher's ability to remain *imperturbable* while chaos erupted in the classroom; even with twenty kindergartners running amuck, she managed to stay calm.
- Bo's usually *imperturbable* nature was put to the test when his roommate spilled cornflakes all over the couch and left without cleaning them up.

IMPETUOUS (im PECH oo us) *adj* hastily or rashly energetic; impulsive and vehement

- We regretted our *impetuous* decision to spend our vacation in Greenland when we realized we hadn't packed any warm clothing.
- John's *impetuous* nature kept him from planning anything in advance, but somehow everything always seemed to work out in the end.

IMPLACABLE (im PLAK uh bul) *adj* not capable of being appeased or significantly changed

- Her anger over her partner's betrayal was *implacable*; nothing anyone said or did would appease her.
- Because I have an *implacable* fear of dentists, I haven't been to see one in twenty years and now only have two teeth left.

IMPORTUNE (imp or TOON) *v* to ask incessantly, beg, nag

- Jerry's constant *importuning* for time off worked in a way; he had plenty of time off once he was fired for nagging his boss about a vacation.

Importunate means persistent in asking.

- Leslie is an *importunate* borrower of clothing; I'm not sure she even owns any of her own clothes since she is always asking to borrow other people's stuff.

IMPUDENT (IM pyuh dunt) *adj* shamelessly bold; insolent, impertinent

- John's *impudent* personality on stage enthralled his fans; unfortunately, it also alienated his fellow band members.

The characteristic of being *impudent* is called *impudence*.

- Adonia was frequently punished in school for her *impudence*.

IMPUGN (im PYOON) *v* attack or assail verbally, censure, execrate, deny

- Although the paper *impugned* his motives for resigning, claiming that he did it to hide his misdeeds, most people still believed he did it for virtuous reasons.

- The candidate's attempt to *impugn* his opponent's voting record backfired when it merely brought to light his own poor attendance record.

IMPUNITY (im PYOON i tee) *n* immunity from punishment, penalty, or harm

- Barry the bully was able to terrorize the schoolyard with *impunity* because he was always able to look completely innocent whenever any authority figures were around.

- It is only possible to lie on a bed of nails with *impunity* if the nails are close enough together that the force per unit area is not enough to break the skin; in other words, don't try this at home without a physicist handy.

IMPUTE (im PYOOT) *v* to attribute to a cause or source, ascribe, assign as a characteristic

- The mechanic *imputed* my car's failure to start to the absence of any gasoline in the tank.

- My dance partner kindly *imputed* by fall to a slippery floor, when in reality my two left feet were the cause.

Quick Quiz #29

Match each word in the first column with its definition in the second column. Check your answers in the back of the book.

1.	imperious	a.	without money
2.	importune	b.	domineering
3.	implacable	c.	extremely calm
4.	impugn	d.	impulsive
5.	impute	e.	incapable of being appeased
6.	impecunious		
7.	imperturbable	f.	beg
8.	impetuous	g.	attack verbally
9.	impudent	h.	immunity from punishment
10.	impunity	i.	ascribe
		j.	impertinent

INALIENABLE (in AYL ee uh bul) *adj* cannot be transferred

Generally, we hear this word with the word "rights," as in *inalienable rights*.

- The Declaration of Independence states that man is endowed with certain *inalienable* rights; unfortunately, the author failed to specify whether those rights were also applicable to woman.

INCHOATE (in KOH ut) *adj* in an initial stage, not fully formed

- Drat, our plan for world domination is still *inchoate*; how will we finalize it before the deadline tomorrow?

- It was amazing to realize that the *inchoate* blob in front of us would become a delicate vase when the glassblower was done.

For a word with a similar definition, see *nascent*.

INCIPIENT (in SIP ee unt) *adj* beginning to come into being or to become apparent

- I could sense the dull throbbing in my head that was the sign of an *incipient* headache; I knew it was only a matter of time before it had developed into a full-fledged migraine.

- Marta rushed to stop the *incipient* unrest that began when the food and drink ran out at the part.

INDECOROUS (in DEK er uhs) *adj* violating generally accepted standards of good taste or propriety, unseemly

- Picking one's nose in public is generally considered *indecorous* behavior.

- Slurping one's soup is considered *indecorous* in the United States, but is considered a sign that one enjoys one's meal in Japan.

INDEFATIGABLE (in di FAT i guh bul) *adj* not easily exhaustible, tireless, dogged

- Her *indefatigable* good humor was legendary; she never seemed out of sorts no matter how annoying everyone around her was.

- Although I tried to convince myself I was *indefatigable*, I started to suspect I would have to be carried the last few miles of the hike.

- His *indefatigability* paid off when he won the dance contest after dancing for fourteen hours straight.

INDEMNIFY (in DEM nuh fahy) *adj* to guard or secure against anticipated loss

- The homeowner's insurance policy *indemnified* him from loss of any property due to inclement weather.

INDIFFERENT (in DIF u runt) *adj* having no interest or concern, apathetic; showing no bias or prejudice

Indifferent is a multifunctional word. It can mean having no interest in something, but it can also mean having no bias, which should remind you of all that confusion around disinterested and uninterested. It can also mean not good or bad, not too much or too little, and neither right nor wrong.

- Maria was *indifferent* about wine and could never understand all that sniffing, swirling, and sipping people seemed to care so much about.

- He may have been an *indifferent* musician, but he was a brilliant composer.

- Her reputation as an *indifferent* judge made all sides trust her; it was her indifference that made the two parties agree to accept her judgment as final.

INDOLENT (IN duh lunt) *adj* lazy, listless, torpid

- Alex was so *indolent* that he hired other people to wash his hands for him.

The noun form of *indolent* is *indolence*.

- It seemed paradoxical that Anna so wished for a life of *indolence* that she worked very hard all the time to be able to afford it.

For a synonym, see *phlegmatic*.

INELUCTABLE (in i LUKT uh bul) *adj* certain, inevitable

- George refused to accept the *ineluctable* reality of death, so he planned to have himself frozen.

- The outcome of the game seemed *ineluctable* once the score was 156 to 14.

INERT (in URT) *adj* unmoving, lethargic, sluggish, not reactive chemically

- Once it hits ninety degrees Fahrenheit and ninety percent humidity, I become completely *inert*; I can't even move at that point.

- Helium and argon are two of the *inert* gases, which do not react with much of anything.

- The bureaucracy had become effectively *inert*; everyone was so bogged down in paperwork that nothing ever moved through the system.

INGENUOUS (in JEN yoo us) *adj* artless, frank and candid, lacking in sophistication

- His *ingenuous* question revealed how naïve he was, but his *ingenuousness* was actually refreshing in this group of cynical, scheming old men.

Disingenuous means lacking in candor, calculating, duplicitous.

- I suspected that his sudden interest in my research was *disingenuous*; he really just wanted an invitation to the party I was hosting.

Be careful not to confuse *ingenuous* with *ingenious*, which means characterized by skill and imagination.

INHERENT (in HEER int) *adj* ingrained within one's nature, intrinsic, firmly established, essential

- His *inherent* skill at spatial relations reasoning was revealed when he solved the Rubik's cube at the age of two.
- Some people believe that self-interest is *inherent* in human nature; others argue that it is a learned characteristic.
- It was *inherent* to the plot that the protagonist dies; without his death, the story would have made no sense.

Inhere means to be *inherent* or innate to something.

- The age-old conflict that *inheres* in the parent-child relationship as the child reaches adolescence was not going to be resolved today.

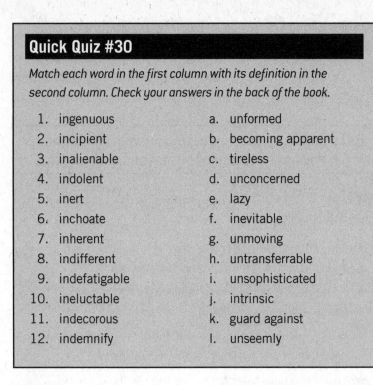

Quick Quiz #30

Match each word in the first column with its definition in the second column. Check your answers in the back of the book.

1.	ingenuous	a.	unformed
2.	incipient	b.	becoming apparent
3.	inalienable	c.	tireless
4.	indolent	d.	unconcerned
5.	inert	e.	lazy
6.	inchoate	f.	inevitable
7.	inherent	g.	unmoving
8.	indifferent	h.	untransferrable
9.	indefatigable	i.	unsophisticated
10.	ineluctable	j.	intrinsic
11.	indecorous	k.	guard against
12.	indemnify	l.	unseemly

INIMICAL (i NIM i kul) *adj* damaging, harmful, injurious, hostile, unfriendly

- While the Antarctic is *inimical* to most animal and plant life, some organisms nevertheless manage to survive there.

- He seemed *inimical* to my overtures of friendship, refusing even to talk to me.

For a synonym for *inimical*, look ahead to *pernicious*.

INIMITABLE (i NIM muh tuh bul) *adj* one of a kind, peerless

- His *inimitable* feats of daring on the trapeze were so audacious that no one else even tried to imitate them.

- She lived up to every expectation when she arrived at the party decked out in ostrich feathers and sequins in her usual *inimitable* style.

INIQUITY (i NIK wuh tee) *n* wickedness, gross injustice

- The *iniquity* of the judgment was so blatant that there was immediate worldwide protest of its unfairness.

- Having suffered under the *iniquity* of the dictator's rule for decades, the citizens understandably celebrated the overthrow of his regime.

Iniquitous means characterized by wickedness.

INJUDICIOUS (in joo DISH us) *adj* showing lack of judgment, unwise, imprudent, indiscreet

- He proved to be so highly *injudicious* in his handling of the affair that the situation soon turned into a disaster.

- She was an *injudicious* friend who could not be trusted to keep a secret.

INNERVATE (i NUR vayt) *v* to supply with nerves, energize

Innervate is usually used to describe a physiological process, as in the fibers that innervate the facial muscles, but it can also be used metaphorically.

- *Innervated* by our coach's pep talk, we were filled with energy for the upcoming game.

Don't confuse this with *enervate*, which is also in this book. Their definitions and pronunciations are very different.

INNOCUOUS (i NAHK yoo us) *adj* harmless; causing no damage

- The poisonous-looking brew turned out to be *innocuous*; it didn't taste very good, but it didn't cause any harm.

- At least her practical jokes are *innocuous*, even if they are annoying.

If you associate this word with *inoculate*, which means to protect, good ear! They don't have the same root, but the association can help you remember the meaning of *innocuous*.

INSCRUTABLE (in SKROOT uh bul) *adj* incapable of being discovered or understood, mysterious

- Her expression was *inscrutable*; I couldn't tell whether she liked the present or not.
- Quantum mechanics is *inscrutable* to me, so I've given up even trying to understand it.

INSENSIBLE (in SENS uh bul) *adj* unconscious, unresponsive, unaware, unaffected, numb

- He lay *insensible* on the field after being hit in the head by a baseball.
- I am not *insensible* of your suffering; I just don't care.
- She was *insensible* to his entreaties, refusing to take him back no matter how much he pleaded.

Note the subtle difference in the last two sentences: *insensible* of your suffering means unaware of it (i.e., "I know you're suffering, but in this case I just don't care.") and *insensible* to his entreaties means unresponsive to them.

INSIPID (in SIP ud) *adj* without taste or flavor, lacking in spirit, dull

- This *insipid* stew is in desperate need of some hot sauce.
- Henry's sense of humor was so *insipid* that he thought all knock-knock jokes were funny.

INSOUCIANT (in SOO see unt) *adj* unconcerned, carefree, nonchalant

- Her *insouciant* attitude toward her schoolwork means that she rarely turned in her papers or bothered to study for a test.
- *Insouciance* may be charming in a friend, but is often annoying in a co-worker if you end up doing his work for him.

INSULAR (IN suh lur) *adj* parochial, narrow-minded, like an island

- The small fishing community have a very *insular* attitude toward outsiders, viewing them as strange and generally distrusting them.

- The *insularity* of his upbringing was reflected in the narrow-mindedness of his views.

The primary definition of *insular* means relating to an island, and *insulate*, meaning to set off in a detached position, comes from the same root.

Quick Quiz #31

Match each word in the first column with its definition in the second column. Check your answers in the back of the book.

1.	insouciant	a.	harmful
2.	iniquity	b.	one of a kind
3.	inscrutable	c.	wickedness
4.	inimitable	d.	supply with nerves
5.	inimical	e.	harmless
6.	insipid	f.	incapable of being understood
7.	innervate		
8.	insular	g.	unconscious
9.	insensible	h.	bland
10.	innocuous	i.	carefree
11.	injudicious	j.	narrow-minded
		k.	unwise

INTERDICT (in tur DIKT) *v* prohibit, forbid, ban, halt

- Although Prohibition attempted to *interdict* the sale of alcohol, it was never entirely successful.

An *interdiction* is a prohibition against something.

- My parents' *interdiction* against my going out on a school night never worked as long as I was able to sneak out the window without getting caught.

INTIMATE (IN tim ayt) *v* to imply, suggest or insinuate

- I'm shocked that you would *intimate* that I borrowed your car without asking; just because I have the keys in my hand doesn't mean I would ever think of doing such a thing!

- The governor *intimated* that he might run for Congress, but coyly refused to commit one way or the other.

An *intimation* is a hint.

- Her *intimations* that I might get the job only made me more nervous.

INTRACTABLE (in TRAK tuh bul) *adj* not easily managed or directed, stubborn, obstinate

- He was the most *intractable* child I have ever met; nothing I tried would get him to brush his teeth or go to bed.

- Poverty remains one of the most *intractable* problems of modern society.

INTRANSIGENT (in TRANS i junt) *adj* refusing to compromise

- He was an *intransigent* supporter of the tax cut, refusing to compromise even the slightest bit.

- Her *intransigence* in the face of all opposing arguments would almost have been impressive if it weren't so darn frustrating.

INTREPID (in TRE pud) *adj* steadfast, courageous

- The *intrepid* explorers continued on despite the harsh conditions.

- Lois Lane and Jimmy Olsen were *intrepid* journalists, daring to investigate under dangerous circumstances, so it was a good thing Superman was around to save them when they got into trouble.

INUNDATE (IN un dayt) *v* to cover or overwhelm, to flood

- Because the village sits in a basin, it is easily *inundated* when river levels rise and there is no escape route for the water.
- Legend has it that the mail-order company was so *inundated* with orders in its early years that it occasionally burned order slips to get rid of them.

Inundation is the noun form of *inundate*.

INURED (in OORD) *adj* accustomed to accepting something undesirable

- I have become *inured* to waking up at 5 a.m.; I still don't like it, but at least I'm used to it.
- Her co-workers were so *inured* to her sarcasm that they no longer took it personally.

INVEIGH (in VAY) *v* to attack verbally, denounce, deprecate

- The students *inveighed* bitterly against the new dress code, complaining that the orange shirt and red pants not only limited their freedom of expression but were also ugly.
- *Inveighing* against the government's policies will do you no good if you don't bother to vote as well.

INVEIGLE (in VAY gul) *v* to obtain by deception or flattery

- I can't believe she *inveigled* a ticket to the concert; I've been trying to get one for weeks.
- Once I realized what he was up to, his attempts to *inveigle* me out of telling his girlfriend where he'd been were unsuccessful.

INVETERATE (in VET u rut) *adj* deep routed, ingrained, habitual

- Tim was such an *inveterate* liar that he lied even when he thought he was telling the truth.

- Her *inveterate* preference for chocolate over vanilla ice cream had stayed the same for fifty years.

Inherent is a close synonym for *inveterate*.

INVIDIOUS (in VID ee us) *adj* tending to arouse envy or ill will in others

- The promotion was important to Sven's career; however, it meant that for a while, he was in the *invidious* position of supervising his former coworkers.

When *invidious* is used to describe a distinction or comparison, it means discriminatory.

- It was *invidious* to give preferential treatment to one group of graduate students over the other, but no one was likely to question the tenured professor.

IRASCIBLE (eer A suh bul) *adj* easily angered; prone to temperamental outbursts

- *Irascible* to the end, the grouchy old man started a fight on his deathbed.

- My roommate is so *irascible* that I always check for the sound of flying objects before I open the door.

GRE Power Vocab

Quick Quiz #32

Match each word in the first column with its definition in the second column. Check your answers in the back of the book.

1.	inveigh	a.	prohibit
2.	intransigent	b.	insinuate
3.	inveterate	c.	stubborn
4.	inveigle	d.	refusing to compromise
5.	intimate	e.	courageous
6.	inundate	f.	accustomed to
7.	irascible	g.	denounce
8.	inured	h.	obtain by deception
9.	interdict	i.	ingrained
10.	intrepid	j.	temperamental
11.	invidious	k.	arousing envy
12.	intractable	l.	overwhelm

ITINERATE (y TIN uh rut) *v* to travel from place to place

- After years of *itinerating*, never staying in one place for more than a couple of months, he finally settled down and bought a house.

Itinerant is an adjective that means traveling from place to place.

- The *itinerant* laborers followed the harvest from county to county.

J

JEJUNE (ji JYOON) *adj* vapid, uninteresting; childish, immature; lacking nutrition

- The *jejune* lecture on various ways to wash clothes had us half-asleep after ten minutes.

- His *jejune* response to our questions revealed how young he was despite his apparent age.

- After surviving on a *jejune* diet of saltines and ginger ale during my illness, I was ready for a more nutritious meal.

JIBE (jyb) *v* to agree, to be in accord

- Since their accounts of the evening's events didn't *jibe*, we knew at least one of them wasn't telling the full truth.

- I was relieved to find that my account balance *jibed* with my calculations so that I didn't bounce a check.

JOCOSE (joh KOHS) *adj* given to joking; humorous

- The *jocose* man could always be counted on for some levity, but it was almost impossible to get him to stop joking even for a minute.

Jocular is very similar to *jocose*, but *jocund* is slightly different in that it means high-spirited rather than specifically humorous. *Jocularity* is fun characterized by humor.

K

KINETIC (ki NET ik) *adj* having to do with motion; lively; active

A *kinetic* personality is a lively, active, moving personality.

- Our new public relations hire has a *kinetic* personality.

L

LABILE (LAY byl) *adj* readily open to change, unstable

- He was so emotionally *labile* that he could be crying one minute and laughing the next.

- Radioactive isotopes are *labile* because they undergo change.

LACHRYMOSE (LAK ri mohs) *adj* causing tears, tearful, showing sorrow

- His *lachrymose* apology didn't move me; he was going to have to do a lot more than shed a few tears before I was ready to forgive him.

- Beth's *lachrymose* portrayal of the heroine didn't work very well since the play was supposed to be a comedy.

LACONIC (luh KAHN ik) *adj* using few words; terse

- We took her "good" as high praise indeed, since that was more than our *laconic* band teacher usually said in a whole week.

- His *laconic* public persona was just a front; once you got to know him he wouldn't shut up.

Need an antonym? *Garrulous* and *loquacious* are both opposites to *laconic*.

LASSITUDE (LAS uh tood) *n* listlessness, languor, weariness

- Those two push-ups I attempted filled me with *lassitude* for the rest of the day.

- It wouldn't be so bad to be in a constant state of *lassitude* as long as I could have someone to wave palm fronds over me and feed me grapes, since I would be too exhausted to do it myself.

LAUD (lahd) *v* to praise highly

- His first novel was so universally *lauded* that it seemed almost impossible that his second book could live up to the expectations.

- It is a good idea to *laud* your partner's skills at house cleaning; otherwise you'll just end up having to do more of it yourself.

LAVISH (LAV ish) *adj* extravagant

- No expense was spared in giving the astronauts a *lavish* homecoming, complete with welcome feasts and a parade down Fifth Avenue, after their arduous mission.

As a verb, to *lavish* is to bestow something in great quantities, or to cover liberally.

LETHARGIC (luh THAR jik) *adj* characterized by lethargy or sluggishness

- Though Ryan loves to run through 18 holes of disc golf in 100-degree weather, I am left too *lethargic* to so much as pick up my bag.

The noun form of *lethargic* is *lethargy*.

- Ben can sit on the balcony for hours doing almost nothing, but his seeming *lethargy* is actually an intense concentration that most people don't reach because of all of their activity.

LIBERTINE (LIB ur teen) *n* someone unrestrained by morality or convention or leading a dissolute life

- We discovered that she was quite the *libertine* when it was revealed that she was having affairs on three different continents at the same time.

- Casanova has become the archetypal *libertine* in popular culture, the very embodiment of a single-minded pursuit of pleasure.

Libertine can also be an adjective, as in his *libertine* disregard for the moral conventions of the day.

Quick Quiz #33

Match each word in the first column with its definition in the second column. Check your answers in the back of the book.

1.	lassitude	a.	travel around
2.	jejune	b.	immature
3.	laud	c.	agree with
4.	labile	d.	joking
5.	jocose	e.	open to change
6.	laconic	f.	tearful
7.	itinerate	g.	lively
8.	lavish	h.	listlessness
9.	libertine	i.	praise highly
10.	jibe	j.	unrestrained by morality
11.	lethargic	k.	sluggish
12.	lachrymose	l.	extravagant
13.	kinetic	m.	terse

LIMN (lim) *v* to draw, outline in detail

- The painter *limned* the old man's face in such exquisite and expressive lines that it almost looked as if he might open his mouth and speak.

- The surveyors *limned* the valley in order to provide an exact topographical map for the construction crew to follow.

LIMPID (LIM pud) *adj* transparent, serene, clear and simple in style, untroubled

- The once-*limpid* pond had become a nasty soup of algae, beer cans, and a random tennis shoe or two.

- The article's *limpid* style was a welcome break from the dense and convoluted theoretical stuff I'd been reading for days' in other words, its *limpidity* was a relief.

LIONIZE (LAHY uh nahyz) *v* to treat something as an object of great interest or importance; to treat a person as a celebrity

- He was *lionized* everywhere after winning the Nobel Prize in medicine.

- Modern society has come to *lionize* wealth and business success.

LIST (list) *v* to tilt or lean to one side

- The ship *listed* to one side after running aground on a rock and filling partially with water.

- After a little too much celebrating, he was *listing* badly to one side and threatening to topple over as he walked up the front steps.

LOQUACIOUS (loh KWAY shus) *adj* extremely talkative

- I knew something had to be wrong when my usually *loquacious* friend didn't say a word for two whole minutes.

- His *loquacity* was legendary; in fact, he held the county record for uninterrupted talking at three days, ten hours and fourteen minutes.

LUCID (LOO sud) *adj* intelligible, sound, clear

- The *lucid* water in the tidepool allowed us to see the bottom clearly.

- Despite the *lucidity* of Lucia's explanation, which allowed me to understand the concept for the first time, I remained skeptical about the method's practicality.

LUMBER (LUM bur) *v* to move heavily and clumsily or with a rumbling sound

- The truck *lumbered* about like a drunken dinosaur.
- His usually *lumbering* gait gave no hint to his remarkable grace as a skater.

LUMINOUS (LOO muh nus) *adj* characterized by brightness and the emission of light, enlightened, clear

- The *luminous* stars and full moon made it as bright as if it were the middle of the day.
- It was amazing that he could write such *luminous* prose when his speech was so confusing and thoughtless.

Many words having to do with light have the same root, such as *illuminate* and even *luster*. Just remember Lumiere, the candle from the animated *Beauty and the Beast*, and you have your word association.

M

MAGNANIMITY (mag nuh NIM i tee) *n* the quality of being generously noble in mind and heart, especially in forgiving

- Her *magnanimity* in forgiving all those who had opposed her ensured that she would be well liked even by her former enemies.
- He was *magnanimous* to a fault; he would give his last penny to anyone who asked for it.

MALEVOLENT (muh LE voh lent) *adj* having or showing often vicious ill will, spite, or hatred

- The *malevolent* villain was so mean that she didn't even like puppies or flowers; now that's mean!

- It's a good thing that his *malevolence* was only matched by his inability to plan things; a lot more of his evil plots would have worked out if he hadn't gotten the timing wrong.

Have you ever noticed how many words beginning with *mal-* mean bad things? *Malevolent*, *malignant*, *malfunction*...the list goes on. Words beginning with *ben-*, on the other hand, tend to have positive meanings. Refer to the entry for *benign* for some examples.

MALFEASANCE (mal FEE zuhns) *n* the performance of a public official of an act that is harmful or illegal

- The police in Ferguson, Missouri, were accused of *malfeasance* after shooting an unarmed man.

- The governor of Illinois was accused of *malfeasance* when he attempted to sell the vacant Senate seat.

MALINGER (muh LING ur) *v* to feign illness so as to avoid work

- Her boss suspected her of *malingering* until she brought a note from her doctor.

- If I were you, I'd take "expert *malingerer*" off my resume.

MALLEABLE (MAL ee uh bul) *adj* capable of being shaped or formed, easily influenced

- I wouldn't put too much importance on his agreement with your argument; he's so *malleable* that he's likely to agree with the next person he meets as well.

- Gold's *malleability* makes it a useful metal for jewelry, since it is so easy to shape.

Quick Quiz #34

Match each word in the first column with its definition in the second column. Check your answers in the back of the book.

1. magnanimity
2. lucid
3. malleable
4. malevolent
5. list
6. malinger
7. limpid
8. limn
9. lumber
10. luminous
11. loquacious
12. lionize
13. malfeasance

a. outline in detail
b. clear
c. lean to one side
d. easily understood
e. move clumsily
f. talkative
g. generously noble
h. spiteful
i. avoid work by pretending illness
j. pliable
k. bright
l. wrongdoing by public official
m. treat as a celebrity

MARTIAL (MAR shul) *adj* associated with war and the armed forces

- When civil war broke out, the military imposed *martial* law for the duration of the conflict.

- Sparta was known for its *martial* culture, in which almost every aspect of life was tied into preparing for battle.

MARTINET (mar ti NET) *n* a rigid disciplinarian

- Sister Paul Marie is a sweet and generous person, but she is a *martinet* when it comes to teaching grammar, and few people passed her class on the first try.

The adjective form of *martinet* is *martinetish*.

- My *martinetish* study hall teacher didn't make my sixth period very relaxing, but boy did I get my homework done!

The word *martinet* is named for Jean Martinet, a seventeenth-century French drillmaster who insisted on absolute adherence to the rules.

MAUNDER (MAHN dur) *v* to talk or move aimlessly, mutter

- After we *maundered* about for over three hours I started to suspect that our guide didn't have the slightest idea where he was going.

- His endless *maundering* on about nothing started to get on my nerves until I wanted to shout, "Get to the point!"

MAVERICK (MAV rik) *n* an independent individual who does not go along with a group or party

- Always the *maverick*, Lola insisted on going right whenever everyone else went left.

Maverick can also be an adjective.

- The *maverick* politician refused to seek safety in numbers by following the consensus; instead, she stuck to her principles regardless of the consequences to her popularity.

Technically, a *maverick* is an unbranded animal such as a cow.

MELANCHOLY (MEL un kahl ee) *adj* tending toward sadness

- Hamlet is the epitome of a *melancholy* character: he dresses in black, talks to skulls, and rambles on at length about whether to kill himself.

According to Aristotle, too much liver bile caused *melancholy* personalities. This book contained vocabulary words based on three other personality types that he identified based on bodily fluids... can you find the rest?

MELLIFLUOUS (mel I floo us) *adj* sweetly flowing, usually used to describe words or sounds

- The *mellifluous* sound of her voice lulled me to sleep, though this wasn't what she had in mind since she was trying to chastise me.

- The *mellifluous* tones of the quartet's performance made the audience smile.

MENDACITY (men DAS uh tee) *n* the condition of being untruthful, dishonesty

- Pinocchio was never able to hide his *mendacity*; whenever he lied his nose grew longer.

Mendacious means false, untruthful.

- I have never met a more *mendacious* child; imagine him telling me that the teapot on my head is silly, when everyone knows it is the height of fashion!

MENDICANT (MEN dih kunt) *n* a beggar, supplicant

- The tourist was horrified to see the number of *mendicants* begging on the streets, not realizing that there were millions of homeless people reduced to *mendicancy* on the streets of his own country as well.

- *Mendicant* orders are religious organizations, such as the Franciscans, that have renounced all material wealth and survive by begging.

MERCURIAL (muh KYOOR ee ul) *adj* characterized by rapid and unpredictable change in mood

- The *mercurial* weather went from sunshine to hail and back in less than an hour.

- Mercutio from Shakespeare's *Romeo and Juliet* is a perfect example of a *mercurial* personality; his moods flit from one extreme to the other in the short time he is on stage.

Things that change rapidly or move quickly are often named after the Greek god Mercury. The metal used in thermometers and the closest planet to the sun are prime examples.

MERETRICIOUS (mer uh TRI shus) *adj* tawdry, pretentious, attractive but false, showy, having to do with prostitution

- His *meretricious* argument had all the false allure of a low-rent Vegas nightclub: showy on the outside, but seedy and desperate on the inside.

METICULOUS (muh TIK yoo lus) *adj* characterized by extreme care and precision, attentive to detail

- Her desk was so *meticulous* that every pen was lined up exactly the same distance apart.

- His *meticulous* planning of every aspect of the conference paid off when the whole week went exactly according to plan.

Quick Quiz #35

Match each word in the first column with its definition in the second column. Check your answers in the back of the book.

1.	meretricious	a.	having to do with war
2.	mellifluous	b.	stray from the path
3.	meticulous	c.	independent individual
4.	maverick	d.	sweetly flowing
5.	martial	e.	dishonesty
6.	mendicant	f.	beggar
7.	mercurial	g.	unpredictable
8.	martinet	h.	cheap, showy
9.	mendacity	i.	extremely precise
10.	maunder	j.	disciplinarian
11.	melancholy	k.	sad

GRE Power Vocab

METTLESOME (MET ul sum) *adj* courageous, high-spirited

- The *mettlesome* doctor risked his own life to try to save the wounded soldiers on both sides.

- She was a *mettlesome* child, always proud and unruly.

Be careful. Not only does this word have the two subtly different meanings of "courageous" and "high-spirited," but it is also very easy to confuse it with other, similar words. Watch out for *meddlesome*, meaning inclined to interfere, and *nettlesome*, meaning prickly or difficult. Remembering that mettle means courage and stamina will help.

MILITATE (MIL i tayt) *v* to have weight or bearing on, to argue (against)

- The president's advisors warned him that the volatility of the situation *militated* against any rash action.

- The presence of polite company *militates* against my telling you exactly what I think of your underhanded scheming, but as soon as we're alone you'd better watch out.

Occasionally *militate* is used to mean arguing for, though it usually used to mean arguing against.

- His phenomenal record *militates* in favor of his consideration for the job.

MILK (milk) *v* to exploit, to squeeze every last ounce of

- I *milked* my sprained ankle for as much sympathy as I could; pretty soon I had people cooking me dinner and cleaning my house.

- My big plans for *milking* my parents' absence for all the fun I could get out of it were thwarted when they returned home before the party even started.

MINATORY (MIN uh tor ee) *adj* menacing, threatening

- Disregarding the *minatory* signs, we opened the door and discovered that the ferocious dog that the sign had warned us about was a dachshund—a fairly assertive dachshund, but only a 20-pound dog nonetheless.

According to an ancient Greek myth, the Minotaur was a creature that guarded the Labyrinth, eating all who dared come inside. Athenian youths were sacrificed to the Minotaur before Theseus killed it, leaving the word *minatory* in its place.

MINCE (mints) *v* pronounce or speak affectedly or too carefully, euphemized, take tiny steps, tiptoe

- Don't *mince* words with me; just come right out and tell me exactly what you think.

- The five-inch heels and straitjacket she wore for Halloween forced her to take little *mincing* steps to keep from falling over.

MISANTHROPE (MIS un throhp) *n* one who hates humankind

- Kate was surprised to discover that she had a reputation as a *misanthrope*, because really she was just very shy.

Misanthropic is an adjective that means "hating humankind."

- Traffic jams tend to bring out the *misanthropic* worst in people, since everyone just starts hating everyone else.

For an antonym, see *philanthropic*.

MISOGYNIST (mis AH jin ist) *n* one who hates women

- The professor had a reputation for being a *misogynist*, which explained why not only none of the female grad students, but also most of the male students didn't want to work with him, despite his supposed brilliance.

- The song's *misogynist* lyrics sparked massive protests by feminists.

Misogynist and *misogynistic* are both regarded as acceptable forms for the adjective.

MITIGATE (MIT uh gayt) *v* to make or become less severe or intense, moderate

- Discovering that I had the date wrong *mitigated* some of the pain of having no one show up to my birthday party.

- Turning on the heater *mitigated* the extreme cold in the living room; why didn't we think of that earlier?

A *mitigating* circumstance doesn't change whether a person is guilty or not, but it may lessen the severity of the punishment (it *mitigates* the severity). *Unmitigated* means absolute or unrelieved.

- My attempt to tango was an *unmitigated* disaster.

MOLLIFY (MAH luh fy) *v* to calm or soothe, reduce in emotional intensity

- After stepping on her tail, I tried to *mollify* the cat by scratching her head and giving her some milk.

- He seemed somewhat *mollified* by my promise to buy him two scoops of ice cream to replace the one that fell on the ground; at least he stopped crying long enough to agree.

Emollient is a related word that can either be an adjective or a noun, and you may well recognize it from advertisements for body lotion; see the entry under *emollient* for more details.

MONOTONY (muh NAHT un ee) *n* tedious lack of variety or change

- One would think that life on a desert island would be filled with *monotony*, but in fact, foraging and hunting for food makes one's days quite exciting.

This word comes from *monotone*, which means one sound. If you think about someone's voice droning on with no change in the pitch, you'll get a pretty good idea of the meaning of *monotony*. The adjective form of this word is *monotonous*.

MOROSE (muh ROHS) *adj* sad, sullen, melancholy

- I knew from the *morose* expression on his face that it would be a bad idea to ask Kent how he did in the competition.
- Although it is easy to be *morose* during the long, cold, wet, gloomy winter in Seattle, it is much more difficult to be sad during the summer when it is sunny and everyone else is happy.

Quick Quiz #36

Match each word in the first column with its definition in the second column. Check your answers in the back of the book.

1.	mollify	a.	courageous
2.	morose	b.	have bearing on
3.	misanthrope	c.	exploit
4.	misogynist	d.	menacing
5.	mince	e.	take tiny steps or speak too carefully
6.	mettlesome	f.	hater of humankind
7.	militate	g.	hater of women
8.	milk	h.	make less severe
9.	monotony	i.	calm
10.	minatory	j.	melancholy
11.	mitigate	k.	lack of change

GRE Power Vocab

MULTIFACETED (mul ty FAS it id) *adj* having many aspects

- It seemed at first to be an open-and-shut robbery case, but soon detectives uncovered so many twists and turns that it seems as *multifaceted* as a dodecahedron.

Literally, *multifaceted* means having many facets or faces, like a diamond. Figuratively, it can mean versatile.

MULTIFARIOUS (mul tuh FER ee us) *adj* varied, motley, greatly diversified

- The objects of his *multifarious* crushes ranged from Katherine Hepburn to the cashier at the grocery store.

- I love to sit and watch the *multifarious* activity at any train station—the variety of people and places they are going is endlessly fascinating.

MUNDANE (mun DAYN) *adj* of the world, typical of or concerned with the ordinary

- Todd was always complaining that he shouldn't have to deal with all the *mundane* details of life, because he was going to be a famous rock star very soon.

- Some people may prefer the lofty philosophical questions about angels dancing on the heads of pins, but I'm more concerned with the *mundane* questions, like where are we going to eat lunch?

N

NADIR (NAY deer) *n* low point, perigee

- Being presented with the "Nice Try" award for finishing in last place was definitely the *nadir* of my professional pinochle career.

- Liver-flavored tapioca with pickled pretzels truly marked the *nadir* of Darryl's cooking experiments.

For an antonym, go to the entry for *apogee*.

NASCENT (NAY sunt) *adj* coming into being; in early developmental stages

- I could always tell when Richard had a *nascent* plan developing, because he got this faraway devious look in his eyes.

- The *nascent* truce between the warring groups was tenuous, and would need intensive diplomatic cooperation in order to grow into a stronger and lasting relationship.

NATTY (NA tee) *adj* trimly neat and tidy, dapper

- My grandmother is always complaining that there are no more *natty* dressers; she just doesn't think that baggy jeans and sneakers can compete with the zoot suits of her adolescence.

NEBULOUS (NEB yoo lus) *adj* vague, cloudy, lacking clearly defined form

- Unfortunately, we were so excited about the prospect of discovering buried treasure that we hadn't noticed how *nebulous* Hannah's plan was for finding it.

- All we could see of the dust storm as it approached was a *nebulous* gray mass.

Nebulous can also mean relating to a nebula, which has several meanings dealing with cloudiness and diffuse particles, but is generally known as a body of interstellar dust or gas.

NEOLOGISM (nee AH luh ji zim) *n* a new word, expression, or usage; the creation or use of new words or senses

- "Eco-chic," "urbanwear," and "technophile" are examples of recent *neologisms*, just as "TV," "bobby socker," and "UFO" once were.

- My least favorite *neologisms* are nouns that have been made into verbs, as in "our team has been tasked with..."

NEOPHYTE (NEE uh fyt) *n* a recent convert; a beginner; novice

- Although only a *neophyte*, Casey was already demonstrating amazing skill at chess.

- As a *neophyte* at archery, I was just happy I didn't put out anyone's eye my first few times.

Tyro is one synonym for *neophyte*.

NETTLE (NET ul) *v* to irritate, annoy, or provoke

- Sarah's habit of picking her teeth right after she ate *nettled* her co-workers.

- Their mother's constant insistence that they clean their rooms *nettled* her children.

NEXUS (NEK sus) *n* a connection, tie, or link; center or focus

- Although many people have studied the *nexus* between reha-bilitation programs for prisoners and rates of recidivism, no one has been able to draw any universally accepted conclu-sions about the relationship.

- The group members' objective is to strengthen the *nexus* between theory and practice by implementing programs based on their ideas about community service.

NICE (nys) *adj* exacting, extremely or even excessively precise; done with delicacy or skill

- The distinction he drew between the two findings was so *nice* that most of his listeners weren't even sure it was there.

- He had so *nice* a sense for chocolate that he could identify the source of the cocoa bean used to make each variety.

Quick Quiz #37

Match each word in the first column with its definition in the second column. Check your answers in the back of the book.

1. nexus
2. neologism
3. nascent
4. nice
5. nadir
6. multifarious
7. neophyte
8. mundane
9. nebulous
10. multifaceted
11. natty
12. nettle

a. varied
b. ordinary
c. low point
d. just beginning
e. neat and tidy
f. vague
g. new word
h. beginner
i. connection, center
j. extremely precise
k. varied
l. annoy

NOISOME (NOY sum) *adj* offensive, especially to one's sense of smell, fetid

- I don't know how anyone with a nose can live in an apartment that *noisome*.

- The *noisome* miasma rising from the swamp was the result of a chemical spill.

NONPLUSSED (nahn PLUST) *adj* baffled, in a quandary, at a loss for what to say, do or think

- Ernest was a little *nonplussed* when Gertrude told him that she loved him but she wasn't in love with him, which is admittedly pretty confusing.

- I was *nonplussed* as to how a dog, a hamster and a turtle could have made such a mess, but once I figured out that they had invited the whole neighborhood menagerie over, it made a lot more sense.

NORMATIVE (NAWR muh tiv) *adj* of or pertaining to an assumed norm regarded as the standard of correctness in behavior, speech, writing

- What is *normative* in terms of social behavior is defined by the surrounding culture.
- In nineteenth century America it was *normative* to leave a calling card when visiting one's neighbors.

NOSTRUM (NAH strum) *n* cure-all, placebo, questionable remedy

- Any *nostrum* that claims to cure both a hangover and bunions is either a miracle or a fraud.
- Spare me your *nostrums* promising the answers to all of life's difficult questions; if it were that easy someone would have found them long ago.

NOXIOUS (NAHK shus) *adj* harmful; injurious

- His speeches advocating intolerance were *noxious*; they spread harm to everyone who hears them.
- That particularly *noxious* shade of pink is making my eyes hurt.
- The school had to be evacuated when the *noxious* gas leak was discovered.

O

OBDURATE (AHB dur ut) *adj* unyielding, hard-hearted, inflexible

- The villain's *obdurate* heart was unmoved by the plight of the villagers; he refused to show any compassion at all.

- Completely unwilling to acknowledge that we might be lost, Anthony was *obdurate* in his insistence that we were going the right way.

OBEISANCE (oh BEE sunts) *n* gesture that expresses deference, such as a bow or curtsy

- In the court of a king or queen, no one would think of dancing without first offering some sort of *obeisance* to the monarch; obviously, rules on other dance floors are more relaxed.

Obeisance shares a root with obey, and it is, in fact, a gesture that shows "obey-ance" to the recipient. An *obeisance* could also be called an *obeisant* gesture.

OBFUSCATE (AHB fus cayt) *v* to deliberately obscure, to make confusing

- He tried to *obfuscate* the issue behind a lot of big words and numbers, but it was obvious that the company was in serious financial straits.

- Magic tricks are based on the art of *obfuscation*; making an audience believe that it sees something other than what is actually occurring.

An *obfuscation* is something that causes confusion.

- Sonya was a genius at removing *obfuscations* and drilling right into the truth of any issue.

OBJURGATE (OB jer geyt) *v* to reproach or vehemently denounce; to scold

- His boss *objurgated* him for his horrible treatment of those he felt were beneath him.

OBSEQUIOUS (ub SEE kwee us) *adj* exhibiting a fawning attentiveness; subservient

- His *obsequious* fawning over Brandy made him seem more like her pet than her peer.

- I suspected that he was only trying to get something from me, and that his *obsequiousness* was not a measure of his adulation, but only of his desire for reward.

OBSTINATE (AHB stin ut) *adj* stubborn; hardheaded; uncompromising

- Stop being so *obstinate* and just admit that I'm right!
- He couldn't get the *obstinate* oxen to move, no matter how much he coaxed.

OBSTREPEROUS (ahb STREP uh rus) *adj* noisy, loudly stubborn, boisterous

- Their *obstreperous* clamor to see their idol didn't quiet down even after he came on stage.
- The entire zoo was kept up all night by the *obstreperous* herd of cranky elephants.

OBTAIN (ub TAYN) *v* to be established, accepted, or customary, prevail

- The customary niceties of polite conversation do not *obtain* in the middle of a tornado.
- The proper conditions for the summit will only *obtain* if all parties agree to certain terms.

OBTUSE (ahb TOOS) *adj* lacking sharpness of intellect, not clear or precise in thought or expression

- Her approach was so *obtuse* that it took me twenty minutes to figure out that she was asking me out.
- The secret agent was so *obtuse* he couldn't remember how to figure out the secret code even after he'd studied it for days.

In geometry, an *obtuse* angle is one that is more than 90 degrees and less than 180 degrees, so it's a pretty dull angle. Perhaps it's not surprising, then, that the definitions of *obtuse* used here also mean dull. For an opposite, see *acumen*.

Match each word in the first column with its definition in the second column. Check your answers in the back of the book.

1.	obsequious	a.	offensive to sense of smell
2.	nonplussed	b.	baffled
3.	obtain	c.	cure-all
4.	obstinate	d.	harmful
5.	noisome	e.	unyielding
6.	obeisance	f.	make confusing
7.	obtuse	g.	subservient
8.	nostrum	h.	stubborn
9.	obstreperous	i.	boisterous
10.	obdurate	j.	prevail
11.	noxious	k.	lacking precision in intellect
12.	obfuscate	l.	deferent gesture
13.	normative	m.	scold
14.	objurgate	n.	correctness in behavior

OBVIATE (AHB vee ayt) *v* to anticipate and make unnecessary

- Finding my keys in my pocket *obviated* the need for the private investigators I just hired to locate them.

- The successful outcome of the most recent experiments *obviated* the need for any additional testing.

OCCLUDE (uh KLOOD) *v* to obstruct or block

- The big bus that parked right in front of us *occluded* our view.

- The path had become *occluded* by years of underbrush growing over the trail.

OCCULT (uh KULT) *adj* hidden, concealed, beyond comprehension

We generally think of the *occult* as having to do with the supernatural. However, it can also mean anything hidden or beyond comprehension.

- The *occult* mysteries of humankind's purpose on earth have yet to be fully solved despite the best efforts of scientists, philosophers and theologians.

Occult can also be a verb, meaning to hide.

- The beam of light from the ranger's station was *occulted* every time we walked behind a tree.

ODIOUS (OH dee us) *adj* hateful; arousing strong feelings of dislike

- As a vegetarian, there are few things more *odious* to Mari than the smell of beef cooking.

- The enmity is so strong between the two competitors that even the thought of being in each other's presence is *odious* to either of them.

OFFICIOUS (uh FISH us) *adj* meddlesome, pushy in offering one's services where they are unwanted

- The *officious* busybody was constantly popping up to offer help when everyone just wished he would go away.

- Our well-intended but *officious* host kept refilling our plates and glasses before we had a chance to take more than a bite or two.

ONEROUS (AH nuh rus) *adj* troubling, burdensome

- We were not looking forward to the *onerous* task of cleaning up after the dance, but it turned out not to be too bad once we brought in the bulldozer.

- Every spring I dread the *onerous* task of filing my income tax return.

OPAQUE (oh PAYK) *adj* impermeable by light; dense in mind

Literally, something *opaque* allows no light through it. Figuratively, *opaque* is similar in meaning to *obtuse*.

- The windows were so dirty that they were almost *opaque*.
- I explained the concept to her the same way I do to everyone; she must just be too *opaque* to understand.

The word comes from a Latin word meaning darkened.

OPPROBRIUM (uh PROH bree um) *n* disgrace, contempt, scorn

- The students couldn't bear to face their teacher's *opprobrium* after they all failed the midterm exam.
- Many terms of *opprobrium* have been reclaimed by their intended targets as a way of fighting back against bigotry.

OSCILLATION (ah suh LAY shun) *n* the act or state of swinging back and forth with a steady, uninterrupted rhythm

- The *oscillation* of the electric fan back and forth was the only sound in the diner mid-afternoon.

The verb *oscillate* can both mean to literally move back and forth and to move back and forth between two ideas or positions.

- As he plucked one petal after another from the flower he *oscillated* between hope and despair, thinking alternately "she loves me, she loves me not."

OSSIFIED (AH suh FYD) *adj* changed into bone; made rigidly conventional and unreceptive to change

- The department had so *ossified* over time that no new ideas were ever introduced; its *ossification* was so advanced that it had become nothing more than a rigid bureaucracy.

OSTENSIBLE (ah STEN suh bul) *adj* seeming, appearing as such, professed

- Even though his *ostensible* reason for coming to all the games was his love of the sport, we knew his crush on the team captain was his real reason.

- Even when they were *ostensibly* written for children, many cartoons are actually more entertaining for adults.

OSTENTATIOUS (ah sten TAY shus) *adj* characterized by or given to pretentiousness

- The *ostentatious* display of his diplomas on the front door of his office backfired whenever anyone noticed that the names of all the schools were spelled incorrectly.

- His house was a shrine to *ostentation*; it had fourteen bathrooms with gold bathtubs.

OVERWEENING (oh vur WEEN ing) *adj* presumptuously arrogant, overbearing, immoderate

- His *overweening* arrogance made everyone want to smack him, which was the only way he got to be the center of attention that he imagined he should be.

- Your *overweening* presumption in asking for my help is stunning, given how many times you have mocked me before.

Quick Quiz #39

Match each word in the first column with its definition in the second column. Check your answers in the back of the book.

1. ostentatious
2. opprobrium
3. officious
4. ostensible
5. occult
6. occlude
7. obviate
8. opaque
9. oscillation
10. overweening
11. onerous
12. odious

a. anticipate and make unnecessary
b. obstruct
c. hidden
d. meddlesome
e. burdensome
f. scorn
g. swinging back and forth
h. rigidly conventional
i. pretentious
j. overbearing
k. hateful
l. dense

P

PAEAN (PEE un) *n* a song or expression of praise and thanksgiving

- The celebratory bonfire was a *paean* to victory.

- The young musician composed a *paean* to his beloved teacher in thanks for her guidance.

PALLIATE (PAL ee ayt) *v* to make something appear less serious, gloss over, mitigate

- His attempts to *palliate* the significance of his plagiarism only made it worse; he would have been better off just owning up to it rather than trying to diminish its importance.

- Nothing could *palliate* the boredom he felt, not even the prospect of a rousing game of ping-pong. If ping-pong had cured his boredom, it would have been an effective *palliative*.

PANACEA (pan uh SEE uh) *n* a remedy for all diseases or ills; an answer or solution for all problems or difficulties

- Aspirin has often been thought of as a *panacea* for most of what ails you.
- The strategy of keeping interest rates low proved to be a *panacea* for the ailing economy.

PANACHE (puh NASH) *adj* a grand or flamboyant manner

- His dress style had a certain *panache*; heads always turned when he walked into a room.
- Liberace showed a great deal of *panache* by always wearing outrageous outfits.

PANDEMIC (pan DEM ik) *adj* widespread; occurring over a large area or affecting an unusually large percentage of the population

- HIV and AIDS together have become *pandemic* throughout much of the world and are likely to be the biggest health crisis of the century.

Pandemic can also be used as a noun.

- The Spanish flu *pandemic* of 1918–1919 killed at least twenty-five million people worldwide within six months.

For a related word with a very different meaning, see *endemic*.

PANEGYRIC (pan uh JYRE ik) *n* formal expression of praise

- Thomas spent months preparing a *panegyric* to his grandfather for his ninetieth birthday.
- The *panegyric* Pliny the Younger delivered before the Roman Senate in honor of Trajan is the only speech of his extant today.

PARADIGM (PAR uh dym) *n* something that serves as a model, example, or pattern; the framework of assumptions and understandings shared by a group or discipline that shapes its worldview

- She is a *paradigm* of studiousness; she spends all of her time studying in the library.

- The move away from the traditional, detached scholarly voice of the critic toward a more engaged, first person narrative represented a major *paradigm* shift. When some academics started talking about how they felt about things rather than being just disembodied voices, it caused a big change in how people thought about academic writing.

PARADOX (PAR uh dox) *n* a contradiction; a seemingly self-contradictory statement that seems true nonetheless

- The most widely used example of a *paradox* is the statement, "Less is more."

Paradoxical is the adjective form.

- Though it seems *paradoxical*, it is actually less tiring to walk than to stand.

Originally, a *paradox* was a statement that conflicted with expectation or accepted opinions.

PARAGON (PAR uh gahn) *n* something regarded as a model of excellence or perfection in some way

- The businessman relied on his reputation as a *paragon* of honesty to become one of the town's most beloved politicians.

- The model was considered such a *paragon* of the perfect female form that the sculptor used her figure for his model of Aphrodite.

The original meaning of *paragon* was a touchstone, or something used to distinguish good from bad. Now it tends to mean a standard by which a certain characteristic is judged.

PARIAH (puh RY uh) *n* an outcast, a rejected and despised person

- The plot of many teen movies revolves around the miraculous transformation of the school nerd from social *pariah* to the most popular boy or girl in school.

- Eating a pound of garlic before bed is likely to make one a *pariah* the next day.

Quick Quiz #40

Match each word in the first column with its definition in the second column. Check your answers in the back of the book.

1.	paradigm	a.	make seem less serious
2.	palliate	b.	formal praise
3.	paradox	c.	model
4.	panegyric	d.	song of praise
5.	paragon	e.	perfect example
6.	pariah	f.	widespread
7.	pandemic	g.	contradiction
8.	paean	h.	outcast
9.	panacea	i.	flamboyant manner
10.	panache	j.	cure-all

PARODY (PAR uh dee) *n* a humorous imitation intended for ridicule or comic effect, especially in literature and art, also something so bad as to be potentially mistaken for an intentional mockery

- The game last night was a *parody* of the game of football; no team could have really played that poorly, so they must have been trying to lose as badly as possible.

- The students' *parody* of the teachers in the talent show skit may have hit a little too close to home; none of the teachers being parodied seemed very amused, but everyone else thought it was hysterical.

PARRY (PAR ee) *v* to block, evade or ward off, as a blow

- Press secretaries are skilled at *parrying* reporters' questions; they can make it seem as if they are answering the question without actually providing any information.

- Chuck was able to *parry* all his opponent's blows, except the last one, which caught him right on the chin.

PARSIMONIOUS (pahr si MOHN ee us) *adj* cheap, miserly

- He was so *parsimonious* that he wouldn't even share the free coupons that came in the mail.

PARTISAN (PAHR tuh zun) *adj* one-sided, committed to a party, biased or prejudiced

- Since *partisan* support for the bill was unlikely to be enough to guarantee its passage, lobbyists were under pressure to persuade members of other parties to vote for it.

- *Partisan* conflict split the club in two as each faction rallied behind its choice for president.

Partisan can also be a noun, meaning supporter, adherent

- *Partisans* of the winning team spilled out of the stadium in loud celebration.

A related word that we hear frequently is *bipartisan*, which means both parties. A very popular bill is likely to have *bipartisan* support.

PASTORAL (PAS ter uhl) *adj* having the simplicity, charm, serenity, or other characteristics generally attributed to rural areas; pertaining to life in the country

- Amy envied the inhabitants of the small town, who seemed so content in their *pastoral* surroundings.

- At 65 he retired and bought a farm so that he could live a life of *pastoral* bliss.

PAUCITY (PAH suh tee) *adj* scarcity, a lacking of

- Carl was very self-conscious about the *paucity* of hair on his head, so he always wore a hat to cover his large bald spot.

- Because he hadn't done laundry in four months, Paul was confronted with a serious *paucity* of clean socks.

- Citing a *paucity* of admissible evidence, the judge dismissed the case.

PECCADILLO (pek uh DIL oh) *n* a slight offense; literally, a minor sin

- Peter's pilfering was hardly a *peccadillo*; he was wanted for grand larceny in thirteen states.

- Using the wrong fork was merely a *peccadillo*, but dumping the tureen of soup over the host's head was a major gaffe.

PEDAGOGY (PED uh goh jee) *n* the art or profession of training, teaching, or instructing

- All his training in *pedagogy* in school hadn't completely prepared Carlos for dealing with 30 manic third graders.

- The Princeton Review trains teachers in a *pedagogical* style based on the Socratic method, in which the teacher asks students questions in order to lead them to a better understanding of the material.

PEDANTIC (pi DAN tik) *adj* ostentatious display of learning, excessive attention to minutiae and formal rules, unimaginative

- The bureaucrat's *pedantic* obsession with rules and regulations ensured that nothing was ever accomplished.

- The author's *pedantic* writing style managed to make a fascinating topic completely boring by including endless fussy details.

One who has a *pedantic* style is called a *pedant*.

- Ever the *pedant*, the professor was more concerned with demonstrating how much he knew than in teaching his students.

PEDESTRIAN (puh DES tree un) *adj* commonplace, trite, unremarkable

- The movie's plot was *pedestrian*, despite the director's brave decision to cast a badger in the role of the hero.

- His dissertation was *pedestrian* at best: thorough but completely unremarkable and not very interesting at all.

PELLUCID (pul loo sid) *adj* clear in meaning, expression, or style; translucent

- Hemingway employed a *pellucid* way of writing, using short sentences and straightforward vocabulary.

- The *pellucid* water of the lake allowed one to see all the way to the bottom.

PENCHANT (PEN chunt) *n* strong inclination, a liking

- I have accepted my cat's *penchant* for climbing on things, so I don't even worry about the state of disrepair of my couch and drapes.

- My *penchant* for fine wines and expensive cars rather exceeds my ability to pay for them.

Quick Quiz #41

Match each word in the first column with its definition in the second column. Check your answers in the back of the book.

1.	penchant	a.	commonplace
2.	parsimonious	b.	art of teaching
3.	partisan	c.	block or evade
4.	pedagogy	d.	committed to a party
5.	parry	e.	humorous imitation
6.	parody	f.	slight offense
7.	pedestrian	g.	scarcity
8.	paucity	h.	ostentatious display of
9.	pedantic		learning
10.	peccadillo	i.	miserly
11.	pastoral	j.	strong inclination
12.	pellucid	k.	clear
		l.	rural charm

PENITENTIAL (pen i TEHN shuhl) *adj* expressive of regret for one's wrongdoing

- In the Middle Ages monks used to flog themselves as a *penitential* act.

PENURIOUS (pen YOOR ee us) *adj* penny-pinching, excessively thrifty; ungenerous

- My *penurious* boss makes us bring toilet paper from home in order to save the company money.

- Mr. Scrooge was so *penurious* that three separate ghostly visitations were required to get him to be even a little bit kind or generous.

Penury is extreme poverty, destitution, or lack of resources.

- Albert's state of *penury* was sufficiently far advanced that he was forced to recycle his coffee grounds each morning.

- The cheerleader was suffering *penury* of spirit; she didn't even care enough to lift her pom-poms during the cheers.

PEREMPTORY (puh REMP tor ee) *adj* admitting of no contradiction, putting an end to further debate, haughty, imperious

- Her *peremptory* tone made it clear that there would be no further discussion of the matter.

- The king dismissed the petitioner with a *peremptory* wave of his hand, not even bothering to say anything more.

PERENNIAL (puh REN ee ul) *adj* recurrent through the year or many years, happening repeatedly

- *Death of a Salesman* was a *perennial* favorite of the community theater; they performed it every season.

- The students' *perennial* complaint was that they had too much homework; the faculty's perennial response was that they should be happy they didn't have more.

- *Perennials* are plants that live for more than one year.

PERFIDY (PUR fuh dee) *n* intentional breach of faith, treachery

- I couldn't believe my campaign manager's *perfidy* in voting for my opponent.

- Kevin was outraged by his brother's *perfidy* when he claimed that it had been Kevin's idea to shave the cat.

PERFUNCTORY (pur FUNK tor ee) *adj* cursory, done without care of interest

- Hilda's *perfunctory* approach to cleaning left dust bunnies the size of small horses in the corners and under the bed.

- His *perfunctory* response to my question confirmed that he hadn't been paying attention to what I said.

PERIPATETIC (per I puh TET ik) *adj* itinerant, traveling, nomadic

- Charlene was unwilling to give up the *peripatetic* life of a sailor for the security of a house with a white picket fence, so she rented an apartment in every port.

- As a *peripatetic* salesman, Frank spent most of his time in his car.

Errant and *itinerant* are two synonyms for *peripatetic*.

PERNICIOUS (pur NI shus) *adj* extremely harmful, potentially causing death

- The *pernicious* venom of the Black Mamba snake will always kill its victim unless an antidote is administered quickly.

- The effect of her *pernicious* sarcasm could be felt at ten paces.

Pernicious is similar in meaning to *inimical*.

PERSONABLE (PUR sun uh bul) *adj* pleasing in appearance, attractive

- I found him quite *personable*, as all those other people flirting with him apparently did as well.

- She was quite *personable* until she revealed that she was a vampire in need of a nightly feeding.

PERSPICACIOUS (pur spuh KAY shus) *adj* acutely perceptive, having keen discernment

- How very *perspicacious* of you to notice that I dyed my hair blue.

- It was quite surprising that his teachers described Kyle as a *perspicacious* student, since he slept through most of their classes; he must have demonstrated great insight in the papers he wrote.

Someone who is *perspicacious* probably has great acumen.

Quick Quiz #42

Match each word in the first column with its definition in the second column. Check your answers in the back of the book.

1.	perfunctory	a.	ungenerous
2.	perspicacious	b.	poverty
3.	penurious	c.	admitting no contradiction
4.	perennial		
5.	penury	d.	happening repeatedly
6.	peripatetic	e.	treachery
7.	peremptory	f.	cursory
8.	personable	g.	traveling
9.	pernicious	h.	extremely harmful
10.	perfidy	i.	attractive
11.	penitential	j.	acutely perceptive
		k.	expressive of regret

PERUSE (pur OOZ) *v* to examine with great care

- Since I didn't have time to *peruse* the entire report with the thoroughness it deserved, I had to settle for reading an abridged version for now.

- She *perused* the shelves for the book, checking each title one by one.

Be careful, many people misuse this word, believing that it means to glance over quickly.

PERVADE (pur VAYD) *v* to permeate throughout

- I was *pervaded* with fear when the stairs creaked in the middle of the night; even the hair on the back of my neck stood up.

Pervasive means having the tendency to permeate or spread throughout.

- The *pervasive* smell of bread baking filled every room in the house and made my stomach rumble.

PETROUS (PET rus) *adj* like a rock; hard, stony

- I wasn't surprised that my *petrous* cake wasn't a big hit, but it did make an excellent doorstop, if I do say so myself.

Petrous technically refers to the hard temporal bone that protects the inner ear. ·

Petrify means to make hard or rocklike, or to paralyze with fear.

- The pores of the wood had been replaced by minerals from the bog in which it was buried, leaving the wood *petrified*.

- We were *petrified* by the dark shape moving toward us; we couldn't even run away because we were frozen with fear.

PETULANT (PET yoo lunt) *adj* impatient, irritable

- It's always easy to tell when Brad is feeling *petulant* because his bottom lip starts to protrude.

- Terrible Tina's babysitters were so afraid of her temper tantrums that they gave her whatever she wanted at the first sign of *petulance*.

PHILANTHROPIC (fil un THRAHP ik) *adj* humanitarian; benevolent

- The mogul eventually turned his attention from making money to more *philanthropic* pursuits, but he will primarily be remembered for his innovations in business.

Philanthropic comes from Greek roots meaning "man-loving"—man meaning humankind. The act of doing humanitarian works is called *philanthropy*.

Remember *misanthrope*? A *philanthropist* is the exact opposite.

PHILISTINE (FIL uh styn) *n* a crass individual guided by material rather than intellectual or artistic values

- The author claimed that his many critics were just *philistines*, who obviously lacked any taste since they didn't appreciate his writing.

PHLEGMATIC (fleg MA tik) *adj* calm, sluggish, unemotional, stoic

- Karen was so *phlegmatic* she didn't even react when Rita stepped on her foot repeatedly.

- His *phlegmatic* response to the question revealed nothing of what he was feeling, if he was feeling anything at all.

According to Aristotle, *phlegmatic* personalities were caused by too much phlegm. This book contains vocabulary words based on three other personality types that he identified based on bodily fluids... can you find the rest?

PICARESQUE (pik uh RESK) *adj* involving clever rogues or adventurers

- Huck Finn is sometimes described as a *picaresque* hero, since the novel follows his roguish adventures.

Be careful not to confuse this with *picturesque*, which means picture-like, charming, or quaint.

PIED (pyd) *adj* multicolored, usually in blotches

- The *pied* goat was easily distinguishable in the herd of solid white and brown coats.

- The jester wore a *pied* coat of many bright colors.

PILLORY (PIL uh ree) *v* to punish, hold up to public scorn

- The politician was *pilloried* in the press for his inability to spell potato.

A *pillory* was a device for punishing people through public humiliation; it consisted of a wooden frame into which someone's neck and hands could be locked, and was usually set up in a town square or other public place. It was very similar in design and purpose to the stocks.

PINE (pyn) *v* to yearn intensely, to languish, to lose vigor

- Johnnie *pined* away for his girlfriend the entire time she was away at camp; he didn't eat or sleep and just stared at her picture all day.

- I *pined* for sunshine all winter until I couldn't stand it any more and had to go buy a sunlamp.

PIOUS (PY us) *adj* extremely reverent or devout

- Cleo was so *pious* that she went to church at least once a day.

Pious can also have the sense of false or hypocritical devotion.

- The evangelist's *pious* preaching was a thin cover for the millions of dollars he was embezzling from the church.

The word *piety* means the state of being *pious*.

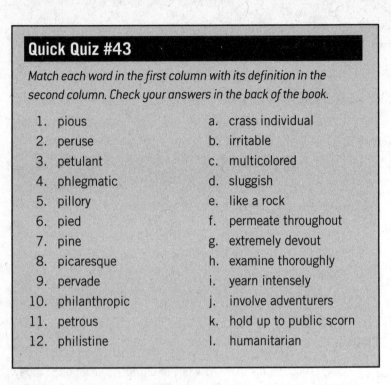

Quick Quiz #43

Match each word in the first column with its definition in the second column. Check your answers in the back of the book.

1.	pious	a.	crass individual
2.	peruse	b.	irritable
3.	petulant	c.	multicolored
4.	phlegmatic	d.	sluggish
5.	pillory	e.	like a rock
6.	pied	f.	permeate throughout
7.	pine	g.	extremely devout
8.	picaresque	h.	examine thoroughly
9.	pervade	i.	yearn intensely
10.	philanthropic	j.	involve adventurers
11.	petrous	k.	hold up to public scorn
12.	philistine	l.	humanitarian

PIQUANT (PEE kunt) *adj* agreeably pungent, spicy, stimulating

- The *piquant* gumbo was a welcome change after days of bland hospital food.

- The *piquancy* of her face with its high cheekbones and arresting eyes made the portrait memorable.

PIQUE (peek) *n* resentment, feeling of irritation due to hurt pride

- In a fit of *pique*, Chelsea threw her boyfriend's bowling ball out the fourth-story window onto his car.

To *pique* can also be a verb, meaning to annoy or irritate, or to provoke or arouse, as in "you've *piqued* my curiousity."

PIRATE (PY rut) *v* to use or reproduce illegally

- *Pirated* copies of the movie were circulated even before its release in theaters.

- U.S. companies are concerned about the widespread *pirating* of software in countries with less strict copyright protection.

PITH (pith) *n* the essential or central part

- The *pith* of his argument seemed to be that he should get a bigger allowance, though it took him an hour to get to the point.

- It's a little strange that the *pith* of an orange is the white spongy stuff under the rind, instead of the part at the center of the orange, but that's the way it goes.

Pithy means precise and brief.

- The *pithy* synopsis of the novel distilled all 1,500 pages into two very concise paragraphs.

PLACATE (PLAY cayt) *v* to appease, to calm by making concessions

- Jesse tried to *placate* the irritable crocodile by feeding it several steaks, but after swallowing these whole, it still seemed to want Jesse for dessert.

- Although my boyfriend seemed somewhat *placated* after I sent him flowers every day for a week, I suspected he was still a little cranky that I had forgotten our anniversary.

Mollify can be a synonym for *placate*.

PLAINTIVE (PLAYN tiv) *adj* mournful, melancholy, sorrowful

- The *plaintive* strains of the bagpipe made everyone feel as mournful as it sounded.

- The dogs' *plaintive* howls effectively expressed their sadness at having been left outside in the rain.

PLANGENT (PLAN junt) *adj* pounding, thundering, resounding

- The *plangent* bells could be heard all over town as they chimed the hour.

- We were awakened from our nap by the *plangent* honking of a flock of migrating geese.

PLASTIC (PLA stik) *adj* moldable, pliable, not rigid

- The supervillain's secret brain control ray rendered its victim's mind *plastic* and easily bendable to his evil plans.
- This foam is highly *plastic* and can be molded to almost any shape.

PLATITUDE (PLAT I tood) *n* a superficial or trite remark, especially one offered as meaningful

- Since Laura loved to say things that seemed profound initially but turned out to be banal once considered, she was a perfect candidate for writing the *platitudes* that go in greeting cards.
- Most people can only offer *platitudes* when faced with someone else's loss; we're just not very good at knowing how to say something meaningful when confronted with grief.

PLETHORA (PLE thor uh) *n* an overabundance, a surplus

- Charles always had a *plethora* of excuses for being late, and they were as imaginative as they were plentiful.
- Since there was still a *plethora* of qualified candidates at the end of the second round of interviews, Michael decided he needed to conduct a third round.
- There was a *plethora* of chimpanzees in our living room, but then even one is usually too many.

PLUCK (pluk) *n* courage, spunk, fortitude

- The audience was impressed by the gymnast's *pluck* in continuing her routine even after she tell off the balance beam.
- The prospect of glory and a hot cup of soup gave the soldiers the *pluck* they needed to keep fighting.

Quick Quiz #44

Match each word in the first column with its definition in the second column. Check your answers in the back of the book.

1.	plastic	a.	appease
2.	placate	b.	spicy
3.	plethora	c.	thundering
4.	piquant	d.	central part
5.	pithy	e.	precise and brief
6.	platitude	f.	superficial remark
7.	pith	g.	use illegally
8.	pirate	h.	resentment
9.	plangent	i.	moldable
10.	pique	j.	courage
11.	pluck	k.	surplus

PLUMB (plum) *v* to measure the depth (as with a plumb line), to examine critically

- It was the exploratory ship's task to *plumb* the depth of a section of the Pacific Ocean.

- Having *plumbed* the viability of the plan, we decided it was too risky to undertake at night.

Plumb as an adjective means exactly vertical. Informally it can also mean directly (as in, "fell *plumb* on his butt") or completely (as in, "*plumb* tuckered out").

PLUMMET (PLUM et) *v* to plunge or drop straight down

- One by one the ostriches *plummeted* to the ground when they remembered that they couldn't fly.

- The company's stock *plummeted* when it failed to get the patent for making money out of thin air.

POIGNANT (POIN yunt) *adj* distressing, pertinent, touching, stimulating, emotional

- The *poignant* final scene between the main character and his pet penguin that was mortally wounded trying to save his owner moved the audience to tears.

- He felt *poignant* anxiety at the thought of what his life would be like now that he no longer had a job.

POLEMICAL (poh LEM i kul) *adj* controversial, argumentative

- Her *polemical* attack on the president's foreign policy was carefully designed to force him into a public debate on the subject.

Polemics are the art or practice of controversy and argumentation.

- Spare me the *polemics*; we need to reach a consensus in the next ten minutes in order to complete this project in time.

PORTENTOUS (pawr TEN tuhs) *adj* ominously significant or indicative

- He gave a *portentous* speech on the power of his enemies the night before he was murdered.

- The recent declines in the stock market are a *portentous* sign that the country is headed toward a recession.

PRAGMATIC (prag MAT ik) *adj* practical rather than idealistic

- I approve of your *pragmatic* decision to wear running shoes to exercise instead of the go-go boots you were considering.

A *pragmatist* is one who is practical.

- I was the *pragmatist* and my business partner was the idealist; she figured out how something should be and I tried to work out whether it was possible.

PRATE (prayt) *v* chatter, babble

- The toddler *prated* on happily to himself though no one else had any idea what he was saying.

Prate is a synonym of *prattle*.

Quick Quiz #45

Match each word in the first column with its definition in the second column. Check your answers in the back of the book.

1.	pragmatic	a.	argumentative
2.	polemical	b.	practical
3.	plumb、	c.	measure depth
4.	poignant	d.	drop straight down
5.	plummet	e.	chatter
6.	prate	f.	touching
7.	portentous	g.	ominous

PRATTLE (PRAT ul) *v* to babble meaninglessly; to talk in an empty and idle manner

- Katrina started to fall asleep as her girlfriend *prattled* on about every little thing that had happened in the previous twenty four hours.

Prattle can also be a noun.

- His interminable *prattle* made me crazy and I just wished he would be quiet for a few minutes.

PRECARIOUS (ri KAYR ee us) *adj* uncertain, risky, dangerous

- The general's hold on power was *precarious*; at any time another coup could overthrow his young regime.

- The house was perched *precariously* on the edge of the cliff, vulnerable to any mudslide.

PRECEPT (PREE sept) *n* rule establishing standards of conduct, a doctrine that is taught

- One of the *precepts* of our criminal justice system is that one is assumed innocent until proven guilty.
- You will violate the *precepts* of fair play if you peek at my cards.

PRECIPITATE (pree SIP uh tut) *adj* acting with excessive haste or impulse

- The captain was forced to take *precipitate* action when the storm arrived earlier than he had expected.

As a verb, *precipitate* means to cause or happen before anticipated or required.

- Be careful, any sudden movement could *precipitate* an avalanche.
- The sale of one of its divisions to its major competitor *precipitated* the company's collapse.

PRECURSOR (PRE kur sur) *n* something that precedes and indicates or announces another

- Overindulgence is often the *precursor* to a nasty hangover the next morning.
- The volleyball team's winning season was a *precursor* to their national championship.

PREDILECTION (pre duh LEK shun) *n* a disposition in favor of something, preference

- Once President Reagan's *predilection* for jellybeans became known, people sent him tons of them.

- Harold's *predilection* for dating older women meant he didn't need to worry as much about getting his driver's license.

PREEMINENT (pree EM uh nuhnt) *adj* superior to others; surpassing

- She is *preeminent* in her field and is often sought by others for her expertise.

- Great Britain was once a *preeminent* world power.

PREEMPT (pree EMPT) *v* to replace, to supersede, to appropriate

- My friends *preempted* my birthday plans by throwing me a surprise party.

Preemption is prior appropriation of or claim to something and *preemptive* means characterized by *preemption*.

- The smaller country launched a *preemptive* strike against its larger neighbor, hoping to diminish its offensive power.

PREEN (preen) *v* to dress up, primp, groom oneself with elaborate care; in animals, to clean fur or feathers

- She was so busy *preening* and posing for the cameras that she didn't pay enough attention to where the edge of the pool was.

- Humans *preen* in front of their chosen mates in much the way some birds do, but birds also preen their feathers to stay warm and watertight.

PREMONITORY (pri MON it tawr ee) *adj* serving to warn beforehand

- Dogs often sense *premonitory* signs of an oncoming tornado.

- She wondered if her fever could be the *premonitory* symptom of a serious illness.

PRESCIENCE (PRE see unts) *n* knowing of events prior to their occurring

- I wish I had had the *prescience* to know it was going to rain today; I would have brought a raincoat.

- Cassandra's unique curse was that she was given the gift of *prescience* but doomed to have no one ever believe her.

PRESUMPTUOUS (pre ZUMP shoo us) *adj* overstepping bounds, as of propriety or courtesy; taking liberties

- I thought it was a little *presumptuous* of Lewis to bring his pajamas and toothbrush with him on our first date.

- Carol couldn't believe her neighbor's *presumption* in borrowing her lawnmower without asking.

PREVARICATE (pri VAT uh kayt) *v* to deliberately avoid the truth, mislead

- The detective began to think the suspect was *prevaricating* about having stayed in all last night when he found mud and grass on her shoes.

- The aging film star had made a lifelong habit of *prevaricating* about his age; he had been thirty five for more than forty years.

PRISTINE (pri STEEN) *adj* pure, uncorrupted, clean

- Never having been explored by humans, the remote wilderness remained a *pristine* natural expanse.
- I feared my *pristine* shirt wouldn't make it through an entire meal of barbecued ribs.

PRIZE (pryz) *v* to pry, press or force with a lever

- His parents had to *prize* the trophy from his sleeping fingers, since he insisted on taking it to bed with him.
- Although I tried to *prize* the information out of him, Arthur refused to reveal his biscuit recipe.

PROBITY (PROHB i tee) *adj* adherence to highest principles, uprightness

- Because the chieftain was known for his *probity* and the soundness of his judgment, people came from miles around to ask him to hear their disputes.

PROCLIVITY (proh CLIV uh tee) *n* a natural predisposition or inclination

- His *proclivity* for napping through movies made his desire to be a movie reviewer a little strange.

PRODIGAL (PRAH duh gul) *adj* recklessly wasteful, extravagant, profuse, lavish

- He was completely *prodigal* in his planning for the party; he hired a 50-piece orchestra and bought 100 cases of champagne for a guest list of ten.
- Linda was *prodigal* with her singing abilities, performing only in karaoke bars.

PRODIGIOUS (pro DI jus) *adj* abundant in size, force, or extent; extraordinary

- The *prodigious* weight of my backpack made me fall over backward.

- The public finally recognized his *prodigious* talent on the kazoo when his album of old kazoo standards topped the charts.

Quick Quiz #47

Match each word in the first column with its definition in the second column. Check your answers in the back of the book.

1.	preen	a.	foreknowledge
2.	prodigious	b.	supersede
3.	prevaricate	c.	uprightness
4.	predilection	d.	taking liberties
5.	proclivity	e.	preference
6.	prize	f.	pure
7.	probity	g.	extravagant
8.	preempt	h.	groom with excessive
9.	prescience		care
10.	presumptuous	i.	mislead
11.	prodigal	j.	pry
12.	pristine	k.	abundant in size
13.	preeminent	l.	natural inclination
14.	premonitory	m.	warning
		n.	superior

PROFLIGATE (PRAH fli get) *adj* excessively wasteful, recklessly extravagant

- The *profligate* ruler emptied the country's treasury to build his many mansions.

PROFUSE (proh FYOOS) *adj* given or coming forth abundantly, extravagant

- Her *profuse* gratitude for my having saved her cat became a little excessive with the fourth sweater she knitted for me.

Profusion means abundance or extravagance.

- The *profusion* of flowers decorating every surface in the room filled the room with color.

PROLIFIC (proh LIF ik) *adj* producing large volumes or amounts, productive

- She was a *prolific* writer, churning out 100 pages a week.
- Opossums are extremely *prolific*, giving birth to up to fourteen babies in each litter.

Proliferate is a related word meaning to grow or increase swiftly and abundantly.

- The termites *proliferated* in the basement until the whole house started to crumble.

Proliferation is the act of increasing quickly.

- The *proliferation* of weeds in the yard suggested it might be time to consider some gardening.

PROLIX (proh LIKS) *adj* long-winded, verbose

- The *prolix* politician was a natural at filibustering; he could talk for hours without stopping.

- His *prolixity* was famous; he could talk for ten minutes before needing to take a breath and for hours before finishing a sentence.

See *verbose* for a synonym of *prolix*.

PROMULGATE (PROM uhl geyt) *v* to make known by open declaration, proclaim formally, or put into operation

- Steve Jobs *promulgated* a vision that technology should not only be useful but also visually appealing.
- During the election the candidate *promulgated* a vision of how the country should be run that was much different from the view espoused by his opponent.

PROPENSITY (pruh PEN suh tee) *n* a natural inclination or tendency, penchant

- His well-known *propensity* for telling tall tales made it unlikely anyone would believe he had really had a conversation with the Abominable Snowman.
- Andy tied strings around his fingers to combat his *propensity* for forgetfulness, but then he just forgot what the strings were for.

PROPINQUITY (pruh PIN kwuh tee) *adj* nearness in time or place, affinity of nature, kinship

- The geographic *propinquity* of the two towns led to a close connection between the two populations.
- His *propinquity* to the object of his affections made him blush.

PROPITIATE (proh PI shi ayt) *v* to appease or pacify

- They tried to *propitiate* the storm gods by dancing in the rain and pouring wine on the ground as an offering.

GRE Power Vocab

Something *propitiatory* is meant to *propitiate*.

- The prime minister sent the emperor a *propitiatory* gift in order to appease his anger over the diplomatic blunder.

PROPITIOUS (proh PI shus) *adj* auspicious, favorable

- They took the clearing of the sky as a *propitious* omen that the storm was passing.

PROPRIETY (pruh PRY uh tee) *n* appropriateness, conformity with standards of acceptable behavior

- Unfortunately, Jean's dinner conversation shocked his new in-laws, whose ideas of *propriety* were significantly more conservative than his.

Be careful; this word is easy to confuse with *proprietary*, which means associated with ownership.

PROSAIC (proh ZAY ik) *adj* dull, unimaginative

- His *prosaic* sensibilities were obvious when in a letter to his wife he described a rainbow as an optical phenomenon caused by the refraction of light through water.

- I was surprised that he should offer so *prosaic* an account of his travels in Spain; it was out of character given his usually poetic descriptions.

PROSCRIBE (proh SKRYB) *v* to outlaw or prohibit

- Attempts to *proscribe* swimming in the old quarry were unsuccessful; people continued to do it despite the new rules.

Proscription is the act of outlawing something. It can also mean to outlaw or banish people, or pass sentence of death. *Prescription* and *proscription* often get mixed up; the former describes what you should do and the latter describes what you are not allowed to do.

Quick Quiz #48

Match each word in the first column with its definition in the second column. Check your answers in the back of the book.

1. prolix
2. proscribe
3. prosaic
4. profligate
5. propriety
6. profuse
7. propensity
8. propinquity
9. prolific
10. propitious
11. propitiate
12. promulgate

a. unimaginative
b. given forth abundantly
c. favorable
d. natural inclination
e. excessively wasteful
f. long-winded
g. appease
h. productive
i. appropriateness
j. nearness
k. outlaw
l. openly declare

PROVIDENT (PRAH vi dunt) *adj* frugal, looking to the future

- His *provident* financial planning allowed him to buy a small tropical island when he retired.

Providential looks similar but means happening as if from divine intervention.

- His *providential* recovery from the accident was nothing short of miraculous.

PUERILE (PYOOR ul) *adj* childish, immature

- His *puerile* humor prominently featured fart jokes.

- Annette's *puerile* response to losing the competition was exactly like that of a small child; she lay down on the ground and started kicking her hands and feet.

PUGNACIOUS (pug NAY shus) *adj* contentious, quarrelsome, given to fighting, belligerent

- That pug is extremely *pugnacious*, biting people's ankles for no reason at all.

- The civil rights attorney was known for her *pugnacious* readiness to fight any injustice.

Bellicose and *querulous* are synonyms for *pugnacious*.

PUNCTILIOUS (punk TIL ee us) *adj* precise, paying attention to trivialities, especially in regard to etiquette

- Although his *punctilious* obsession with etiquette is usually very annoying, it is always handy when royalty comes to dine.

- It was sometimes useful to have an assistant who *punctiliously* recorded where I was and what I did every second of every day; if nothing else, it made it easy to confirm an alibi should one be necessary.

PUNDIT (PUN dit) *n* an authority on a subject, one who gives opinions

- Rob never had any opinions of his own; he just quoted what the *pundits* had said.

- The *pundits* disagreed about what the recently released statistics meant for the prospect of economic recovery.

PUNGENT (PUN junt) *adj* characterized by a strong, sharp smell or taste, penetrating, to the point

- The *pungent* aroma of cinnamon and cloves filled the little tea shop.

- His *pungent* criticism of my paper made me see flaws I hadn't noticed before.

PUSILLANIMOUS (pyoo sil AN uh mus) *adj* cowardly, craven

- His *pusillanimous* refusal to agree to the duel turned out to be wise, if cowardly; his challenger was later revealed to be an Olympic biathlete, and therefore a very good shot.

- The Cowardly Lion thought he was *pusillanimous*, but according to the story he was actually brave all along and just hadn't known it.

PUTREFY (PYOO truh fy) *v* to rot, decay, and give off a foul odor, become gangrenous

- The apples that had fallen on the ground *putrefied* in the warm sun.

- The doctors were forced to amputate the leg in order to prevent *putrefaction*.

Q

QUAFF (kwahf) *v* to drink deeply

- Brett was planning to meet his friends at the pub after work to *quaff* a few pints before heading home.

- The medicine tasted so foul that I had to hold my nose and *quaff* it all in one gulp.

QUAIL (kwayl) *v* to shrink back in fear, lose courage

- The puppy *quailed* at the angry tone in Alicia's voice and put his tail between his legs.

- I *quailed* at the thought of jumping out of a plane as soon as I looked down, which was probably a little late to be having second thoughts.

QUALIFY (KWAH li fy) *v* to limit

- Although she was careful to *qualify* any claims she made about the implications of her discovery, it was clear her research signaled a major breakthrough in the search for a cure.

- He *qualified* the harshness of his criticism by smiling warmly at the students as he delivered it.

QUALMS (kwahm) *n* misgivings, reservations, causes for hesitancy

- Mai had *qualms* about accepting a job so far away from her family, but decided in the end that it was the right option for her.

- Pete had no *qualms* about singing in public, which was a little surprising since he couldn't carry a tune.

Quick Quiz #49

Match each word in the first column with its definition in the second column. Check your answers in the back of the book.

1.	pusillanimous	a.	looking to the future
2.	qualify	b.	childish
3.	provident	c.	quarrelsome
4.	putrefy	d.	precise
5.	puerile	e.	authority
6.	punctilious	f.	having a strong smell
7.	quail	g.	cowardly
8.	pugnacious	h.	rot
9.	pundit	i.	drink deeply
10.	pungent	j.	lose courage
11.	qualms	k.	limit
12.	quaff	l.	reservations

QUERIES (KWE rees) *n* questions, inquiries, reservations

- Liza's *queries* to the Library of Congress for information concerning the old manuscript did not produce the results she had hoped for.

- Although I had some initial *queries* about his sincerity, I decided to trust his proclamations of undying love.

QUERULOUS (KWER yuh lus) *adj* prone to complaining or grumbling, quarrelsome

- Her *querulous* demand to know every five minutes whether we were there yet started to get on my nerves.

- Mitch tended to become *querulous* when he hadn't had his afternoon nap.

QUIESCENCE (kwy ES unts) *n* stillness, motionlessness, quality of being at rest.

- The volcano's *quiescence* was only temporary; it could erupt at any time.

Quiescent means inactive, latent, causing no trouble, being at rest.

- Malaria can remain *quiescent* for years at a time, only to recur at some later point.

- According to Newton, *quiescent* objects tend to remain at rest unless acted upon by an outside force.

QUOTIDIAN (kwoh TID ee un) *adj* occurring or recurring daily, commonplace

- The *quotidian* drag of cornflakes for breakfast, a meaningless job, a TV dinner and the same old shows before going to bed at the same time every night was starting to get Jasper down, so he switched to waffles for breakfast to shake things up a bit.

- Whenever possible, Anita tried to sleep through her *quotidian* train commute home.

R

RAIL (rayl) *v* to complain about bitterly

- He *railed* against the injustice of having not won the lottery yet again.

- After *railing* at the bank teller, she demanded to speak to his manager and then expressed her displeasure to him as well.

RAMIFY (RAM uh fy) *v* to be divided or subdivided, branch out

- Instead of being resolved, the dispute merely *ramified* as more and more people got involved.

- The subject of his book *ramified* in new directions as he began to research all the different branches of the history.

Ramifications are the developments or consequences growing out of something.

- The *ramifications* of the judge's ruling would take years to be fully understood.

RANCOROUS (RAN kuh rus) *adj* characterized by bitter, long-lasting resentment

- The *rancorous* feud between the two sides of the family had been going on for years and had grown completely out of proportion to the missing casserole dish that had started the feud.

Rancor is the bitter, long-lasting resentment itself.

- His *rancor* at having been passed over for promotion was evident in the nasty letters he continued to write to the board of directors for years afterwards.

RAPACIOUS (ruh PAY shus) *adj* voracious, greedy, plundering, subsisting on prey

- The *rapacious* moths ate huge holes in every single one of my socks.

- The Vikings are popularly imagined as *rapacious* warriors, who swept in from the sea and plundered everything in sight. Although this has its truth, it is still a one-dimensional view of their culture.

Rapacity is avarice, or the practice of extorting or exacting by injustice.

- The junta's *rapacity* in despoiling the country of anything of value was only matched by its cruelty to the populace.

RAREFY (RAYR uh fy) *v* to make or become thin, less dense, refine

- Gases condense when they are cooled and *rarefy* when they are heated.

- His sole goal in life was to gain admission to the *rarefied* air of the literary society.

- The air at high elevation is sufficiently *rarefied* that it can be difficult for people with respiratory illnesses to breath.

RECALCITRANT (ri KAL suh trunt) *adj* obstinately defiant of authority or guidance, difficult to manage

- Joe was so *recalcitrant* he refused to do anything he was instructed to do, even something he liked to do, simply because someone told him to do it.

- The bank sent someone to repossess the *recalcitrant* debtor's car and furniture after he refused to make payments for five months.

RECANT (ri KANT) *v* to retract, especially a previously held belief

- After swallowing the first two, Trina *recanted* her earlier boast that she could swallow twenty dead worms.

- Galileo was forced to *recant* his claim that Earth moved around the sun.

Quick Quiz #50

Match each word in the first column with its definition in the second column. Check your answers in the back of the book.

1.	rarefy	a.	complain bitterly
2.	rancorous	b.	voracious
3.	queries	c.	make less dense
4.	quiescence	d.	occurring daily
5.	quotidian	e.	inquiries
6.	recant	f.	branch out
7.	rail	g.	bitterly resentful
8.	ramify	h.	retract
9.	querulous	i.	quarrelsome
10.	recalcitrant	j.	motionlessness
11.	rapacious	k.	defiant of authority

RECAPITULATE (re kuh PITCH oo layt) *v* to summarize, to repeat concisely

- Judy rushed home from work but was still too late to miss the televised debate; she had to settle for the *recapitulated* versions on national news.

Recapitulate is the origin of the shortened form that is more in use today: *recap*.

RECONDITE (rek AHN dyte) *adj* hidden, concealed, difficult to understand, obscure

- Searching for information about the town's *recondite* origins was a lot like doing detective work.
- While it makes perfect sense to physicists, quantum mechanics has always been *recondite* knowledge to me.

RECONNOITER (re kuh NOY tur) *v* to engage in reconnaissance, make a preliminary inspection of

- We sent Bob to *reconnoiter* the party when we first arrived, in order to see who was in the other rooms.
- Our attempts to *reconnoiter* the area for a good camping site were cut short when it grew dark, so we ended up sleeping in the car.

RECUMBENT (ri KUM bunt) *adj* leaning, resting, prone

- I was so comfortable *recumbent* on the picnic blanket that I didn't even stand up when it started raining.
- Wealthy Romans were fond of dining *recumbent* on couches set around a table.

REDOLENT (RED oh lunt) *adj* fragrant, suggestive or evocative

- The dorm rooms were *redolent* with a fragrance of stale beer and cold pizza that brought me back to my college days.
- The city in spring, *redolent* of cherry blossoms, hardly seemed like the same place that had been so gray and uninviting just two months earlier.

REDOUBTABLE (ri DOWT uh bul) *adj* awe-inspiring, worthy of honor

- He came from a *redoubtable* family, just one of many of its members to have served in the highest positions in the country.

- There are many folk songs and stories about the legend of the *redoubtable* John Henry, who beat the steam drill in a tunneling contest in 1872.

REFULGENT (ri FUL junt) *adj* radiant, shiny, brilliant

- The *refulgent* gleam of the motorcycle's chrome was his pride and joy.
- Her *refulgent* smile seemed to light up the evening, though that might just have been the light shining off her braces.

REFUTE (ri FYOOT) *v* to disprove, successfully argue against

- The doctor marshaled any army of statistics to *refute* the critics' claim that his techniques were unsound.
- While no one has successfully *refuted* the existence of a god by scientific means, no one has proven a god's existence either.

REGALE (ri GAYL) *v* to delight or entertain, feast

- Joshua *regaled* his listeners with tales of his world travels while he was the owner of a famous flea circus.
- The visiting dignitaries were *regaled* with a lavish meal and an elaborate dance and musical performance.

RELEGATE (RE luh gayt) *v* to forcibly assign, especially to a lower place or position

- As the youngest member of the troupe, I was *relegated* to the back end of the dancing donkey costume.
- He always *relegated* paying bills to the bottom of his "to do" list, since he hated to be reminded of how little money was in his checking account.

REMONSTRATE (ri MAHN strayt) *v* to protest, object

- When I was a kid, I frequently *remonstrated* with my mom when she made me take my little brother with me to the park.

- My mother *remonstrated* against the city's plan to tear down the park to build a parking lot.

Remonstrations are objections as are *remonstrance's*, though the latter is usually more formal.

- Despite her advisor's *remonstrations*, Linda has decided to take eighteen units of underwater basket weaving next semester, and nothing else.

RENEGE (ri NIG) *v* to fail to honor a commitment, go back on a promise

- I can't believe you *reneged* on your promise to paint the house for the third weekend in a row.

- The government *reneged* on its commitment to provide asylum for the refugees, turning them back at the border instead.

RENT (rent) *v* torn, split apart, pierced as by a sound

- The doll was *rent* limb from limb as the boys fought over it; each combatant was left holding an arm or a leg.

Rend is the present tense. *Rent* can also be a noun, meaning a tear or breach.

- He was determined to *rend* restitution from the company that had destroyed his health, even if it took years of fighting.

- The starship and its valiant crew were hurled through a medium-sized *rent* in the space-time continuum.

REPINE (ri PYNE) *v* to feel or express dejection or discontent, long for

- The old man *repined* for his lost youth, when everything seemed so much more exciting than it was now.

- I got sick of all her *repining* for her former beau; she was the one who dumped him, after all.

REPUDIATE (re PYOO dee ayt) *v* to refuse to have anything to do with, disown

- The psychic *repudiated* his earlier claims when it became clear his client had not in fact won the lottery the day before.

- David threatened to *repudiate* his daughter if she got any more tattoos or had any more body parts pierced, but she knew he was just bluffing.

Quick Quiz #51

Match each word in the first column with its definition in the second column. Check your answers in the back of the book.

1. remonstrate		a.	difficult to understand
2. redoubtable		b.	make preliminary
3. refulgent			inspection
4. repudiate		c.	lying down
5. recondite		d.	fragrant
6. rent		e.	awe-inspiring
7. reconnoiter		f.	shiny
8. refute		g.	disprove
9. regale		h.	entertain
10. relegate		i.	assign to lower position
11. recumbent		j.	protest
12. renege		k.	go back on a promise
13. recapitulate		l.	torn
14. repine		m.	long for
15. redolent		n.	disown
		o.	summarize

RESCIND (ri SIND) *v* to invalidate, repeal, retract

- The headmaster *rescinded* his recent dress code decree when he realized he just couldn't take looking at that many penny loafers every day.

- After the so-called "Espresso Riots," the mayor *rescinded* the tax on lattes.

RESOLUTE (RE zoh loot) *adj* adamant, steadfast, determined

- I remained *resolute* in my decision to give up eating meat, even though I repeatedly awakened in the middle of the night from dreams of bacon cheeseburgers.

Irresolute is the opposite of *resolute*.

- He was *irresolute* about his plans for the summer, wavering between getting a job and learning to be a beach bum.

RESTIVE (RES tiv) *adj* impatient of control, restraint, or delay; restless; uneasy

- She grew so *restive* under the control her husband had over her that eventually divorce was her only option.

- The company president was getting a bit *restive* about the merger negotiations, eager that the deal be inked soon.

RETICENT (RET uh sunt) *adj* quiet, reserved, reluctant to express thoughts and feelings

- She was *reticent* about the party, but we suspected she had had more fun than she was letting on.

- The department head was *reticent* about his plans for filling the new position, giving no clues as to whom he planned to promote.

REVERENT (RE vur unt) *adj* marked by, feeling, or expressing a feeling of profound awe and respect

- As much as she appreciated the compliment, the teacher was a little freaked out by her students' *reverent* attitude toward her, especially when they started wearing robes and calling her their high priestess.
- A moment of *reverent* silence accompanied the unveiling of the magnificent sculpture.

Reverence is a strong feeling of awe or respect, and *irreverence* is the lack thereof.

RHETORIC (RET or ik) *n* the art or study of effective use of language for communication and persuasion

- His study of *rhetoric* made him a powerful public speaker, able to shape his audience's emotions with his words.

Rhetoric can also have a negative connotation, meaning pretentious or insincere language.

- I knew his offer of friendship was mere *rhetoric*, since I'd already been told what he had said behind my back.

Rhetorical means used for persuasive effect, and a *rhetorical* question is one that is used to create an effect and not to get a real answer.

RISIBLE (RYZ uh bul) *adj* hilarious, provoking laughter

- The mating horses created a *risible* sight for Rita, who had never been to a farm before.

Though it is a less common usage, *risible* can also be used to describe people who are inclined to be amused.

- Rita herself, though, is a fairly *risible* individual; the song "I Love to Laugh" could have been written just for her.

RUBRIC (ROO brik) *n* authoritative rule, heading, title, or category

- The *rubric* used to score the writing samples emphasizes structure over content.

- The phenomenon is often examined under the *rubric* of psychology rather than physiology.

Another more obscure version of *rubric* is as an adjective meaning reddish or written in red, and the meanings are actually related. Instructions in church books used to be written in red, so both the color and what it is used for was named for the ruby.

RUE (roo) *v* regret, feel remorse

- I *rued* the day I ever agreed to sublet my apartment to him; now I've got a flooded kitchen and he hasn't even paid the rent.

Rueful means expressing sorrow.

- Her *rueful* apology told me she was really sorry that she had run over my rose bed.

S

SAGACIOUS (suh GAY shus) *adj* having sound judgment, perceptive, wise

- The decision to invest in Brussels sprouts turned out to be a *sagacious* one, since shortly thereafter it was discovered that they contain a powerful aphrodisiac.

Sagacious means like a *sage*, who is a person recognized as having great wisdom. *Sage* can also be an adjective, meaning wise.

- His *sage* advice to grow a beard changed my whole life for the better, since I no longer looked as if I were fourteen.

SALACIOUS (suh LAY shus) *adj* appealing to or causing sexual desire, bawdy

- Magazines containing *salacious* material are kept behind the counter in the bookstore, so you'll have to ask the clerk if you want to see them.

- Tabloids rely in large part on the public's *salacious* curiosity in order to stay in business, and our titillation seems to overcome our outrage often enough for it to work.

SALIENT (SAYL yunt) *adj* prominent, protruding, conspicuous, highly relevant

- The *salient* fact that I had failed to notice at first was that my ride had left me stranded at the club with no way to get home.

- The *salient* root sticking several inches out of the ground caught my foot and caused me to fall unceremoniously on my butt.

SALUBRIOUS (suh LOOB ree us) *adj* promoting health or well-being

- Carrots are *salubrious* for your eyes, since they contain a lot of vitamin A.

- His was not the most *salubrious* of lifestyles, since he lived on donuts and two hours of sleep a night.

Quick Quiz #52

Match each word in the first column with its definition in the second column. Check your answers in the back of the book.

1.	rhetoric	a.	repeal
2.	reticent	b.	determined
3.	salient	c.	quiet
4.	rescind	d.	feeling awe
5.	reverent	e.	art of using language
6.	sagacious	f.	authoritative rule
7.	salubrious	g.	feel remorse
8.	resolute	h.	wise
9.	rue	i.	causing sexual desire
10.	rubric	j.	conspicuous
11.	risible	k.	promoting health
12.	salacious	l.	hilarious
13.	restive	m.	impatient

SALUTARY (SAL yoo ter ee) *adj* remedial, wholesome, causing improvement

- Paul was dismayed to hear the teacher say that she thought summer school would be *salutary* for his math skills.

- The physical therapy she had undergone was having a *salutary* effect on her knees; she could almost walk without discomfort now.

SANCTIMONY (SAYNKT i moh nee) *n* self-righteousness, pretended piety

- His *sanctimony* was laughable, since he was the most self-absorbed, ruthless jerk I'd ever met.

Sanctimonious means hypocritically pretending to be pious or being excessively pious.

- Spare me your *sanctimonious* blather; you're no better than I am.

SANCTION (SAYNK shun) *n* authoritative permission or approval; a penalty intended to enforce compliance

---

This one can be confusing, since it has two, nearly opposite, meanings: approval and penalty.

- Without the *sanction* of the planning commission, we cannot proceed with the renovation.

- Since he received the publisher's *sanction* to reproduce part of the book in his installation, he was able to proceed with the planned opening of the exhibit.

- *Sanctions* were one of the tools used by the international community to pressure South Africa into ending its practice of apartheid.

- After receiving the official *sanction* of the ethics committee, the lawyer was disbarred.

Sanction can also be used as a verb. Up until the last few decades it only meant to encourage or approve, but it has recently come to mean to punish as well.

SANGUINE (SAYN gwun) *adj* cheerful, confident, optimistic

- His *sanguine* attitude was baffling to me, since it seemed clear that he was going to lose the race.

- She was so *sanguine* of success that she booked the honeymoon suite before she had even proposed.

According to Aristotle, *sanguine* personalities were caused by too much blood. This book contains vocabulary words based on three other personality types that he identified based on bodily fluids... can you find the rest?

SAP (sap) *v* to enervate or weaken the vitality of

- Her energy was *sapped* by the wasting fever; every day she felt a little weaker.

As a noun used informally, a *sap* is a gullible person, a fool.

- I can't believe I was such a *sap* that I believed she would call even though I saw her throw my phone number out the window.

A *sap* can also be a blackjack (a short, leather-covered club) or to hit somebody with such a weapon.

SARTORIAL (sahr TAWR ee uhl) *adj* of or pertaining to clothing or style

- Newspapers worldwide commented on the *sartorial* splendor of the royal wedding.

- Her *sartorial* elegance ensured that she was always on the front cover of one fashion magazine or another.

SATIATE (SAY shee ayt) *v* to overindulge, satisfy to excess

- He had a perpetual craving for chocolate that no amount could *satiate*, not even pounds of the stuff.

- After the eight-course meal, I was *satiated*; in fact, I was pretty sure I wouldn't eat again for days.

Sate is a synonym of *satiate*.

SATIRE (SAT yr) *n* a literary work that ridicules or criticizes human vice through humor or derision

- Swift's *Gulliver's Travels* is a famous *satire* in which the protagonist meets strange peoples in his travels, each representing a different aspect of humanity.

- His attempts to *satirize* his boss in the company newsletter were not appreciated. His boss did not like *satirical* work when she was its object.

SATURNINE (SAT ur nyn) *adj* gloomy, dark, sullen, morose

- Pedro's *saturnine* countenance made me think he was either very unhappy or suffering from a bad case of indigestion.

- The *saturnine* principal scared the students with his dark glares, but really he was a pretty nice guy underneath the brooding exterior.

Saturnine is similar in definition to *melancholy*. Like *mercurial*, it draws its name from astrology and the gods associated with certain planets.

SCINTILLATING (SIN ti ley ting) *adj* animated, witty, brilliantly clever

- She had such a *scintillating* personality that she was always the life of the party.

- He was such a *scintillating* conversationalist that all those who heard him were enthralled by his every word.

SCURVY (SKUR vee) *adj* contemptible, despicable

- He felt a little guilty about the *scurvy* trick he had pulled on his friend to get her to loan him a hundred dollars by saying he needed it to visit his dying mother.

"Avast ye *scurvy* dog" is a common comment to hear one pirate say to another. *Scurvy* is a vitamin C deficiency that was a familiar part of a sailor's life before the days of refrigeration, canning and supplements, so it makes sense that pirates would incorporate this into their vocabulary as an insult.

SEDULOUS (SED yoo lus) *adj* diligent, persistent, hardworking

- His *sedulous* efforts to organize the conference were rewarded when the entire event went off perfectly.

- After years of hard work, he found the missing piece to the puzzle he had so *sedulously* sought, which allowed him to solve the mystery of the pilot's disappearance.

SEINE (sayn) *n* a large net hung out and dragged in to catch fish

- The fishermen were extremely surprised when they caught a mermaid in their *seine*.

Seine also means to fish using a *seine*, and the Seine is a river in the middle of Paris in which people might *seine*...or something like that.

Quick Quiz #53

Match each word in the first column with its definition in the second column. Check your answers in the back of the book.

1.	scurvy	a.	causing improvement
2.	sap	b.	self-righteousness
3.	sanguine	c.	cheerful, confident
4.	satire	d.	weaken the vitality of
5.	salutary	e.	diligent
6.	saturnine	f.	work ridiculing human
7.	sanctimony		vice
8.	satiate	g.	gloomy
9.	seine	h.	despicable
10.	sanction	i.	a large net
11.	sedulous	j.	overindulge
12.	sartorial	k.	authoritative approval
13.	scintillating	l.	witty
		m.	pertaining to clothing

SERE (seer) *adj* withered, arid

- Some people have looked at pictures of the *sere* surface of Mars and imagined the possibility of terraforming that might change the arid landscape into something habitable by humans.

- Even the *sere* vegetation at the edge of the desert sent forth new shoots when the brief rains came.

SEMINAL (SEM uh nul) *adj* like a seed, constituting a source, originative

- He wrote the *seminal* text on robotics; people still study it sixty years later.

- The *seminal* idea that had taken root in his mind years earlier grew into the plans for the invention that was to make him a millionaire.

SERENDIPITOUS (ser uhn DIP i tus) *adj* come upon or found by accident; fortuitous

- Running into her at the cafe was completely *serendipitous*; he hadn't expected to see her again.

- Winning the lottery is the ultimate *serendipitous* event.

SHARD (shard) *n* a piece of broken pottery or glass, any small piece or part

- The archaeologist was able to find enough *shards* of pottery at the site that she could piece them together to form the contours of the original bowl.

- He tried to collect the *shards* of his dignity after his pants fell down in the middle of his speech.

SIMPER (SIM pur) *v* to smirk; to say something with a silly, coy smile

- Her *simpering* praise for the famous actress made me want to throw up.

- He *simpered* some feeble attempt at an apology that no one believed.

As a noun, *simper* is the silly smile itself.

SINECURE (SY ni kyoor) *n* position requiring little or no work and usually providing an income

- The evil overlord's sidekick figured he deserved a *sinecure* after years of faithful and often gory service.
- The job was hardly a *sinecure*; not only was there a ton of work, but there was also no job security.

This word was first applied to priests without churches (or without parish duties of curing souls), who were said to have *beneficium sine cura*.

SINGULAR (SING yoo lur) *adj* exceptional, unusual, odd

- The *singular* events of the past week had me thinking I'd lost my mind; first my pet turtle presents me with a list of demands, and then it starts raining humans instead of cats and dogs.
- He was *singularly* ill-suited to ballet since he had two left feet.

SINUOUS (SIN yoo us) *adj* winding, curving, moving lithely, devious

- We were mesmerized by the *sinuous* waving of the cobra as the snake charmer sang to it.
- The *sinuous* pattern on the vase was like a river winding back and forth.
- It became increasingly difficult to follow the argument as her *sinuous* logic wound around and around itself.

SLAKE (slayk) *v* to satisfy, quench, lessen the intensity of

- I was looking forward to getting back to the porch and having a julep to *slake* my thirst.

- His anger *slaked* somewhat when he realized he had simply parked his car in the wrong spot, and that no one had stolen it.

SODDEN (SAHD un) *adj* soaked or drenched, unimaginative, dull

- I managed to get my pants all wet by sitting on the *sodden* ground.

- *Sodden* with drink and sleep, he could barely form a sentence.

Quick Quiz #54

Match each word in the first column with its definition in the second column. Check your answers in the back of the book.

1.	singular	a.	withered
2.	shard	b.	smirk
3.	seminal	c.	exceptional
4.	sinuous	d.	quench
5.	simper	e.	like a seed
6.	sinecure	f.	soaked
7.	sere	g.	position requiring little work
8.	sodden		
9.	slake	h.	broken piece
10.	serendipitous	i.	winding
		j.	fortuitous

SOLDER (SAH dur) *v* to weld, fuse or join, as with a soldering gun

- By *soldering* the broken pieces together, I was able to repair the light fixture.

- The charismatic general managed to *solder* all the factions together into one cohesive army.

SOLICITOUS (suh LI sit us) *adj* concerned and attentive, eager

- It was nice of her to be so *solicitous* of my comfort as to offer me the couch, but I was fine sleeping on the floor.

- Her *solicitous* boyfriend hovered at her elbow all evening, trying to anticipate her every wish, which she started to find somewhat annoying after about five minutes.

SOLVENT (SAHL vunt) *adj* able to meet financial obligations

- After being *solvent* for the first time in years, I celebrated my *solvency* by gambling. After losing, I had once again become *insolvent* and had to borrow rent money from my parents.

SOPHISTRY (SAH fis tree) *n* fallacious reasoning; plausible but faulty logic

- I'm such a sucker for *sophistry*; I can never see through the convincing surface to the false logic underneath.

- The environmentalists claimed that the distinction between "strategic harvesting" and "clear cutting" was merely a political *sophistry* designed to hide the lumber industry's plans.

The Greek root *soph* gave rise to many English words about knowledge—either the love of it, the possession of it, or the lack of it. *Philosophy* is a love or pursuit of knowledge, and someone with great knowledge of the world might be called *sophisticated*. *Sophistry* is somewhat on the opposite path…as is *sophomoric*.

SOPHOMORIC (sahf MOR ik) *adj* exhibiting immaturity, lack of judgment, pretentious

- You may call my humor *sophomoric*, but you laughed at all my jokes, so either I'm funny or you're as immature as I am.

- Her *sophomoric* posturing just made her seem pretentious and silly rather than worldly and wise as she had intended.

Sophomoric literally means of or pertaining to a sophomore.

SOPORIFIC (sahp uh RIF ik) *adj* causing drowsiness, tending to induce sleep

- The economics professor's lectures were amazingly *soporific*; five minutes listening to him would cure any case of insomnia.

Soporific can also be used as a noun.

- She hoped a glass of warm milk would be a sufficient *soporific* to get her daughter to go to sleep at long last.

SORDID (SOR did) *adj* characterized by filth, grime, or squalor, foul

- The *sordid* tale of deceit and betrayal in the criminal underworld became an immediate bestseller.

- Without any sanitation at all, the *sordid* slums at the edge of town were likely to suffer another cholera epidemic.

SPARSE (spars) *adj* thin, not dense, arranged at widely spaced intervals

- Her approval, though *sparsely* given, made me feel I had accomplished something important.

- The *sparsely* wooded hill looked naked in the winter, without the lush growth of the spring and summer to cover it.

SPECIOUS (SPEE shus) *adj* seeming true, but actually false, misleadingly attractive

- The *specious* "get rich quick" promises of pyramid schemes have suckered countless people over the years.

- The teenager's *specious* argument for why she should be allowed to stay out past curfew failed to convince her parents.

Match each word in the first column with its definition in the second column. Check your answers in the back of the book.

1.	sordid	a.	immature
2.	specious	b.	financially sound
3.	solder	c.	faulty logic
4.	solicitous	d.	seeming true but
5.	sophistry		actually false
6.	soporific	e.	concerned and attentive
7.	solvent	f.	join together
8.	sparse	g.	not dense
9.	sophomoric	h.	filthy
		i.	causing drowsiness

SPENDTHRIFT (SPEND thrift) *n* one who spends money wastefully

- Olivia was an incorrigible *spendthrift*; she bought things she would never use and didn't even particularly like.

Spendthrift can also be an adjective.

- Their *spendthrift* extravagance soon exhausted their small bank account.

SPLENETIC (spli NET ik) *adj* bad-tempered, irritable

- The patient became particularly *splenetic* whenever his spleen was bothering him, so the nurses stayed out of his room those days.

- Her boss became *splenetic* whenever anyone asked him about a raise; nothing seemed to irritate him more.

Splenetic also means relating to the spleen, which was the seat of ill temper in classical knowledge.

SPORADIC (spor AD ik) *adj* occurring only occasionally, or in scattered instances

- The *sporadic* nature of the thunderstorms made them very difficult to predict.
- We hoped that the weird appearance of horns on Kurt's forehead would remain *sporadic*, which would help us pretend he wasn't really growing them.

SPURIOUS (SPYOOR ee us) *adj* lacking authenticity or validity, false, counterfeit

- His *spurious* claim that he had found the fountain of youth was soon proven to be the fraud everyone had suspected.
- It was years before anyone discovered that the painting attributed to the young Picasso was *spurious*, having been painted by a not very famous artist who made his living by painting those pictures you find in hotel rooms.

SQUALID (SKWAH lid) *adj* sordid, wretched and dirty as from neglect

- The *squalid* living conditions the migrant laborers were forced to endure were simply inhuman; no one should have to live like that.

Squalor is a wretched or filthy condition.

- Why she was willing to live in *squalor*, no one could figure out, but she seemed happy enough with two months' worth of dishes in the sink and refuse lying all around.

SQUANDER (SKWAHN dur) *v* to waste by spending or using irresponsibly

- I would hate to see you *squander* your talents by making vacuum cleaner bags for the rest of your life instead of the art you really want to create.
- He *squandered* his fortune as quickly as he had made it, ending up exactly where he started.

STANCH (stawnch) *v* to stop the flow of a fluid

- The flow of blood from the cut was so slight that half a tissue was all that was needed to *stanch* it.

- All attempts to *stanch* the hemorrhaging of the company's coffers were futile; the money just kept pouring out as costs increased exponentially.

Don't confuse this with *staunch*, an adjective, meaning firmly committed. To make it really confusing, sometimes *stanch* is spelled *staunch*, and vice versa, but you should be able to figure out the word's meaning from context.

STATIC (STAT ik) *adj* not moving, active or in motion; at rest

- The population of the town had been *static* for years; no one had moved in or out, been born or died in the whole place.

- She couldn't stay *static* for more than five minutes at a time before she started bouncing off the walls again.

Quick Quiz #56

Match each word in the first column with its definition in the second column. Check your answers in the back of the book.

1. splenetic	a.	bad-tempered
2. stanch	b.	occurring occasionally
3. spendthrift	c.	use irresponsibly
4. sporadic	d.	waster of money
5. squander	e.	wretched and dirty
6. squalid	f.	false
7. spurious	g.	not moving or changing
8. static	h.	stop a flow

GRE Power Vocab

STEEP (steep) *v* to saturate or completely soak

- Her plan was to spend three months in Paris and come back *steeped* in French culture, but all she ended up with was a fuchsia beret from the souvenir shop.

- The old castle is *steeped* in history; you can practically feel it oozing out of every corner as you walk around.

STENTORIAN (sten TOR ee un) *adj* extremely loud and powerful

- Her grandfather's *stentorian* voice could be heard from anywhere in the house, and when he issued a command, everyone moved immediately.

- Is it absolutely necessary to keep the stereo on at such a *stentorian* volume that people five blocks away can hear it?

STINT (stint) *v* to restrain, be sparing or frugal

- I hate to *stint* on dessert, so I always save room for at least two portions.

- Since I didn't want to *stint* on her birthday, I got her a cake and a present.

Stinting, and its opposite, *unstinting* are the adjectives that mean restraining and bestowed liberally, respectively.

- Her *unstinting* support for my lemonade stand, both supplier of the product and most loyal customer, gave me my start as an entrepreneur.

Stint as a noun means a length of time spent in a specific way, as in a *stint* in the military, in the White House, or as a roadie.

STOIC (STOH ik) *adj* indifferent to or unaffected by pleasure or pain, steadfast

- Lorelei's *stoic* indifference to the pain of her dislocated shoulder was disconcerting; it was impossible to tell anything was wrong from the expression on her face.

Stoicism is the noun.

- Vulcans, such as Mr. Spock, practice *stoicism*, exercising extremely tight control over their emotions.

STOLID (STAH lid) *adj* calm, impassive

- Ian's *stolid* nature and formidable physique make him perfect for a job as a Buckingham Palace guard.

If you associate this word with *solid*, you have a built-in memory aid; *stolid* people show little animation or emotion.

STRIATED (STRY ayt id) *adj* striped, grooved, or banded

- Our attempt to make a cake with *striated* frosting to look like a beach ball wasn't very successful; all the bands of color ran together until it was just one big blob.

- It was initially a bit strange to drive over the grooves on the roads where the asphalt had been *striated* to provide better traction when it rained.

Striations are the bands themselves.

STRUT (strut) *n* a structural support used to brace a framework

- When one of the *struts* supporting the wing of the old seaplane broke, we thought we were going to be swimming home.

- When the *struts* on our car started to wear, we could feel very tiny bumps on the road.

Strut can also be used as a verb to mean brace or support.

STUPEFY (STOO puh fy) *v* to stun, baffle, or amaze

- *Stupefied* by the blow to his head, Scott just kept bumping into more and more things, getting more and more dazed.

- We were *stupefied* by the sight of a hippopotamus dancing with a kangaroo.

STYMIE (STY mee) *v* to block, thwart

- Rodney planned to *stymie* Jake's chances of winning the cooking contest by switching the salt and sugar when he wasn't looking.

- His plans to become a professional race car driver were *stymied* when he failed his driving test for the third time.

Quick Quiz #57

Match each word in the first column with its definition in the second column. Check your answers in the back of the book.

1.	stint	a.	stun
2.	striated	b.	extremely loud
3.	steep	c.	striped
4.	stolid	d.	be sparing
5.	stupefy	e.	supporting structure
6.	stentorian	f.	completely soak
7.	strut	g.	unaffected by pleasure or pain
8.	stymie	h.	thwart
9.	stoic	i.	impassive

SUBPOENA (suh PEE nuh) *n* a court order requiring appearance and/or testimony

- You could have knocked me over with a feather when my next-door neighbor, the sweet little old grandmother, was served with a *subpoena* to appear in a federal racketeering case.

Subpoena can also be used as a verb.

- The prosecutor *subpoenaed* the kingpin's hairdresser to testify before the grand jury.

SUBTLE (SUH tul) *adj* not obvious, elusive, difficult to discern, crafty or sly

- The *subtle* flavors of the sauce were difficult to detect individually, but together they created a unique and delicious dish.

- We had to admire the *subtlety* of her scheme; she had managed to steal half the gold in the treasury before anyone even knew it was missing.

SUCCINCT (suk SINKT) *adj* brief, concise

- Although he had vowed to keep his introduction *succinct*, he still ended up speaking for a longer time than all of the main speakers combined.

- This sentence is *succinct*.

SUCCOR (SUH kur) *n* assistance, relief in time of distress

- The brief rain did not provide much *succor* to the farmers who were losing their crops to drought.

- The town's inhabitants sought *succor* in the emergency shelters during and after the hurricane.

SUNDRY (SUN dree) *adj* various, miscellaneous, separate

- Of the *sundry* items for sale, the young boy was most interested in the elaborate water pistol.

- My backpack is filled to overflowing with *sundry* items, but somehow I can never find what I need.

If you've heard the phrase torn *asunder*, you are familiar with the etymology of this word. *Sundry* originally meant separate or distinct, but now also means various.

SUPERCILIOUS (soo pur SIL ee us) *adj* disdainful, arrogant, haughty, characterized by haughty scorn.

- The snotty salesperson looked at the clothes I was wearing with a *supercilious* expression and apparently decided I wasn't worth her time, so she went back to filing her nails.

- I was extremely surprised when he told me he had initially taken my shyness for *superciliousness*; luckily he later changed his mind and realized I wasn't stuck-up after all.

SUPERFLUOUS (soo PUR floo us) *adj* exceeding what is sufficient or necessary

- The admonition only to eat one of the cupcakes was *superfluous*; no one would have wanted a second.

- Tim and Shane's new plan for saving money was to stop any *superfluous* spending, but they quickly realized that everything they spent money on was necessary.

SUPINE (SOO pyn) *adj* inactive, lying on one's back, apathetic, mentally or morally slack

- We spent hours *supine* on the floor looking up at the glow-in-the-dark stars we had pasted on the ceiling.

- Our *supine* acceptance of the corruption taking place all around us means we have few to blame for the consequences other than ourselves.

Supine means lying face up and *prone* means lying face down.

SUPPLANT (sup PLANT) *v* to take the place of, supersede

- I was quickly *supplanted* in my ex-girlfriend's affections by her new beau, and a month later she didn't even remember my name.

- Some people have argued that as e-mail *supplants* letter writing, whole new modes of thinking and communicating are being born.

Match each word in the first column with its definition in the second column. Check your answers in the back of the book.

1. sundry	a.	court order
2. subpoena	b.	not obvious
3. supplant	c.	concise
4. succor	d.	relief in time of distress
5. succinct	e.	miscellaneous
6. supercilious	f.	disdainful
7. supine	g.	exceeding what is necessary
8. subtle	h.	inactive
9. superfluous	i.	supercede

SUPPLIANT (sup PLY unt) *adj* asking humbly, beseeching

- The *suppliant* expression on the boy's face would have melted anyone's will to refuse him what he wanted.

- Stubbornly, the band refused the *suppliant* crowd's plea for them to play their hit song; they were simply too sick of playing it night after night.

As a noun, a *suppliant* is the same thing as a *supplicant*.

SUPPLICANT (SUP li kant) *n* beggar, one who prays or begs for something

- A long line of *supplicants* awaited the magistrate each Thursday, which is when he heard petitions for assistance from the very poor.

A *supplicant* is *supplicating* when he or she begs for something. *Supplication* is related to *application*, or the act of bringing yourself close to something. In *supplication*, though, there is the element of folding the legs under, or kneeling, that gives the *sup-* prefix.

SURFEIT (SUR fut) *v* to feed or supply in excess

- The girls *surfeited* themselves with candy and cookies at the birthday party, and all came home with stomachaches.

Surfeit is also a noun, meaning excess, overindulgence.

- A *surfeit* of cooks is said to spoil the broth.

SYCOPHANT (SIK uh funt) *n* someone who tries to flatter or please for personal gain, parasite

- The young basketball player has an entourage of *sycophants*, all hoping to gain his favor and receive expensive gifts when he becomes rich.

- She had been surrounded by *sycophants* her whole life, so she had never received any honest criticism of her behavior.

SYNTHESIS (SIN thuh sus) *n* the combination of parts to make a whole

- Snowboarding is a *synthesis* of skateboarding, surfing, and skiing.

- As much as he tried to find a *synthesis* of his desires to stay up late and wake up early, he was never able to do both.

T

TABLE (TAY bul) *v* to remove (as a parliamentary motion) from consideration

- Unsurprisingly, the council *tabled* the students' motion to reduce the school day by half for the fifth year in a row.

- Because the meeting had already gone two hours longer than scheduled, the remaining agenda items had to be *tabled* until the next month.

TACITURN (TA sit urn) *adj* not talkative, silent

- Although Steve was *taciturn* in public and with people he didn't know, he was very talkative when he was with his friends.

- Their usually *taciturn* boss became downright loquacious whenever she had a couple of drinks.

Taciturn shares a root with the Italian *tacet*, which in music, means to be quiet or rest. *Tacit*, similarly, means implied or not directly stated.

- We chose to understand his failure to say we couldn't go as *tacit* permission to do so.

TALISMAN (TAL iz mun) *n* something believed to have magic power or bestow good luck

- Dumbo's *talisman* was a red feather; he believed that his ability to fly stemmed from carrying it with him.

- Though I am generally not a superstitious person, I keep a rabbit's foot in my pocket as a *talisman* for good luck.

TAMP (tamp) *v* to plug, to drive in or down by a series of blows

- The old man had a very specific ritual for *tamping* the tobacco into his pipe, and he repeated it all day long even though he never actually lit the pipe.

- After placing the saplings in the holes and filling them in with soil, we *tamped* down the ground around each tree.

TAUTOLOGY (taw TAHL uh gee) *n* a repetition, a redundancy, a circular argument

- "There can be no such thing as obscenity in art because art is not obscene" is a *tautology*.

- His argument was *tautological* because he never introduced any support for his claim, he just kept repeating it over and over.

Quick Quiz #59

Match each word in the first column with its definition in the second column. Check your answers in the back of the book.

1. tacit
2. tautology
3. suppliant
4. table
5. supplicant
6. surfeit
7. taciturn
8. sycophant
9. synthesis
10. talisman
11. tamp

a. asking humbly
b. beggar
c. overindulgence
d. flatterer
e. combination of parts into whole
f. remove from consideration
g. not explicitly stated
h. not talkative
i. drive in
j. redundancy
k. good-luck charm

TAWDRY (TAW dree) *adj* cheap, gaudy, showy, tacky, indecent

- Claire bought all sorts of *tawdry* jewelry to complete her Halloween costume when she dressed as an Old West saloon singer.

- The tabloid specialized in revealing the *tawdry* secrets of minor celebrities.

TEMPERANCE (TEM per uhns) *n* moderation of self-restraint; self-control

- Buddhist monks live a life of *temperance* abstaining from most outward pleasures of life.

- He showed remarkable *temperance* by not getting angry at her after she burned his house down.

TENACITY (ten A sit ee) *n* the quality of adherence or persistence to something valued

- His *tenacity* in seeking public office was remarkable; he sought election fifteen different times and even though he never won, he never gave up.

Tenacious means stubborn, refusing to give up or let go of something.

- She was *tenacious* in her refusal to sell her house to the developers, even when they alternately tried to bribe and threaten her.

TENDENTIOUS (ten DEN shus) *adj* biased, showing marked tendencies

- It was difficult to determine what was objective fact and what was *tendentious* opinion, because all the research published thus far had been paid for by one side or the other.

- Although it was clearly a *tendentious* account, I found it very informative, though that may have been because I happened to agree with the author.

TENDER (TEN dur) *v* to offer formally

- We refused the terms of the truce the other side *tendered*, because they wanted us to surrender our water balloons first.

- Frances planned to *tender* her resignation first thing in the morning, though she secretly hoped her boss would talk her out of leaving.

TENUOUS (TEN yoo us) *adj* having little substance or strength, flimsy, weak

- Tyler's grasp on mathematics has always been somewhat *tenuous*; he understands addition fairly well, but subtraction poses some challenges.

- Although the plot of the movie was at best *tenuous*, the performances of the supporting cast were amazing enough to make the movie worth watching.

TEPID (TEP id) *adj* characterized by a lack of force or enthusiasm

- The critics had a *tepid* reaction to the new TV show; seemingly they neither particularly hated nor liked it.

- She gave such a *tepid* response to his invitation that he wasn't sure she really wanted to go with him to the party.

TERSE (turs) *adj* brief and concise in wording

- Keith's *terse*, one-word answers made it clear that he was upset, since he is usually very talkative when he is happy.

TIMOROUS (TIM or us) *adj* timid, fearful, diffident

- Mice are supposed to be *timorous*, but the one living behind the fridge seems very bold and completely unafraid of me.

- His *timorous* request to speak was drowned out by the loud arguing amongst the rest of the members of the panel, and he wasn't confident enough to shout over them.

TIRADE (TYE rayd) *n* a long and extremely critical speech, harsh denunciation

- The students were wary of asking any questions about contemporary literature, afraid that the professor would launch into one of his lengthy *tirades* against the decline of American literature over the last century.

- Alex didn't think he could stand one more *tirade* about the rising cost of toothpaste, so he excused himself from the conference on dental hygiene and went to eat lunch.

TOADY (TOH dee) *n* sycophant, flatterer, yes-man

- Lewis could always rely on his trusty *toady* to tell him what he wanted to hear, even if it didn't match up to reality in any way.

To *toady* is to behave like a *toady*.

- The king trusted his gardener more than anyone else, because the gardener refused to *toady* to him; he could therefore believe that what he said was true, rather than something designed to curry favor.

TORPID (TOR pid) *adj* lethargic, sluggish, dormant

- We were *torpid* with exhaustion and could barely move after walking fifteen miles back to camp.

Torpor is a state of inactivity or lethargy.

- The cat fell into *torpor* after his catnip-induced frenzy and went to sleep in a patch of sunlight in the living room.

TORQUE (tork) *n* a force that causes rotation

- Gary was having a difficult time generating enough *torque* to get the wheel to spin on its own.

- A *torque* wrench measures the amount of force being used to tighten a nut or bolt in order to ensure that it is tight enough not to come loose but not too tight.

Quick Quiz #60

Match each word in the first column with its definition in the second column. Check your answers in the back of the book.

1. tenuous
2. timorous
3. tendentious
4. tawdry
5. terse
6. torque
7. tirade
8. tenacity
9. tender
10. toady
11. torpid
12. temperance
13. tepid

a. a little substance
b. adherence to something valued
c. cheap
d. concise
e. flatterer
f. sluggish
g. fearful
h. harsh denunciation
i. biased
j. offer
k. force causing rotation
l. lack of enthusiasm
m. self-restraint

TORRID (TOR id) *adj* scorching, ardent, passionate, hurried

- Chris was so engrossed in the *torrid* love affair unfolding in the novel that he didn't even notice that he had missed his bus stop.

- Everyone escaped the *torrid* heat of mid-afternoon by taking a siesta.

Perhaps not surprisingly, *torrid* comes from a Latin word meaning burn. So, however, does *torrent*, maybe because a roaring *torrent* looks like its boiling or because a *torrent* of words can burn you.

TORTUOUS (TORT yoo us) *adj* winding, twisting, excessively complicated

- It was unsafe to drive faster than ten miles an hour on the *tortuous* road down the mountain because the turns were so sharp, so most people chose to walk or bicycle down instead.

- Brendan launched into an argument so *tortuous* in its reasoning that he hoped no one would be able to follow it and realize that Brendan had no idea what he was talking about.

Be careful not to mix this one up with *torturous*,
which means relating to or causing torture.

TOUT (towt) *v* to publicly praise or promote

- When the beautiful model went on television *touting* the health benefits of pickle juice, pickle sales quadrupled overnight.

- In the past, many ingredients were *touted* as beneficial that later turned out to be at best ineffective and at worst, toxic.

TRACTABLE (TRAK tuh bul) *adj* docile, obedient, easily led

- The magician was looking for a *tractable* young assistant who would be willing to follow directions such as "get in the box so I can saw you in half."

- The babysitter had thought the children were models of *tractability*, until she discovered they were just very good at hiding their disobedience.

Intractable means unruly.

TRANSIENT (TRAN zee unt) *adj* fleeting, passing quickly, brief

- In June the summer always seemed so long, but by September it always seemed so *transient*.

- Leslie grabbed the *transient* opportunity to join the band on tour, knowing that she only had a brief window in which the offer would be open.

Transience in the state of being *transient*.

- The suitcase that never got unpacked was just one sign of his perpetual *transience*.

TRAVESTY (TRAV est ee) *n* mockery, caricature, parody

- The defendant argued that the proceedings were a *travesty* of a trial since he did not have a lawyer representing him.

As a verb, *travesty* means to imitate in such a way as to ridicule.

- The satire *travestied* the inner circle of the governor's administration.

TRENCHANT (TREN chunt) *adj* sharply perceptive, keen, penetrating, biting, clear cut

- His *trenchant* criticism of the report revealed the fundamentally flawed premise on which it was based.

- Eric could always be counted on to perform the *trenchant* analysis that would unearth what had gone wrong in the project thus far.

- Although she made very *trenchant* distinctions about what was right and wrong in other people's actions, she was less clear cut about her own behavior.

TRITE (TRAHYT) *adj* lacking in freshness or effectiveness because of constant use or excessive repetition

- Her writing was decidedly *trite*; providing nothing original to the body of literature.

- His speech was *trite* and endlessly long.

TRUCULENT (TRUK yoo lunt) *adj* fierce, scathing, eager to fight

- Her *truculent* opposition to the building of a new chemical plant made her a minor celebrity in her hometown, where she was regarded as a fierce crusader for the rights of the townspeople.

- The *truculent* trucker had already been arrested five times this year for starting barroom brawls.

TUMID (TOO mud) *adj* swollen

- The river, *tumid* from the spring rains, overflowed its banks and flooded the surrounding fields.

Tumescence is swelling.

- Elmer put ice on his face to try to reduce the *tumescence* of the black eye he got while fighting with the truculent trucker.

TURBID (TUR bud) *adj* muddy, having sediment stirred up, clouded to the point of being opaque, in a state of turmoil

- The coffee was so *turbid* from the grounds that seeped through the filter that it looked like mud.

- Grace's mind was so *turbid* with anxieties over how she was going to handle the next day that she couldn't sleep all night.

Match each word in the first column with its definition in the second column. Check your answers in the back of the book.

1. transient
2. trenchant
3. travesty
4. torrid
5. tortuous
6. turbid
7. tractable
8. tout
9. tumid
10. truculent
11. trite

a. mockery
b. keen
c. publicly praise
d. brief
e. passionate
f. clouded
g. eager to fight
h. twisting
i. obedient
j. swollen
k. lacking in freshness

TURGID (TUR jid) *adj* swollen, bloated, pompous, excessively ornate

- Her *turgid* prose would have been difficult to take in any context, but it was particularly ill-suited to a computer how-to book.

- The water balloons were so *turgid* that they would pop at the slightest pressure.

Turgid is a synonym for *tumid*.

TURPITUDE (TUR puh tood) *n* depravity, baseness

- Because he had been caught stealing from the orphanage's fund, he was immediately dismissed on the grounds of moral *turpitude*.

- Claiming that shopping malls were marketplaces of *turpitude*, Ms. Snow declared that the morally correct thing to do was to shop exclusively by mail.

TYRO (TY roh) *n* novice, beginner in learning

- Although he was only a *tyro* at the game of chess, he was able to win most of his matches against more experienced players.

- It became clear that he was a *tyro* when he showed the whole table his cards.

Neophyte is a synonym for *tyro*.

U

UBIQUITOUS (yoo BIK wuh tus) *adj* existing everywhere at the same time, constantly encountered, widespread

- Many animals that were once nearly *ubiquitous* in North America, such as the passenger pigeon, are now extinct.

Ubiquity is the state of being everywhere at the same time.

- The *ubiquity* of the ad campaign ended up working against it; people got sick of seeing it everywhere all the time that they vowed never to buy the product it advertised.

UMBRAGE (UM brij) *n* offense, resentment

- I decided not to take *umbrage* at his insults because I know he was just trying to get a response, and ignoring him would be the most satisfying revenge.

UNDULATE (UN dyoo layt) *v* to move in wavelike fashion, fluctuate

- The small snake *undulated* over the twigs in the yard, seeming to flow over them in a way that was unlike the movement of any other animal.

Undulations are the motions something makes when it undulates.

- The audience was hypnotized by the belly dancer's *undulations*.

UNFEIGNED (un FAYND) *adj* genuine, not false or hypothetical

- Constance's surprise when everyone jumped out and said "happy birthday" seemed completely *unfeigned*, which was amazing since I thought at least three people had inadvertently told her about the surprise party.

- Her *unfeigned* warmth as she welcomed us into her home made me feel immediately at ease.

UNTENABLE (un TEN uh bul) *adj* indefensible, not viable, uninhabitable

- The president realized he was in an *untenable* position when even his own cabinet disagreed with him.

- Barry was unsure why his girlfriend was arguing that their long distance relationship was *untenable* when they'd been making it work for two years already.

UNTOWARD (un TOW urd) *adj* troublesome, unruly, unseemly, adverse

- I was always impressed that Shelly managed to remain upbeat under even the most *untoward* situations.

- There was a rumor going around that something *untoward* had occurred in the principal's office the night before.

UPBRAID (up BRAYD) *v* to scold, censure, rebuke, chastise

- Nathan was thoroughly *upbraided* for having gone over his boss's head with a proposal.

An *upbraiding* is a severe scolding.

- When I showed up three hours late without the one thing that I was supposed to bring home for dinner, I suspected I was in for a serious *upbraiding*.

Quick Quiz #62

Match each word in the first column with its definition in the second column. Check your answers in the back of the book.

1. upbraid
2. tyro
3. turgid
4. umbrage
5. untoward
6. unfeigned
7. untenable
8. turpitude
9. ubiquitous
10. undulate

a. swollen
b. depravity
c. novice
d. widespread
e. resentment
f. fluctuate
g. genuine
h. not viable
i. unseemly
j. scold

URBANE (ur BAYN) *adj* sophisticated, refined, elegant

- He was particularly proud of his *urbane* manners, since it was important to him that no one guesses he grew up in a log cabin.

- She was always claiming that her *urbane* tastes could only truly be satisfied back in Paris or Milan, but we suspected she'd never even been there.

USURY (YOO zhuh ree) *n* charging an exorbitant or illegal rate of interest

- Hannah, whenever she got her credit card statements, railed against what she claimed was *usury* on the part of the banks to anyone who would listen.

GRE Power Vocab

Quaint as it may seem now, *usury* used to mean charging interest for a loan, period, and it has been forbidden by law in many religions and cultures. Now that charging interest is a common business practice, its meaning has changed to that of charging an exorbitant rate.

V

VACILLATE (VA sil ayt) *v* to waver indecisively between one course of action or opinion and another, sway from one side to the other

- Harry kept *vacillating* between vanilla and chocolate ice cream for so long that the waiter finally just brought him a scoop of each.

Vacillation is what happens when you vacillate.

- Karen's endless *vacillation* over every minor decision became so annoying to her friends that they just started making all of her decisions for her.

VARIEGATED (VAYR ee uh gay ted) *adj* multicolored, characterized by a variety of patches of different color

- The *variegated* fields of wildflowers in the springtime seemed like they contained every color we'd ever seen.

- His *variegated* coat, with all its different patches of color, made him easy to spot in a crowd.

VAUNT (vahnt) *v* to brag or boast

- Fred has a tendency to *vaunt* his own achievements, even though his friends remind him that it is often more effective to wait for other people to point out when one has done a good job.

- The new model, much *vaunted* before its release by both the reviewers and the manufacturer, turned out to be a total dud.

VENAL (VEE nul) *adj* capable of being bought or bribed, mercenary

- The presence of the *venal* juror who accepted a bribe resulted in an acquittal.

Venality is the use of position for personal gain.

- Rampant *venality* in city politics eroded everyone's trust in the system.

Venal and *venality* share a root with *vendors* and *vending machines*—all refer to people (or machines) to whom we give money in exchange for goods and services. *Venal*, though, has a bad connotation—much worse than even a vending machine that eats your money and gives you nothing in return.

VENERATE (VEN uh rayt) *v* to revere

- The members of the boy band were *venerated* by their young fans, whose parents failed to understand the appeal at all.

Veneration is respect or reverence.

- Food and incense were placed on the shrine to their ancestors as signs of *veneration*.

VERACITY (vuh RAS uh tee) *n* truthfulness, honesty

- I would never have doubted your *veracity* if you hadn't had your fingers crossed and been muttering under your breath.

- A lie detector is a device used to measure the *veracity* of someone's statements.

Be careful not to confuse *veracity* with *voracity*, which means ravenous or very eager. The root *ver* deals with truth, and is shared by *aver, verisimilitude*, and *veritable*, as well as *very*!

Match each word in the first column with its definition in the second column. Check your answers in the back of the book.

1.	venal	a.	waver
2.	vacillate	b.	boast
3.	veracity	c.	mercenary
4.	urbane	d.	multicolored
5.	usury	e.	revere
6.	vaunt	f.	sophisticated
7.	variegated	g.	charging exorbitant interest
8.	venerate	h.	truthfulness

VERISIMILITUDE (ver uh si MIL I tood) *n* appearing true or real

- The *verisimilitude* of the wax figures was uncanny; they looked as if they would start to move and speak at any minute.

- The playwright tried to achieve historical *verisimilitude* by writing dialogue in the dialect of the region and time in which the play was set.

VERITABLE (VER I tuh bul) *adj* authentic, real, genuine

- Once 30 inches of snow had fallen and visibility had been reduced to nothing, we realized we were in the middle of a *veritable* blizzard.

- In this district, for a candidate to receive 60 percent of the vote is a *veritable* landslide.

VESTIGIAL (ve STIJ ee uhl) *adj* possessing a mark or visible evidence of something that is no longer present or in existence; a very slight trace or amount of something

- Paper shredders are useful to destroy *vestigial* photos of exes.
- The dumbwaiter was a *vestigial* reminder of the olden days when the house was serviced by a large staff of butlers and maids.

VEXATION (veks AY shun) *n* annoyance, irritation

- Louise began to suspect that her frequent tardiness was a source of *vexation* to her boss when she saw him pacing around and looking at the clock every morning.

Vexation is a multi-purpose word in that it can mean the act of causing irritation, the irritation itself or the state of being irritated. To *vex* is to annoy or puzzle.

- Shannon was *vexed* by her inability to buy the right lottery ticket and win a million dollars.

VIGILANT (VIJ uh lunt) *adj* alertly watchful

- Jimmy was always particularly *vigilant* around the holidays, watching for any sign of what presents he might get.
- Trina is *vigilant* about Chris's diet, keeping careful track of how much cholesterol he consumes each day.

VILIFY (VIL uh fy) *v* to defame, characterize harshly

- The animal rights activist *vilified* the manufacturers of fur coats for cruelty to animals.
- Although the politicians were *vilified* in the press for their role in the scandal, they received no official sanction.

GRE Power Vocab

When you *vilify* someone, you are engaged in *vilification*.

- Her campaign of *vilification* backfired because it made her look petty to be attacking her opponent in that way.

Anyone who has heard of *villain* has a built-in association to *vilify*.

VIRULENT (VEER uh lunt) *adj* extremely harmful or poisonous, bitterly hostile or antagonistic

- The strain of flu virus that year was particularly *virulent* and caused a national health crisis.

Virulence is extreme harmfulness or bitterness.

- The *virulence* of her response surprised me; I had no idea she was still so angry about something that happened ten years ago.

VISCOUS (VIS kus) *adj* thick, sticky

- The *viscous* cold medicine was designed to coat the throat, but its stickiness made it very unpleasant to swallow.

- Pitcher plants, among other carnivorous plants, catch their prey in *viscous* fluids in which the insects get stuck.

Viscosity is the state of being *viscous*.

- The apple juice had reached a disturbing level of *viscosity* after sitting out for a few days.

VITIATE (VI shee ayt) *v* to reduce the value of, debase, spoil, make ineffective

- His failure to live up to his end of the deal *vitiated* the entire agreement as far as I was concerned.

- The usefulness of the experimental results was *vitiated* by the lack of a control group against which to measure them.

Quick Quiz #64

Match each word in the first column with its definition in the second column. Check your answers in the back of the book.

1.	veritable	a.	make ineffective
2.	vigilant	b.	annoyance
3.	verisimilitude	c.	characterize harshly
4.	vitiate	d.	sticky
5.	vilify	e.	watchful
6.	vexation	f.	appearing true
7.	virulent	g.	extremely harmful
8.	viscous	h.	authentic
9.	vestigial	i.	very small amount

VITUPERATE (vy TOOP ur ayt) *v* to use harsh condemnatory language; abuse or censure severely

- Don't you *vituperate* me, missy, when you know you're every bit as much to blame.

- After they had spent most of the day *vituperating* each other in the harshest terms possible, it was a little strange to see them settle their differences so easily and walk off arm in arm to get lunch.

VOCIFEROUS (voh SIF er us) *adj* crying out noisily

- She was *vociferous* in maintaining her innocence, crying out to anyone willing to listen.

- The *vociferous* activist insisted that the politician hear her complaint.

VOLATILE (VAHL uh tul) *adj* readily changing to a vapor; changeable, fickle, explosive

- It was a *volatile* situation, with both parties to the negotiations changing their positions frequently, and each threatening to walk out if the other side didn't agree to the terms.

- Liquids are *volatile* if they evaporate, or change to a vapor, rapidly. Alcohol and kerosene are examples of *volatile* liquids.

VOLUBLE (VOL yuh bul) *adj* characterized by a ready and continuous flow of words; fluent; talkative

- After she drinks a martini she becomes *voluble* and will not stop talking.

- The spokesman was known for his *voluble* manner of speaking; he could get any message out in under a minute.

VORACIOUS (vor AY shus) *adj* having an insatiable appetite for an activity or pursuit, ravenous

- Michelle was a *voracious* reader; as a kid she read under the covers at night with a flashlight.

- The *voracious* mosquitoes were so hungry for our blood that no amount of citronella would keep them away, so we had to go inside.

W

WAFT (wahft) *n* a light breeze, a puff

- I must not have been holding on to the kite string very tightly, because just a single, gentle *waft* of air was enough to send it floating away over the rooftops.

Waft as a verb means to send floating through the air or over water.

- The ant *wafted* down the creek on a leaf raft.

WAVER (WAY vur) *v* to move to and fro, to sway; to be unsettled in opinion

- Ted *wavered* over whether or not to report the ten thousand dollars he found on the park bench to the police, but then he started thinking about who might come looking for it and decided to turn it in to the authorities.

- Enid never *wavered* in her conviction that her pet goose would lay golden eggs, despite its repeated failures to do so.

WELTER (WEL tur) *v* to writhe, to toss about, to be in turmoil

- The lake *weltered* in the storm, tossing the boat up on huge waves.

Welter is also a noun, meaning a state of turmoil or chaotic jumble.

- He'd searched through the *welter* of papers on his desk for the contract but couldn't find it.

WEND (wend) *v* to go, proceed, walk

- We *wended* our way through the market, buying vegetables for dinner.

- As Fritz *wended* his long way home from work, he thought again about moving closer to town.

WHET (wet) *n* to sharpen or stimulate

- The appetizers were intended to *whet* our hunger, but they were so high in fat that they completely satiated any appetite I had.

Whet is derived from a Germanic word meaning sharp. In literature, you may see *whet* used as a noun (meaning something that has the effect of *whetting*), but that meaning is not prevalent in common speech today.

WHIMSICAL (WIM zi kul) *adj* imaginative; unpredictable

While you usually see this word used in a fanciful, playful way, it can have a bad connotation.

- When Iris was a child, she dreamt of living in a *whimsical* world not unlike that in the fantasy cartoons she saw on television.

Whim and *whimsy* are related nouns.

- The entrepreneur ran her company like a dictatorship; everyone was subject to the *whims* of the boss.

Z

ZEALOUS (ZEL us) *adj* fervent, ardent, impassioned

- The team's *zealous* fans stormed the field at the end of each game, even the ones the team lost.
- She started to suspect she had become a little *overzealous* when she realized she was stalking five different Elvis impersonators at the same time.

To be *zealous* is to be filled with *zeal*.

- Have you gained a new *zeal* for learning vocabulary yet?

Quick Quiz #65

Match each word in the first column with its definition in the second column. Check your answers in the back of the book.

1. zealous
2. waft
3. waver
4. vituperate
5. wend
6. whet
7. welter
8. voracious
9. whimsical
10. volatile
11. vociferous
12. voluble

a. be in turmoil
b. ravenous
c. be unsettled in opinion
d. censure severely
e. impassioned
f. go
g. light breeze
h. changeable
i. imaginative
j. sharpen
k. very talkative
l. crying out noisily

Chapter 5

Word Roots

As we mentioned in Chapter 2, learning word roots is a great way to learn new words. In this chapter, we've included a list of the most important roots for you to know. Some of these can have more than one spelling, so we have listed the most common variations. Beneath each root are examples of words in which it is contained. Of course, these are not exhaustive lists; they are just designed to give you a sense of what the root looks like "in action."

Rather than try to memorize the roots themselves, the key is to gain familiarity with them. Get a sense of how the roots connect to each word's definition. Many people mistakenly think that roots are best used for guessing the meaning of new words. Unfortunately, English comes from a variety of linguistic origins, which means that parts of words that look similar might not actually have the same source. Misidentifying roots in that way could lead you to guess the wrong definition for the word. For instance, the root *vid* in the word *viduity* might tempt you into thinking that the definition has something to do with seeing (as in *evident* or *video*). However, *viduity* means widowhood, and comes from the Latin word *viduitas*, meaning want or widowhood.

Just because you can't rely on roots to help you guess a definition reliably, however, doesn't mean they won't help you learn the word. Roots can act as a link between the word and its definition, the same as any other mnemonic device. If you see the *lum* in *luminescent* and remember that it has to do with light, it will help you remember the word's full definition.

As we've said throughout the book, use this root list the way that works best for you. Some people choose to focus on one root at a time, learning all the words in that list. If you use this approach, you can make the most of it by noting how the root's meaning appears in each word's definition.

Once you've learned the words in these lists, go through Chapter 4 and add any words you find there that seem to contain these roots. It's a good idea to check the words in a dictionary that contains information on word origins to make sure. If you identify a word with one of these (or any other) common roots, add the root to the back of the word's flashcard. Another exercise you might find useful involves opposite-meaning roots. Identify pairs of roots having anti- thetical meaning and learn words with these roots together. For instance, learning words that contain *ben/bon* (*meaning "good"*) with those that contain *mal/male* (*meaning "bad," "evil"*) will help reinforce their meanings.

You can also play "Six Degrees of Separation" with roots. Start with one word and see how far you can get by linking common roots between adjoining words. For example, if you started with *euphony*, you could link it to *eulogy*, then to *anthropology*, *anthropocentric*, *concentric*, and end up with *convivial*.

In the end, it all comes down to trying different strategies and seeing what works for you. Do we sound like a broken record? It's because the only way to make these tools effective is to use them, and you will only use what you find at least somewhat enjoyable. The bottom line is to have fun with these. You never know; you might end up discovering a hidden passion for etymology!

A (WITHOUT)
amoral
atheist
atypical
anonymous
apathy
amorphous
atrophy
apartheid
anomaly
agnostic

AB/ABS (OFF, AWAY FROM, APART, DOWN)
abduct
abhor
abolish
abstract
abnormal
abdicate
abstinent
absolution
abstruse
abrogate
abscond
abjure
abstemious
ablution
abominate
aberrant

AC/ACR (SHARP, BITTER)
acid
acute
acerbic
exacerbate

acrid
acrimonious
acumen

ACT/AG (TO DO, TO DRIVE, TO FORCE, TO LEAD)
act
agent
agile
agitate
exacting
pedagogue
demagogue
synagogue
cogent
exigent

AD/AL (TO, TOWARD, NEAR)
adapt
adjacent
addict
admire
address
adhere
administer
adore
advice
adjoin
adultery
advocate
allure
alloy

AL/ALI/ALTER (OTHER, ANOTHER)

alternative
alias
alibi
alien
alter ego
alienation
altruist
altercation
allegory

AM (LOVE)

amateur
amatory
amorous
enamored
amity
paramour
inamorata
amiable
amicable

AMB (TO GO, TO WALK)

ambitious
amble
preamble
ambulance
ambulatory
perambulator
circumambulate

AMB/AMPH (AROUND)

amphitheater
ambit
ambiance
ambient

AMB/AMPH (BOTH, MORE THAN ONE)

ambiguous
amphibian
ambivalent
ambidextrous

ANIM (LIFE, MIND, SOUL, SPIRIT)

unanimous
animosity
equanimity
magnanimous
pusillanimous

ANTE (BEFORE)

ante
anterior
antecedent
antedate
antebellum
antediluvian

ANTHRO/ANDR (MAN, HUMAN)

anthropology
android
misanthrope
philanthropy
anthropomorphic
philander
androgynous
anthropocentric

ANNU/ENNI (YEAR)

annual
anniversary
biannual
biennial

centennial
annuity
perennial
annals
millennium

ANTI (AGAINST)
antidote
antiseptic
antipathy
antipodal

APO (AWAY)
apology
apostle
apocalypse
apogee
apocryphal
apotheosis
apostasy
apoplexy

APT/EPT (SKILL, FITNESS, ABILITY)
adapt
aptitude
apt
inept
adept

ARCH/ARCHI (CHIEF, PRINCIPAL)
architect
archenemy
archetype
archipelago

ARCHY (RULER)
monarchy
matriarchy
patriarchy
anarchy
hierarchy
oligarchy

ART (SKILL, CRAFT)
art
artificial
artifice
artisan
artifact
artful
artless

AUC/AUG/AUX (TO INCREASE)
auction
auxiliary
augment
august

AUTO (SELF)
automatic
autopsy
autocrat
autonomy

BE (TO BE, TO HAVE A CERTAIN QUALITY)
belittle
belated
bemoan
befriend
bewilder
begrudge

bequeath
bespeak
belie
beguile
beset
bemuse
bereft

BEL/BELL (WAR)
rebel
belligerent
bellicose
antebellum

BEN/BON (GOOD)
benefit
beneficiary
beneficent
benefactor
benign
benevolent
benediction
bonus
bon vivant
bona fide

BI (TWICE, DOUBLY)
binoculars
biannual
biennial
bigamy
bilateral
bilingual
bipartisan

BRI/BREV (BRIEF, SHORT)
brief
abbreviate
abridge
brevity

CAD/CID (TO FALL, TO HAPPEN BY CHANCE)
accident
coincidence
decadent
cascade
recidivism
cadence

CAND (TO BURN)
candle
incandescent
candor

CANT/CENT/CHANT (TO SING)
chant
enchant
accent
recant
incantation
incentive

CAP/CIP/CEPT (TO TAKE, TO GET)
capture
anticipate
intercept
susceptible
emancipate
recipient
incipient
percipient
precept

CAP/CAPIT/CIP (HEAD, HEADLONG)

capital
cape
captain
disciple
principle
principal
precipice
precipitate
precipitous
capitulate
capitalism
precipitation
caption
recapitulate

CARD/CORD/COUR (HEART)

cardiac
courage
encourage
concord
discord
accord
concordance
cordial

CARN (FLESH)

carnivorous
carnival
carnal
carnage
reincarnation
incarnation

CAST/CHAST (CUT)

caste
castigate
chastise
chaste

CAUST (TO BURN)

caustic
holocaust

CED/CEED/CESS (TO GO, TO YIELD, TO STOP)

exceed
precede
recess
concede
cede
access
predecessor
precedent
antecedent
recede
abscess
cessation
incessant

CENTR (CENTER)

central
concentrate
eccentric
concentric
centrifuge
egocentric

CERN/CERT/CRET/CRIM/CRIT (TO SEPARATE, TO JUDGE, TO DISTINGUISH, TO DECIDE)

concern
critic
secret
crime
discreet
ascertain
certitude
hypocrite
discriminate
criterion
discern
recrimination

CHRON (TIME)

synchronize
chronicle
chronology
chronic
chronological
anachronism
chronometer

CIRCU (AROUND, ON ALL SIDES)

circumference
circumstances
circuit
circumspect
circumvent
circumnavigate
circumambulate
circumlocution
circumscribe
circuitous

CIS (TO CUT)

scissors
precise
exorcise
excise
incision
incisive
concise

CIT (TO SET IN MOTION)

excite
incite
solicit
solicitous

CLA/CLO/CLU (SHUT, CLOSE)

closet
enclose
conclude
claustrophobia
disclose
exclusive
recluse
preclude
seclude
cloister
foreclose

CLAIM/CLAM (TO SHOUT, TO CRY OUT)

exclaim
proclaim
acclaim
clamor
disclaim
reclaim
declaim

CLI (TO LEAN TOWARD)

decline
recline
climax
proclivity
disinclination

CO/COL/COM/CON (WITH, TOGETHER)

connect
confide
concede
coerce
cohesive
cohort
confederate
collaborate
compatible
coherent
comply
conjugal
connubial
congenial
convivial
coalesce
coalition
contrite
conciliate
conclave
commensurate

CRAT/CRACY (TO GOVERN)

bureaucracy
democracy
aristocracy
theocracy
plutocracy
autocracy

CRE/CRESC/CRET (TO GROW)

creation
increase
crescendo
increment
accretion
accrue

CRED (TO BELIEVE, TO TRUST)

incredible
credibility
credentials
credit
creed
credo
credence
credulity
incredulous

CRYP (HIDDEN)

crypt
cryptic
apocryphal
cryptography

CUB/CUMB (TO LIE DOWN)

cubicle
succumb
incubate
incumbent
recumbent

CULP (BLAME)

culprit
culpable

exculpate
inculpate
mea culpa

COUR/CUR (RUNNING, A COURSE)
occur
recur
current
curriculum
courier
cursive
excursion
concur
concurrent
incur
incursion
discourse
discursive
precursor
recourse
cursory

DE (AWAY, OFF, DOWN, COMPLETELY, REVERSAL)
descend
detract
decipher
deface
defile
defraud
deplete
denounce
decry
defer
defame

delineate
deferential

DEM (PEOPLE)
democracy
epidemic
endemic
demagogue
demographics
pandemic

DI/DIA (APART, THROUGH)
dialogue
diagnose
diameter
dilate
digress
dilatory
diaphanous
dichotomy
dialectic

DIC/DICT/DIT (TO SAY, TO TELL, TO USE WORDS)
dictionary
dictate
predict
contradict
verdict
abdicate
edict
dictum
malediction
benediction
indict
indite

diction
interdict
obiter dictum

DIGN (WORTH)
dignity
dignitary
dignify
deign
indignant
condign

DIS/DIF (AWAY FROM, APART, REVERSAL, NOT)
disperse
disseminate
dissipate
dissuade
diffuse

DAC/DOC (TO TEACH)
doctor
doctrine
indoctrinate
doctrinaire
docile
didactic

DOG/DOX (OPINION)
orthodox
paradox
dogma
dogmatic

DOL (SUFFER, PAIN)
condolence
indolence

doleful
dolorous

DON/DOT/DOW (TO GIVE)
donate
donor
pardon
condone
antidote
anecdote
endow
dowry

DUB (DOUBT)
dubious
dubiety
indubitable

DUC/DUCT (TO LEAD)
conduct
abduct
conducive
seduce
induct
induce
ductile

DUR (HARD)
endure
durable
duress
dour
obdurate

DYS (FAULTY)
dysfunction
dystopia

dyspepsia
dyslexia

EPI (UPON)

epidemic
epilogue
epidermis
epistle
epitome
epigram
epithet
epitaph

EQU (EQUAL, EVEN)

equation
adequate
equivalent
equilibrium
equable
equidistant
equity
iniquity
equanimity
equivocate
equivocal

ERR (TO WANDER)

err
error
erratic
erroneous
errant
aberrant

ESCE (BECOMING)

adolescent
obsolescent

iridescent
luminescent
coalesce
quiescent
acquiescent
effervescent
incandescent
evanescent
convalescent
reminiscent

EU (GOOD, WELL)

euphoria
euphemism
eulogy
eugenics
euthanasia
euphony

E/EF/EX (OUT, OUT OF, FROM, FORMER, COMPLETELY)

evade
exclude
extricate
exonerate
extort
exhort
expire
exalt
exult
effervesce
extenuate
efface
effusion
egregious

EXTRA (OUTSIDE OF, BEYOND)

extraordinary
extrasensory
extraneous
extrapolate

FAB/FAM (SPEAK)

fable
fabulous
affable
ineffable
fame
famous
defame
infamous

FAC/FIC/FIG/FAIT/FEIT/FY (TO DO, TO MAKE)

factory
facsimile
benefactor
facile
faction
fiction
factitious
efficient
deficient
proficient
munificent
prolific
soporific
figure
figment
configuration
effigy
magnify

rarefy
ratify
ramification
counterfeit
feign
fait accompli
ex post facto

FER (TO BRING, TO CARRY, TO BEAR)

offer
transfer
confer
referendum
infer
fertile
proffer
defer
proliferate
vociferous

FERV/FERM (TO BOIL, TO BUBBLE, TO BURN)

fervor
ferment
fervid
effervescent

FID (FAITH, TRUST)

confide
confident
confidant
affidavit
diffident
fidelity
infidelity

perfidy
fiduciary
infidel
semper fidelis
bona fide

FIN (END)

final
finale
confine
define
definitive
infinite
affinity
infinitesimal

FLAG/FLAM (TO BURN)

flame
flamboyant
flammable
inflammatory
flagrant
conflagration
in flagrante delicto

FLECT/FLEX (TO BEND)

deflect
flexible
inflect
reflect
genuflect

FLICT (TO STRIKE)

afflict
inflict
conflict
profligate

FLU/FLUX (TO FLOW)

fluid
influence
fluent
affluent
fluctuation
influx
effluence
confluence
superfluous
mellifluous

FOR (BEFORE)

foresight
foreshadow
forestall
forgo
forebear

FORT (CHANCE)

fortune
fortunate
fortuitous

FRA/FRAC/FRAG/FRING (TO BREAK)

fracture
fraction
fragment
fragile
refraction
fractious
infraction
refractory
infringe

FRUIT/FRUG (FRUIT, PRODUCE)
fruitful
fruition
frugal

FUND/FOUND (BOTTOM)
foundation
fundamental
founder
profound

FUS (TO POUR)
confuse
transfusion
profuse
effusive
diffuse
suffuse
infusion

GEN (BIRTH, CREATION, RACE, KIND)
generous
generate
genetics
photogenic
degenerate
homogenous
genealogy
gender
genre
genesis
carcinogenic
genial
congenial
ingenuous

ingénue
indigenous
congenital
progeny
engender
miscegenation
sui generis

GN/GNO (KNOW)
ignore
ignoramus
recognize
incognito
diagnose
prognosis
agnostic
cognitive
cognoscenti
cognizant

GRAND (BIG)
grand
grandeur
grandiose
aggrandize
grandiloquent

GRAT (PLEASING)
grateful
ingrate
ingratiate
gratuity
gratuitous

GRAV/GRIEV (HEAVY, SERIOUS)
grave
grief

aggrieve
gravity
grievous

GREG (HERD)
congregation
segregation
aggregation
gregarious
egregious

GRAD/ GRESS (TO STOP)
progress
graduate
gradual
aggressive
regress
degrade
retrograde
transgress
digress
egress

HER/HES (TO STICK)
coherent
cohesive
adhesive
adherent
inherent

(H)ETERO (DIFFERENT)
heterosexual
heterogeneous
heterodox

(H)OM (SAME)
homogeneous
homonym
homosexual
homeostasis

HYPER (OVER, EXCESSIVE)
hyperactive
hyperbole

HYPO (UNDER, BENEATH, LESS THAN)
hypodermic
hypochondriac
hypothesis
hypocritical

ID (ONE'S OWN)
idiot
idiom
idiosyncrasy

IM/IN/EM/EN (IN, INTO)
embrace
enclose
ingratiate
intrinsic
influx
incarnate
implicit
indigenous

IM/IN (NOT, WITHOUT)
inactive
indifferent
innocuous
insipid

indolence
impartial
inept
indigent

INFRA (BENEATH)

infrastructure
infrared
infrasonic

INTER (BETWEEN, AMONG)

interstate
interim
interloper
interlude
intermittent
interplay
intersperse
intervene

INTRA (WITHIN)

intramural
intrastate
intravenous

JECT (TO THROW, TO THROW DOWN)

inject
eject
project
trajectory
conjecture
dejected
abject

JOIN/JUNCT/JUG (TO MEET, TO JOIN)

junction
joint
adjoin
subjugate
juxtapose
injunction
rejoinder
conjugal
junta

JUR (TO SWEAR)

jury
perjury
abjure
adjure

LECT/LEG (TO SELECT, TO CHOOSE)

collect
elect
select
electorate
predilection
eclectic
elegant

LEV (LIFT, LIGHT, RISE)

elevator
relieve
lever
alleviate
levitate
relevant
levee
levity

LOC/LOG/LOQU (WORD, SPEECH)

dialogue
eloquent
elocution
locution
interlocutor
prologue
epilogue
soliloquy
eulogy
colloquial
grandiloquent
philology
neologism
tautology
loquacious

LUC/LUM/LUS (LIGHT)

illustrate
illuminate
luminous
luminescent
illustrious
lackluster
translucent
lucid
elucidate

LUD/LUS (TO PLAY)

illusion
ludicrous
delude
elude
elusive
allude
collusion

prelude
interlude

LUT/LUG/LUV (TO WASH)

lavatory
dilute
pollute
deluge
antediluvian

MAG/MAJ/MAX (BIG)

magnify
magnitude
major
maximum
majestic
magnanimous
magnate
maxim
magniloquent

MAL/MALE (BAD, ILL, EVIL, WRONG)

malfunction
malodorous
malicious
malcontent
malign
malaise
dismal
malapropism
maladroit
malevolent
malinger
malfeasance
malefactor
malediction

MAN (HAND)

manual
manufacture
emancipate
manifest
mandate
mandatory

MATER/MATR (WOMAN, MOTHER)

matrimony
maternal
maternity
matriculate
matriarch

MIN (SMALL)

minute
minutiae
diminution
miniature
diminish

MIN (TO PROJECT, TO HANG OVER)

eminent
imminent
prominent
preeminent

MIS/MIT (TO SEND)

transmit
manumit
emissary
missive
intermittent
remit
remission
demise

MISC (MIXED)

miscellaneous
miscegenation
promiscuous

MON/MONIT (TO WARN)

monument
monitor
summons
admonish
remonstrate

MORPH (SHAPE)

amorphous
metamorphosis
polymorphous
anthropomorphic

MORT/MOR (DEATH)

immortal
morgue
morbid
moribund
mortify

MUT (CHANGE)

commute
mutation
mutant
immutable
transmutation
permutation

NAM/NOM/NOUN/NOWN/NYM (RULE, ORDER)

astronomy
economy
autonomy

gastronomy

taxonomy

NAT/NAS/NAI (TO BE BORN)

natural

native

naïve

cognate

nascent

innate

renaissance

NEC/NIC/NOC/NOX (HARM, DEATH)

innocent

noxious

obnoxious

pernicious

internecine

innocuous

necromancy

NOM/NYM/NOUN/NOWN (NAME)

synonym

anonymous

nominate

pseudonym

misnomer

nomenclature

acronym

homonym

nominal

ignominy

denomination

noun

renown

nom de plume

nom de guerre

NOV/NEO/NOU (NEW)

novice

novel

novelty

renovate

innovate

neologism

neophyte

nouvelle cuisine

nouveau riche

NOUNC/NUNC (TO ANNOUNCE)

announce

pronounce

denounce

renounce

OB/OC/OF/OP (TOWARD, TO, AGAINST, COMPLETELY, OVER)

obese

object

obstruct

obstinate

obscure

obtrude

oblique

oblivious

obnoxious

obstreperous

obtuse

opprobrium

obsequious

obfuscate

OMNI (ALL)

omnipresent
omniscient
omnipotent

PAC/PEAC (PEACE)

peace
appease
pacify
pacifist
pacifier
pact

PAN (ALL, EVERYWHERE)

panorama
panacea
panegyric
pantheon
panoply
pandemic

PAR (EQUAL)

par
parity
disparity
disparate
disparage

PARA (NEXT TO, BESIDE)

parallel
paraphrase
parasite
paradox
parody
paragon
parable
paradigm

paramilitary
paranoid
paranormal
parapsychology
paralegal

PAS/PAT/PATH (FEELING, SUFFERING, DISEASE)

apathy
sympathy
empathy
antipathy
passionate
compassion
compatible
dispassionate
impassive
pathos
pathology
sociopath
psychopath

PATER/PATR (FATHER, SUPPORT)

patron
patronize
paternal
paternalism
expatriate
patrimony
patriarch
patrician

PAU/PO/POV/PU (FEW, LITTLE, POOR)

poor
poverty

paucity
pauper
impoverish
puerile
pusillanimous

PED (CHILD, EDUCATION)
pedagogue
pediatrician
encyclopedia

PED/POD (FOOT)
pedal
pedestal
pedestrian
podiatrist
expedite
expedient
impede
impediment
podium
antipodes

PEN/PUN (TO PAY, TO COMPENSATE)
penal
penalty
punitive
repent
penance
penitent
penitentiary
impunity

PEND/PENS (TO HANG, TO WEIGH, TO PAY)
depend
dispense

expend
stipend
spend
expenditure
suspense
compensate
propensity
pensive
indispensable
impending
pendulum
appendix
append
appendage
ponderous
pendant

PER (COMPLETELY, WRONG)
persistent
perforate
perplex
perspire
peruse
pervade
perjury
perturb
perfunctory
perspicacious
permeate
pernicious
perennial
peremptory
pertinacious

PERI (AROUND)
perimeter
periscope

peripheral
peripatetic

PET/PIT (TO GO, TO SEEK, TO STRIVE)

appetite
compete
petition
perpetual
impetuous
petulant
propitious

PHIL (LOVE)

philosophy
philanthropy
philatelist
philology
bibliophile

PHONE/PHONY (SOUND)

telephone
symphony
megaphone
euphony
cacophony

PLAC (TO PLEASE)

placid
placebo
placate
implacable
complacent

PLE (TO FILL)

complete
deplete

complement
supplement
implement
plethora
replete

PLEX/PLIC/PLY (TO FOLD, TO TWIST, TO TANGLE, TO BEND)

complex
complexion
complicate
duplex
replica
ply
comply
implicit
implicate
explicit
duplicity
complicity
supplicate
accomplice
explicate

PON/POS/POUND (TO PUT, TO PLACE)

component
compound
deposit
dispose
expose
exposition
expound
juxtapose
depose
proponent

repository
transpose
superimpose

PORT (TO CARRY)

import
portable
porter
portfolio
deport
deportment
export
portmanteau
portly
purport
disport
importune

POST (AFTER)

posthumous
posterior
posterity
ex post facto

PRE (BEFORE)

precarious
precocious
prelude
premeditate
premonition
presage
presentiment
presume
presuppose
precedent
precept

precipitous
preclude
predilection
preeminent
preempt
prepossess
prerequisite
prerogative

PREHEN/PRISE (TO TAKE, TO GET, TO SEIZE)

surprise
comprehend
enterprise
reprehensible
apprehension
comprise
apprise
apprehend
comprehensive
reprisal

PRO (MUCH, FOR, A LOT)

prolific
profuse
propitious
prodigious
profligate
prodigal
protracted
proclivity
proliferate
propensity
prodigy
proselytize
propound

provident
prolix

PROB (TO PROVE, TO TEST)
probe
probation
approbation
probity
opprobrium
reprobate

PUG (TO FIGHT)
pugilism
pug
pugnacious
impugn
repugnant

PUNC/PUNG/POIGN/POINT (TO POINT, TO PRICK)
point
puncture
punctual
punctuate
pungent
poignant
compunction
expunge
punctilious

QUE/QUI (TO SEEK)
acquire
acquisition
exquisite
acquisitive
request
conquest

inquire
inquisitive
inquest
query
querulous
perquisite

QUI (QUIET)
quiet
disquiet
tranquil
acquiesce
quiescent

RID/RIS (TO LAUGH)
ridicule
derision
risible

ROG (TO ASK)
interrogate
arrogant
prerogative
abrogate
surrogate
derogatory
arrogate

SAL/SIL/SAULT/SULT (TO LEAP, TO JUMP)
insult
assault
somersault
salient
resilient
desultory

SACR/SANCT/SECR (SACRED)

sacred

sacrifice

sanctuary

sanctify

sanction

sacrament

sacrilege

SCI (TO KNOW)

science

conscious

conscience

unconscionable

omniscient

prescient

conscientious

nescient

SCRIBE/SCRIP (TO WRITE)

scribble

describe

script

postscript

prescribe

proscribe

ascribe

inscribe

conscription

scripture

transcript

circumscribe

manuscript

scribe

SE (APART)

select

separate

seduce

seclude

segregate

secede

sequester

sedition

SEC/SEQU (TO FOLLOW)

second

prosecute

sequel

sequence

consequence

inconsequential

obsequious

non sequitur

SED/SESS/SID (TO SIT, TO BE STILL, TO PLAN, TO PLOT)

preside

resident

sediment

session

dissident

obsession

residual

sedate

subside

subsidy

subsidiary

sedentary

dissident

insidious

assiduous
sedulous

SENS/SENT (TO FEEL, TO BE AWARE)
sense
sensual
sensory
sentiment
resent
consent
dissent
assent
consensus
sentinel
insensate
dissent
sentient
presentiment

SOL (TO LOOSEN, TO FREE)
dissolve
soluble
solve
resolve
resolution
irresolute
solvent
dissolution
dissolute
absolution

SPEC/SPIC/SPIT (TO LOOK, TO SEE)
perspective
aspect
spectator

specter
spectacles
speculation
suspicious
auspicious
spectrum
specimen
introspection
retrospective
perspective
perspicacious
circumspect
conspicuous
respite
specious

STA/STI (TO STAND, TO BE IN A PLACE)
static
stationary
destitute
obstinate
obstacle
stalwart
stagnant
steadfast
constitute
constant
stasis
status
status quo
homeostasis
apostasy

GRE Power Vocab

SUA (SMOOTH)

suave
assuage
persuade
dissuade

SUB/SUP (BELOW)

submissive
subsidiary
subjugate
subliminal
subdue
sublime
subtle
subversive
subterfuge
subordinate
suppress
supposition

SUPER/SUR (ABOVE)

surpass
supercilious
superstition
superfluous
superlative
supersede
superficial
surmount
surveillance
survey

TAC/TIC (TO BE SILENT)

reticent
tactic
taciturn

TAIN/TEN/TENT/TIN (TO HOLD)

contain
detain
pertain
pertinacious
tenacious
abstention
sustain
tenure
pertinent
tenant
tenable
tenet
sustenance

TEND/TENS/TENT/TENU (TO STRETCH, TO THIN)

tension
extend
tendency
tendon
tent
tentative
contend
contentious
tendentious
contention
contender
tenuous
distend
attenuate
extenuating

THEO (GOD)

atheist
apotheosis

theocracy

theology

TOM (TO CUT)
tome

microtome

epitome

dichotomy

TORT (TO TWIST)
tort

extort

torture

tortuous

TRACT (TO DRAG, TO PULL, TO DRAW)
tractor

attract

contract

detract

tract

tractable

intractable

protract

abstract

TRANS (ACROSS)
transfer

transaction

transparent

transport

transition

transitory

transient

transgress

transcendent

intransigent

translucent

US/UT (TO USE)
abuse

usage

utensil

usurp

utility

utilitarian

VEN/VENT (TO COME, TO MOVE TOWARD)
adventure

convene

convenient

event

venturesome

avenue

intervene

advent

contravene

circumvent

VER (TRUTH)
verdict

verify

veracious

verisimilitude

aver

verity

VERS/VERT (TO TURN)
controversy

revert

subvert

invert

divert
diverse
aversion
extrovert
introvert
inadvertent
versatile
traverse
covert
overt
avert
advert

VI (LIFE)
vivid
vicarious
convivial
viable
vivacity
joie de vivre
bon vivant

VID/VIS (TO SEE)
evident
television
video
vision
provision
adviser
provident
vista
visionary
visage

VOC/VOK (TO CALL)
vocabulary
vocal
provocative
advocate
equivocate
equivocal
vocation
avocation
convoke
vociferous
irrevocable
evocative
revoke
invoke

VOL (TO WISH)
voluntary
volunteer
volition
malevolent
benevolent

Chapter 6

Final Exam

All of the drills in this chapter include words defined in Chapter 4. We recommend that you take this exam on scratch paper, so that you can redo the test later if you do more studying. You should shoot for at least 80–90 percent accuracy on each individual drill. Keep in mind here that the GRE does not have sections that are matching words, antonyms, synonyms, or analogies. The GRE tests vocabulary in text completion, sentence equivalence, or reading comprehension format. However, the drills in this section are valuable as learning tools for vocabulary words. Answers to these questions appear along with the Quick Quiz answers in Chapter 11.

Final Exam Drill #1

Pair 'Em Up

In each of these lists, circle the two words that are most similar in meaning. The other word may be an opposite, or may not be related at all.

1.	philistine	boor	martinet
2.	lachrymose	punctilious	melancholy
3.	insipid	jejune	tawdry
4.	subpoena	laud	aggrandize
5.	obsequious	soporific	reverent
6.	picaresque	acumen	perspicacity
7.	paean	elegy	tirade
8.	aver	assuage	mitigate
9.	chic	natty	venal
10.	oscillate	recapitulate	waffle

Final Exam Drill #2

Synonyms

Match each word in the first column with the word in the second that is most nearly THE SAME in meaning.

1.	illusion	a.	chimera
2.	blithe	b.	omen
3.	malleable	c.	courage
4.	pluck	d.	errant
5.	supine	e.	indolent
6.	augury	f.	plastic
7.	voracious	g.	rapacious
8.	intractable	h.	obdurate
9.	axiomatic	i.	insouciant
10.	itinerant	j.	self-evident

Final Exam Drill #3

Antonyms

Match each word in the first column with the word in the second that is most nearly OPPOSITE in meaning.

1.	distrait	a.	active
2.	dearth	b.	agree
3.	audacious	c.	agreeable
4.	aberrant	d.	attentive
5.	fallow	e.	bounty
6.	demur	f.	castigation
7.	divulge	g.	clumsy
8.	contentious	h.	conceal
9.	adroit	i.	conforming
10.	accolade	j.	craven

Final Exam Drill #4

Synonyms

Match each word in the first column with the word in the second that is most nearly THE SAME in meaning.

1. milk	a. splenetic
2. grouse	b. exploit
3. inveterate	c. complain
4. homily	d. silly
5. morose	e. habitual
6. harrow	f. supercede
7. fatuous	g. sermon
8. supplant	h. torment
9. forswear	i. renounce
10. inimitable	j. peerless

Final Exam Drill #5

Antonyms

Match each word in the first column with the word in the second that is most nearly OPPOSITE in meaning.

1. felicitous	a. exacerbate
2. auspicious	b. flattery
3. chicanery	c. fragment
4. labile	d. guilelessness
5. ameliorate	e. humility
6. forbearance	f. ill-omened
7. amalgamate	g. immutable
8. culpable	h. impatience
9. derision	I. inappropriate
10. hubris	j. innocent

Final Exam Drill #6

Complete the Sentence

Based on clues within each sentence, choose the answer choice that, when placed in the blank, best completes the meaning of the sentence.

1. Although the story was probably _____, many people believed it to be true.
    a) eclectic
    b) idolatrous
    c) mellifluous
    d) apocryphal
    e) eloquent

2. Since the police had failed to _____ the suspect of his rights, his conviction was overturned in court.
    a) harangue
    b) apprise
    c) jibe
    d) militate
    e) vilify

3. The _____ of his remarks was a harsh reminder that he still remembered our previous lapse in judgment.
    a) asperity
    b) umbrage
    c) rent
    d) stint
    e) insouciance

4. Thomas had an amazing _____ for learning new languages; it came very easily to him and he enjoyed it tremendously.

a) chimera

b) dross

c) paradigm

d) fell

e) bent

5. Before she received the flowers, Christina was still very angry; afterwards, however, her feelings were somewhat _____.

a) garnered

b) mollified

c) groused

d) imputed

e) remonstrated

6. The recruiter was impressed by how _____ Franklin's work experience was, remarking that he had done everything from perform in an orchestra to run his own company.

a) presumptuous

b) turbid

c) suppliant

d) virulent

e) multifarious

7. It took three people and a crowbar to _____ the stove out of the ground where it had become wedged during the tornado.

   a) prize

   b) interdict

   c) limn

   d) milk

   e) cajole

8. Her lack of _____ caused innumerable problems because everyone now knew details of the story that were never meant to be public.

   a) apotheosis

   b) cynicism

   c) grandiloquence

   d) discretion

   e) idyll

9. Although he tried to hide his _____ toward his fellow board members, it nonetheless became very obvious that he couldn't stand them.

   a) antipathy

   b) platitude

   c) query

   d) tenacity

   e) turpitude

10. The _____ problem facing the students was the same one they dealt with every year: how they were going to spend their summer vacation.

a) meretricious

b) polemical

c) officious

d) perennial

e) voracious

Final Exam Drill #7

Make a Sentence

Write a sentence that begins with the first word in each pair, ends with the second, and which defines the relationship between the two. (In some cases, it may be easier to start with the second word and end with the first.)

1. EMPIRICAL : EXPERIMENT
2. CANON: LAW
3. PLUMB : DEPTH
4. FORESTALL : ACTION
5. SUCCOR : NEED
6. PERUSE : CARE
7. EXHORT : APPEAL
8. INHERENT : NATURE
9. BROACH : SUBJECT
10. STATIC : MOVEMENT

Final Exam Drill #8

Make a Sentence

Write a sentence that begins with the first word in each pair, ends with the second, and which defines the relationship between the two. (In some cases, it may be easier to start with the second word and end with the first.)

1. INNOCUOUS : DAMAGE
2. ALCHEMY : GOLD
3. CONVENTION : PRACTICE
4. PICARESQUE : ROGUE
5. SUPERFLUOUS : NECESSARY
6. EFFRONTERY : BOLDNESS
7. RECALCITRANT : DEFIANCE
8. TABLE : MOTION
9. IMPLACABLE : CHANGE

Final Exam Drill #9

Antonyms

Match each word in the first column with the word in the second that is most nearly OPPOSITE in meaning.

1.	assiduous	a.	integration
2.	diaphanous	b.	lazy
3.	dissolution	c.	minor
4.	derivative	d.	opaque
5.	plethora	e.	open-minded
6.	dogmatic	f.	original
7.	cardinal	g.	paucity
8.	apogee	h.	prodigal
9.	evanescent	i.	perigee
10.	parsimonious	j.	permanent

Final Exam Drill #10

Make a Sentence

Write a sentence that begins with the first word in each pair, ends with the second, and which defines the relationship between the two. (In some cases, it may be easier to start with the second word and end with the first.)

1. TAMP : TIGHTLY
2. DILATORY : DELAY
3. LUMBER : MOVE
4. PECCADILLO : SIN
5. DIFFIDENT : CONFIDENCE
6. SOPORIFIC : SLEEP
7. CONDEMN : DISLIKE

8. PEDAGOGY : TEACHING

9. DAMP : INTENSIFY

10. STANCH : FLOW

Final Exam Drill #11

Antonyms

Match each word in the first column with the word in the second that is most nearly OPPOSITE in meaning.

1.	feckless	a.	mild
2.	ennui	b.	endorse
3.	ebullience	c.	modest
4.	astringent	d.	apathy
5.	evince	e.	excitement
6.	facetious	f.	disguise
7.	censure	g.	serious
8.	foment	h.	responsible
9.	consequential	i.	earnest
10.	flip	j.	calm

Final Exam Drill #12

Make a Sentence

Write a sentence that begins with the first word in each pair, ends with the second, and which defines the relationship between the two. (In some cases, it may be easier to start with the second word and end with the first.)

1. STRUT : SUPPORT
2. ARREST : ATTENTION
3. MINCE : SPEAK
4. MISANTHROPE : HUMAN
5. FLOUT : RULE
6. OBSEQUIOUS : FAWN
7. QUALIFY : LIMITATION
8. PARRY : BLOW
9. DOGGEREL : VERSE

Final Exam Drill #13

Make a Sentence

Write a sentence that begins with the first word in each pair, ends with the second, and which defines the relationship between the two. (In some cases, it may be easier to start with the second word and end with the first.)

1. VENAL : BOUGHT
2. APPROPRIATE : USE
3. OSCILLATION : PENDULUM
4. INURED : UNPLEASANT
5. UNTOWARD : BEHAVIOR
6. ANATHEMA : CURSE

7. MAVERICK : GROUP

8. INSULAR : ISOLATION

9. HEGEMONY : IDEOLOGY

10. ARABESQUE : ORNATE

Final Exam Drill #14

Make a Sentence

Write a sentence that begins with the first word in each pair, ends with the second, and which defines the relationship between the two. (In some cases, it may be easier to start with the second word and end with the first.)

1. RECONNOITER : RECONNAISSANCE

2. ABROGATE : RESPONSIBILITY

3. OBTUSE : SHARPNESS

4. PRECEPT : CONDUCT

5. IMPECUNIOUS : MONEY

6. CONTIGUOUS : BORDER

7. EPITHET : WORD

8. PHILISTINE : MATERIAL

9. BOOR : CHURLISH

10. OSTENTATIOUS : PRETENSION

Final Exam Drill #15

Make a Sentence

Write a sentence that begins with the first word in each pair, ends with the second, and which defines the relationship between the two. (In some cases, it may be easier to start with the second word and end with the first.)

1. DIDACTIC : INSTRUCT
2. PERSPICACIOUS : PERCEPTION
3. CODA : COMPOSITION
4. LIBERTINE : RESTRAINT
5. ENDEMIC : REGION
6. LUMINOUS : LIGHT
7. EXILE : PARIAH
8. IMPORTUNE : ASK
9. ELEGY : DEAD
10. INTREPID : COURAGE

Final Exam Drill #16

One of These Is not Like the Others

In each of these lists, three of the words have something in common. Circle the word that does NOT fit with the others.

1. heretical   canonical   heterodox   iconoclastic
2. denigrate   depredate   disparage   deprecate
3. archaic   enigmatic   recondite   arcane
4. artless   felicitous   credulous   ingenuous
5. toady   fawn   blandish   excoriate
6. seminal   irascible   bellicose   pugnacious
7. vituperate   inveigh   precipitate   excoriate
8. panegyric   encomium   eulogy   satire
9. laconic   loquacious   reticent   terse
10. admonish   undulate   chasten   upbraid

Final Exam Drill #17

Antonyms

Match each word in the first column with the word in the second that is most nearly OPPOSITE in meaning.

1. calumniate   a. planned
2. extemporaneous   b. praise
3. dissemble   c. predictable
4. burgeon   d. wither
5. effusive   e. purify
6. furtive   f. reluctance
7. alloy   g. restrained
8. capricious   h. reveal
9. alacrity   i. similar
10. disparate   j. straightforward

Final Exam Drill #18

Pair 'Em Up

In each of these lists, circle the two words that are most similar in meaning. The other word may be an opposite, or may not be related at all.

1.	fanatical	filibuster	fervent
2.	salubrious	giving succor	glib
3.	dirge	eulogy	coda
4.	obtuse	diffident	timorous
5.	didactic	pedagogical	risible
6.	static	hermetic	insular
7.	inundate	malinger	importune
8.	pirate	attenuate	rarefy
9.	lavish	ostentatious	exigent
10.	erudite	imminent	sagacious

Final Exam Drill #19

Synonyms

Match each word in the first column with the word in the second that is most nearly THE SAME in meaning.

1.	baleful	a.	rubbish
2.	exculpate	b.	loud
3.	pedestrian	c.	malevolent
4.	indolent	d.	torpid
5.	mendacity	e.	dishonesty
6.	dross	f.	noisome
7.	fetid	g.	austere
8.	ascetic	h.	partisan
9.	boisterous	i.	quotidian
10.	chauvinist	j.	exonerate

Final Exam Drill #20

Antonyms

Match each word in the first column with the word in the second that is most nearly OPPOSITE in meaning.

1.	accretion	a.	stubbornness
2.	refulgent	b.	stygian
3.	acerbic	c.	success
4.	complaisance	d.	sweet
5.	garrulous	e.	taciturn
6.	debacle	f.	unconvincing
7.	bucolic	g.	unrepentant
8.	estimable	h.	unworthy
9.	cogent	i.	urban
10.	contrite	j.	shrinkage

Final Exam Drill #21

Antonyms

Match each word in the first column with the word in the second that is most nearly OPPOSITE in meaning.

1.	brook	a.	remain
2.	coalesce	b.	curse
3.	abscond	c.	resist
4.	corrigible	d.	fragment
5.	approbation	e.	simple
6.	beatify	f.	irreparable
7.	desiccate	g.	embolden
8.	convoluted	h.	moisten
9.	disabuse	i.	detraction
10.	daunt	j.	deceive

Final Exam Drill #22

Synonyms

Match each word in the first column with the word in the second that is most nearly THE SAME in meaning.

1.	puerile	a.	prone
2.	rail	b.	fulminate
3.	inchoate	c.	obstreperous
4.	stentorian	d.	disinterested
5.	germane	e.	foreshadow
6.	recumbent	f.	jejune
7.	maunder	g.	apposite
8.	indifferent	h.	nebulous
9.	adumbrate	i.	digress
10.	enervate	j.	sap

Final Exam Drill #23

Antonyms

Match each word in the first column with the word in the second that is most nearly OPPOSITE in meaning.

1.	ineluctable	a.	conventional
2.	nadir	b.	goodness
3.	inert	c.	substantial
4.	mettlesome	d.	uncertain
5.	enormity	e.	active
6.	eccentric	f.	cowardly
7.	arrant	g.	zenith
8.	adulation	h.	criticism
9.	gossamer	i.	respectful
10.	aspersion	j.	compliment

Final Exam Drill #24

Synonyms

Match each word in the first column with the word in the second that is most nearly THE SAME in meaning.

1.	color	a.	cacophony
2.	meticulous	b.	prevaricate
3.	acumen	c.	incipient
4.	discomfit	d.	entertain
5.	din	e.	disprove
6.	nascent	f.	discernment
7.	regale	g.	nice
8.	refute	h.	numb
9.	insensible	i.	imply
10.	intimate	j.	thwart

Final Exam Drill #25

Make a Sentence

Write a sentence that begins with the first word in each pair, ends with the second, and which defines the relationship between the two. (In some cases, it may be easier to start with the second word and end with the first.)

1. PIRATE: USE
2. OBVIATE : NECESSARY
3. LACHRYMOSE : CRY
4. EXPIATE : AMENDS
5. STRIATED : GROOVES
6. PAEAN : PRAISE
7. TORQUE : ROTATION
8. HYPERBOLE : EXAGGERATE
9. INSCRUTABLE : UNDERSTOOD

Final Exam Drill #26

Make a Sentence

Write a sentence that begins with the first word in each pair, ends with the second, and which defines the relationship between the two. (In some cases, it may be easier to start with the second word and end with the first.)

1. BYZANTINE : DESIGN
2. SLAKE : THIRST
3. SODDEN : WATER
4. SOPHISTRY : REASONING
5. ABATE : DEGREE
6. CAUSTIC : BURN

7. INSOUCIANT : CARE

8. DESUETUDE : USE

9. EDIFYING : ENLIGHTENMENT

10. GLIB : DEPTH

Final Exam Drill #27

Make a Sentence

Write a sentence that begins with the first word in each pair, ends with the second, and which defines the relationship between the two. (In some cases, it may be easier to start with the second word and end with the first.)

1. INVEIGLE : DECEPTION

2. SPEECH : EULOGY

3. CHANGE : CATALYST

4. TAUTOLOGY : ARGUMENT

5. PILLORY : PUNISHMENT

6. RAREFY : DENSE

7. REDOUBTABLE : HONOR

8. FROWARD : YIELD

9. DENOUEMENT : PLOT

10. PERNICIOUS : DEATH

Final Exam Drill #28

Make a Sentence

Write a sentence that begins with the first word in each pair, ends with the second, and which defines the relationship between the two. (In some cases, it may be easier to start with the second word and end with the first.)

1. WAFFLE : POSITION
2. INSIPID : FLAVOR
3. DESULTORY : PLAN
4. EQUIVOCATE : LANGUAGE
5. FORD : RIVER
6. VERISIMILITUDE : TRUTH
7. PITH : ARGUMENT
8. FORTUITOUS : CHANCE
9. PAIN : ANODYNE

Final Exam Drill #29

Make a Sentence

Write a sentence that begins with the first word in each pair, ends with the second, and which defines the relationship between the two. (In some cases, it may be easier to start with the second word and end with the first.)

1. SINECURE : WORK
2. IMPUNITY : PENALTY
3. SIMPER : SMILE
4. INTRANSIGENT : COMPROMISE
5. SAGACIOUS : WISDOM
6. SYNTHESIS : WHOLE

7. EPICURE : LUXURY

8. JEJUNE : MATURITY

9. SHARD : POTTERY

10. NOSTRUM : REMEDY

Final Exam Drill #30

Make a Sentence

Write a sentence that begins with the first word in each pair, ends with the second, and which defines the relationship between the two. (In some cases, it may be easier to start with the second word and end with the first.)

1. LAUD : PRAISE

2. PRODIGIOUS : SIZE

3. EMOLLIENT : HARSH

4. HERMETIC : AIR

5. DECORUM : POLITE

6. RAMIFY : BRANCHES

7. JOCOSE : HUMOR

8. REDOLENT : FRAGRANCE

9. MALINGER : WORK

10. FETTER : CHAINS

Final Exam Drill #31

Make a Sentence

Write a sentence that begins with the first word in each pair, ends with the second, and which defines the relationship between the two. (In some cases, it may be easier to start with the second word and end with the first.)

1. RELEGATE : LOWER
2. IMMINENT : OCCUR
3. FILIBUSTER : LEGISLATION
4. PREEN : FEATHERS
5. ANACHRONISM : TIME
6. NEOLOGISM : WORD
7. RHETORIC : LANGUAGE
8. AGGRANDIZE : POWER
9. PARODY : IMITATION
10. AESTHETIC: ART

Final Exam Drill #32

Make a Sentence

Write a sentence that begins with the first word in each pair, ends with the second, and which defines the relationship between the two. (In some cases, it may be easier to start with the second word and end with the first.)

1. MERCURIAL : MOOD
2. EXPURGATE : OBSCENE
3. FERVENT : EMOTION
4. QUIESCENCE : REST
5. GAUCHE : TASTE
6. BURNISH : SHINY

7. MITIGATE : SEVERITY
8. FLAG : SPIRITS
9. UBIQUITOUS : PLACES
10. ERUDITE : LEARNING

Final Exam Drill #33

Make a Sentence

Write a sentence that begins with the first word in each pair, ends with the second, and which defines the relationship between the two. (In some cases, it may be easier to start with the second word and end with the first.)

1. TENUOUS : STRENGTH
2. ASSUAGE : LESSEN
3. SEINE : NET
4. AMENABLE : SUGGESTION
5. INIMICAL : HARM
6. PUNDIT : OPINION
7. ATTENUATE : THICKNESS
8. PUNCTILIOUS : DETAILS
9. SATIATE : EXCESS
10. ABSCISSION : CUT

Final Exam Drill #34

Make a Sentence

Write a sentence that begins with the first word in each pair, ends with the second, and which defines the relationship between the two. (In some cases, it may be easier to start with the second word and end with the first.)

1. IMPERTURBABLE : CALM
2. HIRSUTE : HAIR
3. ADULTERATE : PURITY
4. MISOGYNIST : WOMEN
5. MARTIAL : WAR
6. RENEGE : PROMISE
7. WAFT : AIR
8. AVER: FACT
9. PETROUS : ROCK
10. BOLSTER : SUPPORT

Final Exam Drill #35

Synonyms

Match each word in the first column with the word in the second that is most nearly THE SAME in meaning.

1. surfeit   a. avoid
2. remonstrate   b. turmoil
3. welter   c. object
4. vitiate   d. mendicant
5. supplicant   e. tyro
6. gambol   f. ascribe

7. eschew   g. frolic
8. impute   h. debase
9. neophyte   i. excess
10. placate   j. propitiate

Final Exam Drill #36

Antonyms

Match each word in the first column with the word in the second that is most nearly OPPOSITE in meaning.

1. ignominious   a. serenity
2. gainsay   b. good-humored
3. imbroglio   c. agree
4. halcyon   d. turbulent
5. imperious   e. honorable
6. felicitous   f. submissive
7. impugn   g. support
8. iniquity   h. unfortunate
9. fractious   i. virtue
10. innervate   j. sap

Final Exam Drill #37

Synonyms

Match each word in the first column with the word in the second that is most nearly THE SAME in meaning.

1.	mendicant	a.	link
2.	florid	b.	beggar
3.	nexus	c.	waste
4.	mundane	d.	ruddy
5.	lucid	e.	comprehensible
6.	squander	f.	atone
7.	sanctimony	g.	ordinary
8.	garner	h.	self-righteousness
9.	expiate	i.	gather

Final Exam Drill #38

Antonyms

Match each word in the first column with the word in the second that is most nearly OPPOSITE in meaning.

1.	perfidy	a.	vigor
2.	lassitude	b.	opaque
3.	obfuscate	c.	benign
4.	noxious	d.	clarify
5.	palliate	e.	exacerbate
6.	personable	f.	wealth
7.	limpid	g.	fidelity
8.	perfunctory	h.	thorough
9.	penury	i.	unattractive
10.	petulant	j.	patient

Final Exam Drill #39

Synonyms

Match each word in the first column with the word in the second that is most nearly THE SAME in meaning.

1.	gregarious	a.	category
2.	squalid	b.	sordid
3.	opprobrium	c.	affable
4.	antithetical	d.	consecrate
5.	salacious	e.	obscene
6.	hallow	f.	scorn
7.	rubric	g.	vilify
8.	fulminate	h.	revoke
9.	rescind	i.	contradictory
10.	impetuous	j.	impulsive

Final Exam Drill #40

Antonyms

Match each word in the first column with the word in the second that is most nearly OPPOSITE in meaning.

1.	discordant	a.	destroyed
2.	chary	b.	dilettante
3.	extant	c.	disproportionate
4.	egress	d.	dulcet
5.	ephemeral	e.	eager
6.	connoisseur	f.	easy
7.	commensurate	g.	embrace
8.	arduous	h.	encomium
9.	abjure	i.	enduring
10.	diatribe	j.	entrance

Final Exam Drill #41

Antonyms

Match each word in the first column with the word in the second that is most nearly OPPOSITE in meaning.

1.	prescience	a.	excitable
2.	plummet	b.	ascent
3.	precarious	c.	idealistic
4.	phlegmatic	d.	secure
5.	querulous	e.	hindsight
6.	pristine	f.	corrupted
7.	quixotic	g.	meager
8.	pragmatic	h.	cheerful
9.	profuse	i.	pragmatic
10.	rancorous	j.	harmonious

Final Exam Drill #42

Synonyms

Match each word in the first column with the word in the second that is most nearly THE SAME in meaning.

1.	polemical	a.	generosity
2.	exemplar	b.	paradigm
3.	torrid	c.	baffled
4.	interdict	d.	controversial
5.	magnanimity	e.	prohibit
6.	nonplused	f.	ardent
7.	onerous	g.	solidified
8.	precursor	h.	arduous
9.	ossified	i.	harbinger
10.	occult	j.	hidden

Final Exam Drill #43

Match each word in the first column with the word in the second that is most nearly OPPOSITE in meaning.

1.	singular	a.	embrace
2.	saturnine	b.	undecided
3.	salient	c.	irrelevant
4.	repudiate	d.	unwholesome
5.	salutary	e.	pessimistic
6.	scurvy	f.	amiable
7.	sere	g.	laudable
8.	resolute	h.	lush
9.	solder	i.	commonplace
10.	sanguine	j.	separate

Final Exam Drill #44

Synonyms

Match each word in the first column with the word in the second that is most nearly THE SAME in meaning.

1.	sporadic	a.	hackneyed
2.	proclivity	b.	cocky
3.	tender	c.	apparent
4.	putrefy	d.	offer
5.	prosaic	e.	propensity
6.	ostensible	f.	attentive
7.	probity	g.	rot
8.	solicitous	h.	occasionally
9.	supercilious	i.	uprightness
10.	peremptory	j.	imperious

Final Exam Drill #45

Match the Definition

For each definition, circle the word that best fits.

1. one who hates women
   a. maverick
   b. misogynist
   c. misanthrope
   d. advocate

2. the appearance of truth
   a. denouement
   b. desuetude
   c. corroboration
   d. verisimilitude

3. a pain-killing drug or medicine
   a. prescription
   b. anodyne
   c. epicure
   d. dilation

4. to dismiss or demote
   a. marshal
   b. relegate
   c. reconnoiter
   d. exhort

5. having mixed feelings
   a. ambivalent
   b. ambiguous
   c. multifaceted
   d. provident

6. a mark to indicate an insertion
   a. abscission
   b. deleterious
   c. chary
   d. shard

7. smile or gesture in a coy way
   a. belie
   b. repine
   c. abstain
   d. simper

8. language designed to have a persuasive effect on its audience
   a. rhetoric
   b. doggerel
   c. epithet
   d. tirade

9. atone
   a. lumber
   b. damp
   c. condemn
   d. expiate

10. expert

    a. apostate

    b. pundit

    c. catalyst

    d. profligate

Final Exam Drill #46

Antonyms

Match each word in the first column with the word in the second that is most nearly OPPOSITE in meaning.

1. spendthrift	a.	destitute
2. stymie	b.	mature
3. stygian	c.	dense
4. solvent	d.	miser
5. stoic	e.	arrogant
6. sophomoric	f.	passionate
7. overweening	g.	sunny
8. subtle	h.	enable
9. sparse	i.	obvious
10. succinct	j.	verbose

Final Exam Drill #47

Synonyms

Match each word in the first column with the word in the second
that is most nearly THE SAME in meaning.

1.	quaff	a.	touching
2.	stupefy	b.	drink
3.	tumid	c.	curving
4.	poignant	d.	meddlesome
5.	extirpate	e.	variegated
6.	sinuous	f.	stun
7.	vaunt	g.	brag
8.	meretricious	h.	tawdry
9.	pied	i.	turgid
10.	officious	j.	destroy

Final Exam Drill #48

Synonyms

Match each word in the first column with the word in the second
that is most nearly THE SAME in meaning.

1.	wend	a.	proximity
2.	pique	b.	proceed
3.	prodigal	c.	attempt
4.	essay	d.	profligate
5.	prate	e.	adorn
6.	preempt	f.	provoke
7.	propinquity	g.	replace
8.	tacit	h.	delineate
9.	filigree	i.	prattle
10.	limn	j.	implicit

Final Exam Drill #49

Antonyms

Match each word in the first column with the word in the second that is most nearly OPPOSITE in meaning.

1.	tendentious	a.	indifferent
2.	volatile	b.	dishonesty
3.	tortuous	c.	inattentive
4.	unfeigned	d.	thin
5.	zealous	e.	constant
6.	vigilant	f.	unbiased
7.	viscous	g.	straight
8.	veracity	h.	permanent
9.	urbane	i.	false
10.	transient	j.	unsophisticated

Final Exam Drill #50

Synonyms

Match each word in the first column with the word in the second that is most nearly THE SAME in meaning.

1.	minatory	a.	unimaginative
2.	prolific	b.	threatening
3.	cadge	c.	patronage
4.	pedantic	d.	mooch
5.	steep	e.	productive
6.	tout	f.	praise
7.	auspice	g.	saturate
8.	tractable	h.	approve
9.	countenance	i.	obedient
10.	engender	j.	cause

GRE Power Vocab

Final Exam Drill #51

Synonyms

Match each word in the first column with the word in the second that is most nearly THE SAME in meaning.

1.	esoteric	a.	coax
2.	specious	b.	cower
3.	cajole	c.	recondite
4.	truculent	d.	pugnacious
5.	dynamo	e.	obstruct
6.	quail	f.	festoon
7.	occlude	g.	vacillate
8.	vexation	h.	spurious
9.	bedizen	i.	irritation
10.	waver	j.	powerhouse

Final Exam Drill #52

Make a Sentence

Write a sentence that begins with the first word in each pair, ends with the second, and which defines the relationship between the two. (In some cases, it may be easier to start with the second word and end with the first.)

1. FALLACY : BELIEF
2. TIMOROUS : CONFIDENCE
3. TIRADE : SPEECH
4. ACUMEN : INSIGHT
5. EXIGENT : ACTION
6. USURY : INTEREST
7. AUGUST : DIGNITY
8. PROSCRIBE : RESTRICTIONS
9. SUBPOENA : TESTIFY
10. PROVIDENT : FUTURE

Final Exam Drill #53

Make a Sentence

Write a sentence that begins with the first word in each pair, ends with the second, and which defines the relationship between the two. (In some cases, it may be easier to start with the second word and end with the first.)

1. APOSTATE : FAITH
2. UNTENABLE : DEFENDED
3. RECANT : BELIEF
4. AXIOM : PRINCIPLE
5. RUE : REMORSE
6. PROLIX : WORDS

7. TAWDRY : TASTE

8. BOMBASTIC : SPEECH

9. NATTY : DRESS

10. PUSILLANIMOUS : COURAGE

Final Exam Drill #54

Synonyms

Match each word in the first column with the word in the second that is most nearly THE SAME in meaning.

1.	obstinate	a.	penetrating
2.	veritable	b.	stubborn
3.	qualms	c.	predilection
4.	piquant	d.	various
5.	pious	e.	pungent
6.	penchant	f.	hesitancy
7.	sundry	g.	itinerant
8.	peripatetic	h.	authentic
9.	trenchant	i.	devout
10.	venerate	j.	revere

Final Exam Drill #55

Pair 'Em Up

In each of these lists, circle the two words that are most similar in meaning. The other word may be an opposite, or may not be related at all.

1. intransigent   recalcitrant   amenable
2. axiom   fallacy   tautology
3. inimical   impecunious   deleterious
4. erratic   mercurial   impudent
5. impassive   implacable   imperturbable
6. exile   arrest   forestall
7. slake   satiate   whet
8. fetter   obviate   table
9. abrogate   renege   waft

Final Exam Drill #56

Synonyms

Match each word in the first column with the word in the second that is most nearly THE SAME in meaning.

1. exact   a. yearn
2. travesty   b. permeate
3. pervade   c. toady
4. pine   d. require
5. plangent   e. resounding
6. equanimity   f. mockery
7. sycophant   g. sporadic
8. epitome   h. self-possession
9. episodic   i. deceive
10. cozen   j. quintessence

Final Exam Drill #57

Make a Sentence

Write a sentence that begins with the first word in each pair, ends with the second, and which defines the relationship between the two. (In some cases, it may be easier to start with the second word and end with the first.)

1. REVERENT : AWE
2. BELIE : REPRESENT
3. HACKNEYED : WORN
4. AVARICE : WEALTH
5. REPINE : DISCONTENT
6. LIST : SIDE
7. BANE : HARM
8. IMPASSIVE : EMOTION
9. INDEFATIGABLE : TIRE
10. SALUBRIOUS : HEALTH

Chapter 7
Foreign Words

This chapter is designed to increase your familiarity with words or phrases that are commonly used in American culture that may not have originated from English words. The first definition listed is generally how the word is used in American speech.

APARTHEID (uh PART yt) *n* [Afrikaans] the policy of racial segregation and oppression in the Republic of South Africa

Though *apartheid* does refer to a specific policy in a certain place and time, it can be used more generally to mean any strict system of segregation and discrimination by race. The literal meaning in Afrikaans is "apartness."

BLITZKRIEG (BLITS kreeg) *n* [German] a swift, overwhelming attack employing speed and surprise

The literal translation means lightning war, and in WWII, *blitzkriegs* referred to the massive air attacks that the Germans carried out. Today the word is often shortened to *blitz*.

CHAI (chye) *n* [Swahili and many South Asian dialects] tea

To Westerners, *chai* denotes particular kinds of spiced black tea, but in many places in Africa and India, it is the generic word for tea [so to say *chai tea* is actually redundant].

CHI (chee) *n* [Chinese] life force

Traditional Chinese philosophy holds that *chi* is inherent in everything, and a proper balance of positive and negative forms is essential for good physical health. You may also see this word spelled *qi*.

CHUTZPAH (HUTS puh) *n* [Yiddish] audacity, gall

Generally *chutzpah* connotes brashness, in a negative sense; however, it is often used admiringly in English speech.

COUP D'ÉTAT (KOO day TAH) *n* [French] a sudden, violent overthrow of the government

The literal meaning in French is blow of the state. You may already be familiar with the word *coup* on its own, and it's often used to mean any victory; *coup d'état* is used more for governmental and organizational overthrows.

DOPPELGÄNGER (DAHP el gang ur) *n* [German] a wraith or ghostlike twin of a living person; an alter ego

German for double, *doppelgänger* usually refers to an alter ego, or haunted version of a living person.

FIESTA (fee EST uh) *n* [Spanish] party

Though we generally use the term to mean any party, in Spanish it often connotes a religious festival or large celebration.

GESTALT (geh SHTALT) *n* [German] shape or form

While there is no direct translation from German for *gestalt*, we generally use the term to mean anything having to do with shape, form, or arrangement.

INTIFADA (in ti FAH dah) *n* [Arabic] rebellion, uprising

While the generic meaning of *intifada* is the throwing off of oppression, it can also specifically refer to the Palestinian uprisings in the late 1980s.

KANBAN (KAHN bahn) *n* [Japanese] the means by which JIT [just-in-time] manufacturing is managed

The original meaning of *kanban* is sign or card, and it refers to a system of just-in-time (JIT) manufacturing created to minimize the need to store anything during the manufacturing process. It can also refer to the signaling system used to indicate that something is needed at each step in the process.

KUDOS (KOO dohz) *n* [Greek] praise, accolades

In Greek this word means that which is heard of, and we suppose that if your boss (finally!) gave you *kudos* for a job well done, you'd probably want the world to hear about it, too.

MAHATMA (mah HOT mah) *n* [Sanskrit] a title of respect for a holy or wise man

Perhaps the most familiar use of the word *mahatma* to Westerners is in reference to Mohandas Karamchand Gandhi, who is often referred to as Mahatma Gandhi out of respect.

MENSCH (mensh) *n* [Yiddish] a decent human being

Literally human in the German variants that influenced Yiddish, a *mensch* is a complimentary term that means someone who can always be counted on to do the right thing.

OMBUDSMAN (AHM buds mun) *n* [Swedish] one who is appointed to investigate complaints against organizations and public officials

Most universities have an *ombudsman*, though many students may not know what his or her official duties are. NGOs private companies, and other organizations may have them, as well.

PATOIS (pah TWAH) *n* [French] jargon or specialized language

The original meaning was clumsy or nonstandard speech, such as the provincial speech you might have that marked you as being from a certain region.

SCHADENFREUDE (SHAH den froy duh) *n* [German] pleasure derived from the misfortunes of others

A person might feel *schadenfreude* when she didn't get a desired promotion, but the person who got the job is having an awful experience. This comes from the German *Schaden* (destruction) and *Freude* (joy).

SHALOM (shuh LOM) *n* [Hebrew] hello, good-bye

The literal meaning is peace, which has become a greeting in the English-speaking world, as well. Other languages have related words, such as the Arabic *salam* and city names such as Salem and Jerusalem share roots with this word, as well.

SIESTA (see EST uh) *n* [Spanish] nap

Though we tend to just use *siesta* to mean a nap, *siesta* in the Spanish tradition is a nap after the midday meal, and the word shares a root with the Spanish word for sixth, because the *siesta* would take place in the sixth hour or midday.

TAPAS (TAH pahs) *n* [Spanish] appetizers or small servings of food

Tapas are generally ordered and shared among a group, and can be anything from plates of olives to more elaborate or substantial side dishes.

Tapa is actually Spanish for cover, and the etymology of the term is under dispute. To add to the confusion, with the increasing popularity of *tapas* bars throughout the world, we've heard more than one conversation in which someone mistakenly thought someone else suggested going to a topless bar to eat.

TSCHOTCHKE (CHAHCH kee) *n* [Yiddish] inexpensive trinket

Originally from a Slavic word for toys, *tschotchkes* can be a variety of knickknacks, baubles, or souvenirs. The spelling on this word can vary significantly.

YOGA (YOH guh) *n* [Sanskrit] a type of physical exercise imported from India

In Sanskrit, *yoga* means union, and the physical exercise is meant to join the body with the mind, or with the divine.

Chapter 8
Science Words

Even people who've put time and effort into improving their vocabulary tend to have a spotty knowledge of science terms; it's hard to pick them up outside of bio or pre-med courses. So familiarize yourself with the following list and you may get more out of your next trip to the doctor—or, at least, your favorite TV medical drama. You'll also spot a number of terms that have roots in common with other kinds of vocabulary words.

It is important to note here that highly specialized medical terminology is rarely tested on the GRE's Sentence Equivalence or Text Completion question types. However, by knowing these types of words you will be able to understand more clearly many of the science passages that are found in the Reading Comprehension section. In this light, the science terms found in this chapter are very useful.

In this chapter, we've included several parts of words that people commonly confuse. See how many you can identify!

ADRENALINE (uh DREN uh lun) *n* a hormone secreted by the adrenal glands, especially in conditions of stress; also called epinephrine

Adrenaline is often released by the body to prepare for fight or flight. Taking a test is an *adrenaline* trigger if it is a stressful situation. This leads to anxiety in some point and increased focus and stamina in others.

ANTERIOR (an TEER err or) *adj* situated near the front of the body (opposite of posterior)

When a word starts with *ant-*, it usually means something that is before or in front. *Antebellum*, *ante* (in poker), and even *antlers* are some examples.

AORTA (ay OR tah) *n* the main artery of the body, which supplies oxygen-rich blood to the heart

ARTERY (AR tuh ree) *n* tube by which blood is carried from the heart to other parts of the body

In common speech, *arteries* can refer to waterways, highways, or basically anything by which something is carried from one place to another.

ATROPHY (AT roh fee) *v* waste away, particularly because of disuse

In medicine and sports, *atrophy* is something that happens to muscles when they aren't used, but the word can also refer figuratively to skills and abilities.

AXON (AK sahn) *n* a projection of a nerve cell that sends electric stimulation to other nerve cells

BACTERIA (bak TEER ee uh) *n* a group of microscopic, one-celled microorganisms

While some bacteria can make us sick, there are many beneficial kinds as well, some of which we actually need in order for our bodies to function properly. The singular form of the word *bacteria* is *bacterium*.

CALORIE (KAL or ee) *n* a unit of energy-producing potential that is contained in food.

The word *calorie*, when used in the context of food, actually refers to what scientists called a *kilocalorie*. A *kilocalorie* is the amount of energy needed to raise the temperature of 1 kilogram of water 1 degree Celsius.

CAPILLARY (KAP uh ler ee) *n* any of the fine-branching blood vessels that form a network between the arteries and veins

CARPAL (KAR pul) *adj* relating to the bones in the wrist

Carpal tunnel syndrome is one usage that might make this word familiar.

CARTILAGE (KAR tuh lej) *n* firm, whitish, flexible tissue that often connects bones

Babies are born with more *cartilage* than adult humans have, because it is replaced by bone as their skeletons become fully formed. Some creatures (such as sharks) maintain a high amount of *cartilage* throughout their lives.

CEREBRUM (sur EE brum) *adj* the largest part of the brain,, responsible for higher mental functions, such as thought, emotion, and memory

The *cerebrum* is divided into left and right hemispheres which are joined by the *corpus callosum*. When people or experiences are described as *cerebral, that* means they are characterized by deep or plentiful mental activity.

CONGENITAL (kun JEN uh tul) *adj* present from birth

While this word deals primarily with defects and other anatomical conditions in the field of medicine, it is used in ordinary English as a synonym for innate or inveterate; a *congenital* liar is someone who cannot break the habit of telling untruths.

CORTEX (KOR teks) *n* outer layer of a tissue or organ (such as the cerebral cortex)

Cortex originally meant bark in Latin, and it serves the same function as bark does for trees: to protect what's inside. The *cerebral cortex* is that layer of gray matter that protects your *cerebrum*, in which all your higher mental functions are controlled.

CPR *n* abbreviation for cardiopulmonary resuscitation; the practice of reviving someone who has no pulse for breath

DENDRITE (DEN dryt) *n* a projection of a nerve cell that receives electric stimulation from other nerve cells

DISTAL (DIS tul) *adj* farther from the body or point of attachment (opposite of proximal)

The *distal* end of your arm bone is the part your hand is attached to, because that end is farthest from the center of your body. *Distal*, of course, shares a root with *distant*, and means about the same thing; something *distal* to the body is farther away from it than something else.

DORSAL (DOR sul) *adj* on the upper side of an animal, plant, or organ (opposite of ventral)

Movies with shark attacks often focus on the shark's *dorsal* fin, exposed above the water, in order to build suspense.

EKG *n* abbreviation for electrocardiogram; a record or display of a person's heartbeat produced by electrocardiography

Some people use the abbreviation, *ECG*, because those are the letters derived from *ElectroCardioGram*. Others use *EKG*, perhaps because the "k" sound is heard in *electrocardiogram*, or maybe it's because words having to do with the heart, such as *cardiac*, come from the Greek *kardiakos*. Both spellings are correct.

ENDORPHINS (en DOR funs) *n* any of a group of hormones that occur naturally in the brain and have pain-relieving qualities

Endorphins can be released by a good workout, and some studies show that love can also be a powerful *endorphin* trigger.

GENETIC (jen ET ik) *adj* relating to or caused by heredity; that which is passed along through our genes

Genetics is a field of science that has received more and more press over the years, as new discoveries are made in the field. Many people with *congenital* diseases hope to find treatments that can repair the *genetic* cause of their illness rather than control symptoms using medicines.

HORMONE (HAWR mohn) *n* a substance that regulates the growth or functioning of a bodily organ or tissue

Hormones are secreted by the body, but this term can also refer to synthetic substances that function like natural hormones.

INSULIN (IN suh lin) *n* a hormone naturally secreted by the pancreas that regulates the metabolism of carbohydrates and fats

The term *insulin* also refers to the pharmaceutical preparation taken by diabetics, who do not produce adequate levels of *insulin* naturally. Without *insulin*, glucose remains in the blood rather than being taken up by the tissues. This increased blood-sugar level can damage organs if left untreated.

KERATIN (KER uh tin) *n* a fibrous protein forming the main structural constituent of hair, feathers, hoofs, claws, horns, etc.

KETOSIS (kee TOH sis) *n* an abnormal increase of ketones in the body; a stage of metabolism in which the liver switches to fasting mode

Ketosis can be an unfortunate effect of diets that are extremely low in carbohydrates. When undergoing *ketosis*, the body converts fats into energy, which sounds like a great way to get rid of any of that extra cellulite you might have lying around. This process can be harmful, however, because the *ketones* that are released in your blood during *ketosis* are acidic and can do damage to your liver and kidneys.

LATERAL (LAT uh rul) *adj* on one side of a body or organ, farthest from the median plane or "core" of the body (opposite of medial)

Lateral is similar to *distal*, in that it refers to the area away from the center of the body.

In everyday speech, *lateral* can also mean on the side or to the side. If you take a new job doing pretty much the same thing you were doing before, with no change in responsibility or title, that is a *lateral* move.

LIGAMENT (LIG uh ment) *n* a tough connecting tissue that holds bones or organs in place

Ligaments are often confused with tendons, because both help hold internal parts of the body together. *Ligate* and *ligature* are related words that also have to do with connecting similar things.

MEDIAL (MEE dee ul) *adj* near the median plane or center of a body or organ (opposite of lateral)

Many words with *med* in them, such as *median* and *medium*, mean middle. *Medial* is similar to *proximal* as both words refer to the area near the center or core of the body.

MELANIN (MEL uh nin) *n* a dark brown or black pigment occurring in the hair, skin, and iris of the eye in people and animals

Melanin is responsible for skin's tanning when it is exposed to sunlight.

METABOLISM (meh TAB oh lizm) *n* the processes by which new material is assimilated and fuel is provided for vital activities in the body.

MRI n abbreviation for magnetic resonance imaging; medical imaging used to produce images of the internal organs

PITUITARY (pit OO i ter ee) *n* the major endocrine gland, which controls growth and development and the functioning of the other endocrine glands

If you've ever heard a linebacker referred to as a pituitary case, you know that the *pituitary* gland regulates growth.

POSTERIOR (pahs TEER ee ur) *adj* situated near the back of the body (opposite of anterior)

Chances are that you've heard this word before, as a noun that means backside. In fact, many words with *post* in them—such as *posthumous* and *postpartum*—have something to do with the being after.

PROXIMAL (PRAHKS uh mul) *adj* nearer the body or point of attachment (opposite of distal)

The *proximal* end of your arm bone is at your armpit, because that end is nearest to the center of your body. This word shares a root with the word *proximity*, which describes how close something is.

SYNAPSE (SIN aps) *n* a "space" between an axon of one nerve cell and a dendrite of another nerve cell, through which electric stimulation is passed.

If you've ever heard someone say that her "synapses just aren't firing today," that means that she's not making connections in thought, or her thinking is slow.

TENDON (TEN dun) *n* a tough connecting tissue that holds muscles to bones

Tendons are often confused with ligaments, but *tendons* connect only muscle to bone.

THYROID (THY roid) *n* a large gland in the neck that secretes hormones affecting the rate of metabolism

VEIN (vayn) *n* tube by which blood is carried from other parts of the body back to the heart

VENTRAL (VEN trul) *adj* on the underside of an animal, plant, or organ (opposite of dorsal)

The root for *ventral* comes from the Latin, meaning to split open. The reproductive and excretive openings in some animals, such as chicken and fish, are called *vents*. And, since these *vents* happen to be on the underside of the animal, near the stomach, the underside is referred to as the *ventral* area.

VIRUS (VY rus) *n* a microscopic parasite that reproduces by invading and controlling host cells

Our immune systems attempt to shut down any *viruses* that enter the body and prevent them from replicating. The body's fight against these invaders is what causes the symptoms we associate with a *viral* illness.

Viruses are not classified as living organisms because they cannot replicate on their own; they require a host to do so. *Viruses* are often confused with *bacteria*.

VISCERAL (VIS uh rul) *adj* relating to the internal organs in the main body cavity, especially the stomach

A *visceral* experience is one that someone connects with on an instinctual or bodily level, rather than mentally. To *eviscerate* an animal is to remove the guts, but the word is also used figuratively, as in "the television host *eviscerated* his guest."

Chapter 9
Literature 101

Why do freshman literature classes all seem to start at 8:00 A.M.? We don't know the answer to that, but we do know plenty of people who rarely managed to make it to class. If you're one of them, be sure to review this glossary of literary terms and allusions that have become part of common speech. It'll allow you to hang with the English majors—even if you studied the backs of your eyelids more than your literature texts as an undergrad.

ALLUSION (uh LOO zhun) *n* the act of referring to something—often a literary text—without mentioning it directly

Example: In a fit of optimism, the novice playwright chose William Bard as his pen name.

CATCH-22 (KACH twen tee too) *n* a situation that is characterized by absurdity, or impossible to get out of because of conflicting conditions.

Though the term is frequently used today to describe any difficult situation, in *Catch-22*, a novel by Joseph Heller, the term referred to a "catch" imposed by the U.S. Army to keep pilots flying combat missions. This "catch-22" was that the only way to get excused from flying combat missions was insanity, but only a sane person would be in fear of his life and request to be removed from flying combat missions. Therefore, the request to be removed would always be turned down.

DRAMATIC IRONY (druh MAT ik EYE ruh nee) *n* the condition in which the reader's understanding of a character's situation is more accurate than the character's own understanding of his or her situation; also called situational or tragic irony

Example: In O. Henry's short story, "The Gift of the Magi," a man pawns his watch to buy a gift of hair combs for his wife. Meanwhile, his wife has cut off and sold her hair to buy him a watch chain.

FAUSTIAN (FOW stee un) *adj* done without regard for future consequences

In German legend, Johann Faust is a magician and alchemist who sells his soul to the devil in return for power and knowledge. A common use of the term today is in the term "Faustian bargain."

GARGANTUAN (gar GAN choo un) *adj* huge

Though many people (and even dictionaries) have forgotten the literary etymology of this word, its origin is in the book *Gargantua and Pantagruel*, by François Rabelais. The character Gargantua is a voracious giant.

HYPERBOLE (hy PUR boh lee) *n* an extreme exaggeration for dramatic effect

Example: When my mom comes home and sees this mess, she's going to kill me!

LILLIPUTIAN (lil uh PYOO shun) *adj* trivial or small

In Jonathan Swift's *Gulliver's Travels*, Gulliver travels to many strange places, one of which is Lilliput, an imaginary country inhabited by people who are six inches tall.

MACHIAVELLIAN (mah kee ah VEL ee un) *adj* characterized by deceit, cunning, and bad faith

Niccolo Machiavelli was a philosopher, political advisor, and writer. He wrote *The Prince*, a political treatise in which he advocates cruelty, fraudulence, and the idea that the end justifies the means.

METAPHOR (MET uh for) *n* figure of speech likening two dissimilar things

Example: Juliet is the sun.

ORWELLIAN (or WEL lee un) *adj* relating to or similar to works of George Orwell, particularly with respect to a vision of a totalitarian future

George Orwell's *1984* and *Animal Farm* are some of the most chilling tales of all-powerful governments ever told. In Orwell's best-known novel, *1984*, all people were under constant surveillance by Big Brother, and were reminded of it in the omnipresent slogan, "Big Brother is watching you." (TV addicts may be familiar with the term "Big Brother" from a reality TV show of the same name, which started in the late '90s.) Other terms that originated in *1984* include *groupthink*, *newspeak*, and *thought police*.

PARADOX (PAR uh dahks) *n* a literally false statement that only has meaning if interpreted figuratively

Example: Less is more.

PERSONIFICATION (pur SAHN i fi cay shun) *n* the attribution of human qualities to something that is not human

Example: The yellow fog rubs its back upon the windowpanes.

PYGMALION (pig MAY lee un) *n* a character, particularly a man, who creates a person to fit his liking

Pygmalion was a mythical king of Cyprus who carved a statue of ivory that was so lovely, he prayed to Aphrodite to make it come alive. The term also refers to a type of story in which a similar plot plays out, such as *My Fair Lady* and *The Taming of the Shrew*.

QUIXOTIC (kwik SAH tik) *adj* idealistic to the point of being impractical

This word is derived from the novel *Don Quixote*, by Miguel de Cervantes. The title character is a low-ranking member of Spanish nobility who—after reading too many tales about knights and their noble endeavors—decides to journey the countryside looking for adventures and righting wrongs. His actions are well-intentioned but often end in disaster—hence, the meaning of the word *quixotic*.

SATIRE (SAT y ur) *n* a form of writing, usually involving irony, which makes fun of people or events in order to bring about social or political change

Example: In the essay "A Modest Proposal," the narrative voice argues that the children of poor Catholics in Ireland should be fattened up and fed to rich landowners.

SIMILE (SIM uh lee) *n* figure of speech using "like" or "as" to draw a comparison

Example: My love is like a red, red rose.

SIREN SONG (SY ren song) *n* an enchanting appeal, especially if it is deceptive and will lead to a bad result

Sirens were mythical creatures in *The Odyssey* who enticed sailors to their island by singing a luring song. The island had rocky cliffs, though, and sailors who attempted to land were always dashed upon the rocks and drowned. Odysseus overcame this by plugging his sailors' ears with wax and having them tie him to the mast, so that he could hear the *siren song* but would be unable to succumb to it.

STYGIAN (STI jee un) *adj* very dark

The River Styx in Greek mythology is the river that leads to the underworld, or Hades. Naturally, it's pretty dark, and that is the origin of the word *stygian*.

VERBAL IRONY (VUR bul EYE ruh nee) *n* the use of words to express something other than their literal intent

Example: How brilliant do you have to be to lock your keys in the car twice in one day?

Chapter 10

Theories and Concepts

Here's your chance to brush up on some of the theories and concepts that seem to pop up all the time when people are discussing "the big issues." Our list is drawn from the fields of philosophy, psychology, mathematics, and beyond.

AGNOSTICISM (ag NAHS ti sizm) *n* the idea that nothing can be definitely known about a given area, particularly about the existence of God

Agnosticism is often confused with *atheism*, the belief that God does not exist. It is also commonly thought to refer to indecisiveness about whether or not God exists, but that is not really correct either.

ATHEISM (AY thee izm) *n* the idea that God does not exist

Atheists generally hold the belief that God is an invention of mankind's imagination, and many even hold that "blind faith" goes against reason, particularly in the face of increasing scientific discovery.

BEHAVIORISM (bee HAY vyor izm) *n* the theory that animal (and therefore, human) behavior is due entirely to responses by stimuli

The term *behaviorism* was coined by John Broadus Watson, and it is also known as the stimulus-response model. *Behaviorism* was deeply influenced by the work of Ivan Petrovich Pavlov, who performed famous experiments to "teach" dogs that they would be fed after a bell was rung, causing them to salivate upon hearing the bell ring.

BIRTH ORDER THEORY (burth OR dur THEE oh ree) *n* the theory that children born in a certain order in the same household experience different environments and therefore develop different tendencies in their personalities

This controversial idea was proposed by Alfred Adler, and some more commonly held components of it include the belief that "oldest" siblings tend to be responsible and mature, "youngest" siblings tend to be self-centered, and "middle" siblings tend to be peacemakers.

CATEGORICAL IMPERATIVE (kat eh GOR ik ul im PER uh tiv) *n* the idea that if one is acting in a consistent manner, one must act in a way that he or she would want everyone else to act, as well

The concept of the *categorical imperative* was introduced by Immanuel Kant, who sought to derive morality from reason.

COLLECTIVE MEMORY (kul EK tiv MEM uh ree) *n* a hypothetical unconscious memory shared by all of humanity

This idea of *collective memory*, also called the *collective unconscious* or *racial memory*, was proposed by Carl Gustav Jung. It is difficult to prove or disprove because of the difficulty of testing it; however, it is an idea that has sparked much public imagination and interest.

DEISM (DEE izm) *n* the idea that God created the universe and then left mankind to operate by his own free will

Deists believe that the idea of a creator-God is compatible with reason, though some still refer to an unknowable, supernatural faith. Voltaire and Rousseau are some of the most well-known philosophers associated with *deism*, though many founding fathers of the United States—including Thomas Jefferson and Benjamin Franklin—espoused *deism* as well.

DETERMINISM (deh TUR min izm) *n* the idea that every event, physical and mental, has a specific cause

Put forth by Pierre-Simon, Marquis de Laplace, *determinism* covers a wide range of beliefs about the existence of free will and freedom of choice.

EGOISM (EE goh izm) *n* the idea that everyone should act to maximize his or her own welfare

In plain speech we call this selfishness or egotism, but it is also a concept that has undergone serious philosophical study. One problem with it is that one cannot be a proponent of *egoism* without encouraging others to act in their own best interests, which may conflict with one's own.

EPICUREANISM (ep uh KYUR ee an izm) *n* a materialistic belief that pleasure should be maximized and pain minimized

Though today's definition has more to do with self-indulgence, particularly in the areas of wine and food, this school of thought created by Epicurus of Samos was originally a rival school to the Stoics.

GAME THEORY (gaym THEE oh ree) *n* the analysis of conflicts to find optimal strategies

This type of study was created by mathematician John von Neumann, through the study of games of poker. It is frequently used in high-stakes decision-making, such as in business and war.

GESTALT THEORY (geh SHTALT THEE oh ree) *n* the idea that phenomena should be treated holistically rather than individually

The word *gestalt* comes from German and has no direct English translation, but is generally translated as form, shape, arrangement, or essence. In *gestalt theory*, a whole is not necessarily the same as the sum of its parts.

HERMENEUTICS (hur min OO tiks) *n* the study of interpretation

Hermeneutics is largely concerned with the way in which interpretation is developed between the reader and a text and holds that there is no single correct interpretation of any text. *Hermeneutics* has its origins in biblical studies, but has expanded into the study of all literature, other art forms, and even human actions and events.

IDEALISM (y DEEL izm) *n* the idea that holds that reality is, at least in part, dependent on the mind.

This idea is often contrasted with realism, and it covers a wide range of beliefs about the degree to which the mind determines reality.

NIHILISM (NYE uh li zum) *n* literally "nothingism," the belief that all knowledge is impossible

This term can also mean the complete rejection of all traditional values. It was popularized by Ivan Sergeyevich Turgenev in the novel *Fathers and Sons.*

OCKHAM'S RAZOR (AH kumz RAY zor) *n* the idea that one should adopt the simplest hypothesis

Also known as the principle of parsimony, this idea is often appealing but problematic, partly because there is little scientific evidence that the simplest hypothesis has a greater claim to truth.

PHRENOLOGY (fren AH luh jee) *n* the theory that observations of the skull were sufficient to determine the individual's personality and mental capacity

This discredited theory was first proposed by Franz Josef Gall, but the word remains and commonly refers to ideas that internal characteristics can be measured by external ones.

POSITIVISM (PAHZ i ti vizm) *n* a movement that involves approaching the natural world in a scientific fashion and classifying it accordingly

Pioneered by Auguste Comte, *positivism* had a profound impact on psychology and sociology. The sciences and human thought are both classified in hierarchical structures according to this idea.

PRAGMATISM (PRAG muh tizm) *n* a theory that assesses theories and concepts based on their effects on experiences and practices

Charles Sanders Peirce was the developer of this theory, and mainly focused on intellectual concepts, but William James expanded the theory to cover senses and emotions.

RELATIVISM (REL uh tiv izm) *n* the idea that anything exists or is defined relative to anything else

Cognitive relativism seeks to ascertain that all beliefs are true for their holders, and *moral relativism* seeks to establish that right and wrong to some degree depend on the situation and circumstances in which a decision is made.

SOCIAL DARWINISM (SOH shul DAHR win izm) *n* the idea that the theory of natural selection can be applied to human society

Social Darwinism is based on the evolutionary theory put forth by Charles Darwin. *Social Darwinism* believe that humans—like the members of all other species—are in direct competition with one another, and that humans with certain qualities are more likely to survive and flourish than others. According to this theory, social programs such as welfare prevent society as a whole from growing stronger because they mitigate the effects of this competition.

SOLIPSISM (SAH lip sizm) *n* the idea that nothing exists beyond oneself and one's immediate experiences

Solipsism is often a starting point for exploration into some other inquiry than a logical conclusion that one eventually reaches.

STOICISM (STOH ih sizm) *n* a way of thinking that divides philosophy into the three branches of logic, physics, and ethics

Founded by Zeno of Citium, this school of philosophy was named for the "stoa" or portico where its adherents met. *Stoicism* was a rival school of *Epicureanism* and ancient *Scepticism* and it treated self-sufficiency and acceptance of fate as the aim. In modern language, a stoic is one who does not have or display emotions.

THEISM (THEE izm) *n* the idea that God is the creator and supreme authority of the universe

Theism is the idea on which most major religions are based. Philosophers who claim that *theism* is flawed cite problems such as unknown nature of the supreme being, the conflict between the will of God and the expression of free will, and the presence of evil.

Chapter 11

Answers

Answers to Warm-Up Quizzes

Warm-up Quiz #1
1. h
2. d
3. a
4. c
5. g
6. i
7. f
8. j
9. b
10. e

Warm-up Quiz #2
1. dogmatic and intransigent
2. didactic and pedagogical
3. synthesize and conjoin
4. iconoclastic and heretical
5. inherent and inveterate
6. accolade and elegy
7. hackneyed and trite
8. sophomoric and puerile
9. inchoate and nascent
10. renege and rescind

Warm-up Quiz #3

1. f
2. h
3. i
4. a
5. g
6. c
7. j
8. b
9. d
10. e

Warm-up Quiz #4

1. c
2. a
3. e
4. d
5. a
6. b
7. e
8. b
9. d
10. b

Warm-up Quiz #5

1. d
2. c
3. e
4. a
5. h
6. i
7. j
8. g
9. f
10. b

Warm-up Quiz #6

1. avaricious and penurious
2. indolent and phlegmatic
3. pithy and fundamental
4. plaintive and melancholy
5. quaff and satiate
6. cacophony and din
7. stymie and filibuster
8. loquacious and prolix
9. inimical and malevolent
10. beguile and dupe

Warm-up Quiz #7

1. e
2. f
3. h
4. i
5. a
6. d
7. j
8. b
9. c
10. g

Warm-up Quiz #8

1. d
2. e
3. a
4. e
5. c
6. d
7. a
8. c
9. d
10. d

Answers to Quick Quizzes

Quick Quiz #1

1. k
2. j
3. a
4. d
5. f
6. b
7. e
8. i
9. g
10. h
11. c
12. l

Quick Quiz #2

1. b
2. j
3. a
4. f
5. c
6. i
7. g
8. h
9. d
10. e

Quick Quiz #3

1. d
2. c
3. l
4. j
5. b
6. e
7. g
8. i
9. h
10. f
11. a
12. k

Quick Quiz #4

1. h
2. g
3. c
4. j
5. b
6. d
7. i
8. f
9. e
10. a

Quick Quiz #5

1. b
2. e
3. f
4. h
5. g
6. d
7. i
8. j
9. a
10. c

Quick Quiz #6

1. g
2. c
3. d
4. e
5. a
6. i
7. f
8. h
9. b

Quick Quiz #7

1. f
2. h
3. e
4. g
5. d

6. c
7. a
8. b

Quick Quiz #8

1. d
2. a
3. g
4. f
5. h
6. c
7. b
8. j
9. i
10. e
11. k

Quick Quiz #9

1. h
2. a
3. e
4. c
5. g
6. i
7. d
8. b
9. f
10. j

Quick Quiz #10

1. l
2. g
3. a
4. b
5. m
6. e
7. d
8. i
9. j
10. f
11. h
12. c
13. k

Quick Quiz #11

1. f
2. e
3. h
4. i
5. k
6. g
7. d
8. a
9. c
10. j
11. b
12. m
13. l

Quick Quiz #12

1. i
2. h
3. g
4. j
5. c
6. e
7. a
8. d
9. b
10. k
11. f

Quick Quiz #13

1. b
2. h
3. a
4. g
5. i
6. f
7. k
8. c
9. e
10. j
11. d

Quick Quiz #14

1. f
2. g
3. e
4. c
5. a
6. h
7. i
8. d
9. b
10. j

Quick Quiz #15

1. e
2. f
3. g
4. b
5. c
6. d
7. a

Quick Quiz #16

1. j
2. i
3. h
4. g
5. f
6. e
7. d

8. l
9. c
10. b
11. k
12. a

Quick Quiz #17

1. f
2. j
3. a
4. k
5. l
6. i
7. h
8. c
9. b
10. n
11. d
12. e
13. g
14. o
15. m
16. p

Quick Quiz #18

1. g
2. i
3. d
4. e
5. f

6. b
7. c
8. j
9. a
10. h
11. k

Quick Quiz #19

1. e
2. f
3. i
4. g
5. c
6. h
7. b
8. d
9. a

Quick Quiz #20

1. h
2. d
3. f
4. c
5. b
6. e
7. i
8. k
9. a
10. g
11. j

Quick Quiz #21

1. i
2. c
3. j
4. g
5. f
6. h
7. a
8. d
9. e
10. k
11. b

Quick Quiz #22

1. h
2. d
3. b
4. e
5. g
6. f
7. a
8. i
9. j
10. c

Quick Quiz #23

1. e
2. c
3. j

4. i
5. a
6. g
7. b
8. f
9. k
10. d
11. h

Quick Quiz #24

1. f
2. j
3. h
4. e
5. b
6. c
7. i
8. a
9. d
10. g
11. k

Quick Quiz #25

1. h
2. c
3. a
4. i
5. b

6. j
7. f
8. g
9. e
10. d
11. l
12. k

Quick Quiz #26

1. c
2. i
3. j
4. g
5. a
6. h
7. e
8. f
9. b
10. d

Quick Quiz #27

1. g
2. i
3. d
4. h
5. e
6. a
7. f

8. c
9. j
10. b
11. k

Quick Quiz #28

1. d
2. h
3. g
4. f
5. l
6. b
7. a
8. m
9. e
10. n
11. j
12. i
13. c
14. k
15. q
16. p
17. o

Quick Quiz #29

1. b
2. f
3. e
4. g

5. i
6. a
7. c
8. d
9. j
10. h

Quick Quiz #30

1. i
2. b
3. h
4. e
5. g
6. a
7. j
8. d
9. c
10. f
11. l
12. k

Quick Quiz #31

1. i
2. c
3. f
4. b
5. a
6. h
7. d

8. j
9. g
10. e
11. k

Quick Quiz #32

1. g
2. d
3. i
4. h
5. b
6. l
7. j
8. f
9. a
10. e
11. k
12. c

Quick Quiz #33

1. h
2. b
3. i
4. e
5. d
6. m
7. a
8. l
9. j

10. c
11. k
12. f
13. g

Quick Quiz #34

1. g
2. d
3. j
4. h
5. c
6. i
7. b
8. a
9. e
10. k
11. f
12. m
13. l

Quick Quiz #35

1. h
2. d
3. i
4. c
5. a
6. f
7. g
8. j

9. e
10. b
11. k

Quick Quiz #36

1. i
2. j
3. f
4. g
5. e
6. a
7. b
8. c
9. k
10. d
11. h

Quick Quiz #37

1. i
2. g
3. d
4. j
5. c
6. a
7. h
8. b
9. f

10. k
11. e
12. l

Quick Quiz #38

1. g
2. b
3. j
4. h
5. a
6. l
7. k
8. c
9. i
10. e
11. d
12. f
13. n
14. m

Quick Quiz #39

1. i
2. f
3. d
4. h
5. c
6. b
7. a
8. l

9. g
10. j
11. e
12. k

Quick Quiz #40

1. c
2. a
3. g
4. b
5. e
6. h
7. f
8. d
9. j
10. i

Quick Quiz #41

1. j
2. i
3. d
4. b
5. c
6. e
7. a
8. g
9. h
10. f

11. l
12. k

Quick Quiz #42

1. f
2. j
3. a
4. d
5. b
6. g
7. c
8. i
9. h
10. e
11. k

Quick Quiz #43

1. g
2. h
3. b
4. d
5. k
6. c
7. i
8. j
9. f
10. l
11. e
12. a

Quick Quiz #44

1. i
2. a
3. k
4. b
5. e
6. f
7. d
8. g
9. c
10. h
11. j

Quick Quiz #45

1. b
2. a
3. c
4. f
5. d
6. e
7. g

Quick Quiz #46

1. b
2. d
3. a
4. c
5. e

Quick Quiz #47

1. h
2. k
3. i
4. e
5. l
6. j
7. c
8. b
9. a
10. d
11. g
12. f
13. n
14. m

Quick Quiz #48

1. f
2. k
3. a
4. e
5. i
6. b
7. d
8. j
9. h
10. c
11. g
12. l

Quick Quiz #49

1. g
2. k
3. a
4. h
5. b
6. d
7. j
8. c
9. e
10. f
11. l
12. i

Quick Quiz #50

1. c
2. g
3. e
4. j
5. d
6. h
7. a
8. f
9. i
10. k
11. b

Quick Quiz #51

1. j
2. e
3. f
4. n
5. a
6. l
7. b
8. g
9. h
10. i
11. c
12. k
13. o
14. m
15. d

Quick Quiz #52

1. e
2. c
3. j
4. a
5. d
6. h
7. k
8. b
9. g

10. f
11. l
12. i
13. m

Quick Quiz #53

1. h
2. d
3. c
4. f
5. a
6. g
7. b
8. j
9. i
10. k
11. e
12. m
13. l

Quick Quiz #54

1. c
2. h
3. e
4. i
5. b
6. g
7. a
8. f

9. d

10. j

Quick Quiz #55

1. h
2. d
3. f
4. e
5. c
6. i
7. b
8. g
9. a

Quick Quiz #56

1. a
2. h
3. d
4. b
5. c
6. e
7. f
8. g

Quick Quiz #57

1. d
2. c
3. f
4. i

5. a
6. b
7. e
8. h
9. g

Quick Quiz #58

1. e
2. a
3. i
4. d
5. c
6. f
7. h
8. b
9. g

Quick Quiz #59

1. g
2. j
3. a
4. f
5. b
6. c
7. h
8. d
9. e
10. k
11. i

Quick Quiz #60

1. a
2. g
3. i
4. c
5. d
6. k
7. h
8. b
9. j
10. e
11. f
12. m
13. l

Quick Quiz #61

1. d
2. b
3. a
4. e
5. h
6. f
7. i
8. c
9. j
10. g
11. k

Quick Quiz #62

1. j
2. c
3. a
4. e
5. i
6. g
7. h
8. b
9. d
10. f

Quick Quiz #63

1. c
2. a
3. h
4. f
5. g
6. b
7. d
8. e

Quick Quiz #64

1. h
2. e
3. f
4. a
5. c
6. b
7. g
8. d
9. i

Quick Quiz #65

1. e
2. g
3. c
4. d
5. f
6. j
7. a
8. b
9. i
10. h
11. l
12. k

Answers to Final Exam Drills

Final Exam Drill #1

1. philistine and boor
2. lachrymose and melancholy
3. insipid and jejune
4. laud and aggrandize
5. obsequious and reverent
6. acumen and perspicacity
7. paean and elegy
8. assuage and mitigate
9. chic and natty
10. oscillate and waffle

Final Exam Drill #2

1. a
2. i
3. f
4. c
5. e
6. b
7. g
8. h
9. j
10. d

Final Exam Drill #3

1. d
2. e
3. j
4. i
5. a
6. b
7. h
8. c
9. g
10. f

Final Exam Drill #4

1. b
2. c
3. e
4. g
5. a
6. h
7. d
8. f
9. i
10. j

Final Exam Drill #5

1. i
2. f
3. d
4. g
5. a
6. h
7. c
8. j
9. b
10. e

Final Exam Drill #6

1. d
2. b
3. a
4. e
5. b
6. e
7. a
8. d
9. a
10. d

Final Exam Drill #7

1. EMPIRICAL means based on EXPERIMENT
2. CANON is religious LAW
3. PLUMB means to determine the DEPTH
4. FORESTALL means to prevent an ACTION

5. SUCCOR means providing aid in time of NEED

6. PERUSE means to examine with CARE

7. EXHORT means to make a strong APPEAL

8. INHERENT means ingrained in one's NATURE

9. BROACH means to introduce a SUBJECT

10. STATIC means having no MOVEMENT

Final Exam Drill #8

1. INNOCUOUS means causing no DAMAGE

2. ALCHEMY is the study of trying to make GOLD

3. CONVENTION is an agreed upon PRACTICE

4. PICARESQUE is a story of a ROGUE

5. SUPERFLUOUS means beyond what is NECESSARY

6. EFFRONTERY is extreme BOLDNESS

7. RECALCITRANT means characterized by DEFIANCE

8. TABLE is to prevent the discussion of a MOTION

9. IMPLACABLE means unable to CHANGE

Final Exam Drill #9

1. b

2. d

3. a

4. f

5. g

6. e

7. c

8. i

9. j

10. h

Final Exam Drill #10

1. TAMP means to pack TIGHTLY
2. DILATORY means causing DELAY
3. LUMBER is clumsily to MOVE
4. PECCADILLO is a minor SIN
5. DIFFIDENT means lacking CONFIDENCE
6. SOPORIFIC means causing SLEEP
7. CONDEMN is to strongly DISLIKE
8. PEDAGOGY is the art or practice of TEACHING
9. DAMP is to lessen something's INTENSITY
10. STANCH is to stop a FLOW

Final Exam Drill #11

1. h
2. e
3. d
4. a
5. f
6. g
7. b
8. j
9. c
10. i

Final Exam Drill #12

1. STRUT is used to SUPPORT
2. ARREST is to hold one's ATTENTION
3. MINCE is too carefully to SPEAK
4. MISANTHROPE hates any HUMAN

5. FLOUT is to disregard a RULE
6. OBSEQUIOUS means tending to FAWN
7. QUALIFY is to place a LIMITATION
8. PARRY is to block a BLOW
9. DOGGEREL is a trivial type of VERSE

Final Exam Drill #13

1. VENAL means able to be BOUGHT
2. APPROPRIATE is to take for one's USE
3. OSCILLATION is the movement of a PENDULUM
4. INURED means accustomed to accepting the UNPLEASANT
5. UNTOWARD means displaying unseemly BEHAVIOR
6. ANATHEMA is a religious CURSE
7. MAVERICK is someone not part of the GROUP
8. INSULAR means characterized by ISOLATION
9. HEGEMONY is the dominance of one IDEOLOGY
10. ARABESQUE is a design that is ORNATE

Final Exam Drill #14

1. RECONNOITER means to engage in RECONNAISSANCE
2. ABROGATE means to disregard RESPONSIBILITY
3. OBTUSE means lacking SHARPNESS
4. PRECEPT is a rule for CONDUCT
5. IMPECUNIOUS means lacking MONEY
6. CONTIGUOUS means sharing a BORDER
7. EPITHET is a disparaging WORD
8. PHILISTINE only cares about the MATERIAL
9. BOOR is characterized by being CHURLISH
10. OSTENTATIOUS means having a lot of PRETENSION

Final Exam Drill #15

1. DIDACTIC means intended to INSTRUCT
2. PERSPICACIOUS means having keen PERCEPTION
3. CODA is the end of a COMPOSITION
4. LIBERTINE acts without moral RESTRAINT
5. ENDEMIC means particular to a REGION
6. LUMINOUS means filled with LIGHT
7. EXILE is the state of a PARIAH
8. IMPORTUNE means incessantly to ASK
9. ELEGY is a poem for the DEAD
10. INTREPID means having COURAGE

Final Exam Drill #16

1. canonical
2. depredate
3. archaic
4. felicitous
5. excoriate
6. seminal
7. precipitate
8. satire
9. loquacious
10. undulate

Final Exam Drill #17

1. b
2. a
3. h
4. d

5. g
6. j
7. e
8. c
9. f
10. i

Final Exam Drill #18

1. fanatical and fervent
2. salubrious and giving succor
3. dirge and eulogy
4. diffident and timorous
5. didactic and pedagogical
6. hermetic and insular
7. inundate and importune
8. attenuate and rarefy
9. lavish and ostentatious
10. erudite and sagacious

Final Exam Drill #19

1. c
2. j
3. i
4. d
5. e
6. a
7. f
8. g
9. b
10. h

Final Exam Drill #20

1. j
2. b
3. d
4. a
5. e
6. c
7. i
8. h
9. f
10. g

Final Exam Drill #21

1. c
2. d
3. a
4. f
5. i
6. b
7. h
8. e
9. j
10. g

Final Exam Drill #22

1. f
2. b
3. h
4. c

5. g
6. a
7. i
8. d
9. e
10. j

Final Exam Drill #23

1. d
2. g
3. e
4. f
5. b
6. a
7. i
8. h
9. c
10. j

Final Exam Drill #24

1. b
2. g
3. f
4. j
5. a
6. c
7. d
8. e
9. h
10. i

Final Exam Drill #25

1. PIRATE is illegally to USE
2. OBVIATE is to make no longer NECESSARY
3. LACHRYMOSE means causing to CRY
4. EXPIATE is to make AMENDS
5. STRIATED means marked by GROOVES
6. PAEAN is a song of PRAISE
7. TORQUE is a force causing ROTATION
8. HYPERBOLE is used to EXAGGERATE
9. INSCRUTABLE means incapable of being UNDERSTOOD

Final Exam Drill #26

1. BYZANTINE means complex in DESIGN
2. SLAKE is to satisfy THIRST
3. SODDEN means filled with WATER
4. SOPHISTRY is faulty REASONING
5. ABATE is to lessen the DEGREE
6. CAUSTIC means causing to BURN
7. INSOUCIANT means having no CARE
8. DESUETUDE means lack of USE
9. EDIFYING means causing ENLIGHTENMENT
10. GLIB means lacking DEPTH

Final Exam Drill #27

1. INVEIGLE is to obtain by DECEPTION
2. SPEECH honoring the dead is a EULOGY
3. CHANGE is accelerated by a CATALYST
4. TAUTOLOGY is a circular ARGUMENT
5. PILLORY is used for PUNISHMENT

6. RAREFY is to make less DENSE
7. REDOUBTABLE means worthy of HONOR
8. FROWARD means unwilling to YIELD
9. DENOUEMENT is the resolution of a PLOT
10. PERNICIOUS means potentially causing DEATH

Final Exam Drill #28

1. WAFFLE is to shift in POSITION
2. INSIPID means lacking FLAVOR
3. DESULTORY means done without a PLAN
4. EQUIVOCATE is to deceive through the use of ambiguous LANGUAGE
5. FORD is to cross a RIVER
6. VERISIMILITUDE means having the appearance of TRUTH
7. PITH is the center of an ARGUMENT
8. FORTUITOUS means happening by CHANCE
9. PAIN is soothed by something ANODYNE

Final Exam Drill #29

1. SINECURE is a job that requires little or no WORK
2. IMPUNITY is immunity from PENALTY
3. SIMPER is to talk with a silly SMILE
4. INTRANSIGENT means unwilling to COMPROMISE
5. SAGACIOUS means having great WISDOM
6. SYNTHESIS is the merging of parts into a WHOLE
7. EPICURE seeks LUXURY
8. JEJUNE means lacking MATURITY
9. SHARD is a broken piece of POTTERY
10. NOSTRUM is a questionable REMEDY

Final Exam Drill #30

1. LAUD is to highly PRAISE
2. PRODIGIOUS means large in SIZE
3. EMOLLIENT soothes something HARSH
4. HERMETIC means impervious to AIR
5. DECORUM is behavior that is POLITE
6. RAMIFY is to spend out in BRANCHES
7. JOCOSE is characterized by HUMOR
8. REDOLENT means full of FRAGRANCE
9. MALINGER is to avoid WORK
10. FETTER is to restrain in CHAINS

Final Exam Drill #31

1. RELEGATE is to assign to a position that is LOWER
2. IMMINENT means about to OCCUR
3. FILIBUSTER is to stall LEGISLATION
4. PREEN is to groom FEATHERS
5. ANACHRONISM means in the wrong TIME
6. NEOLOGISM is a new WORD
7. RHETORIC is the effective use of LANGUAGE
8. AGGRANDIZE is to increase in POWER
9. PARODY is a humorous work using IMITATION
10. AESTHETIC means dealing with ART

Final Exam Drill #32

1. MERCURIAL means frequently changing in MOOD
2. EXPURGATE is to remove everything OBSCENE
3. FERVENT means filled with EMOTION
4. QUIESCENCE is a state of REST

5. GAUCHE means lacking good TASTE

6. BURNISH means to rub until SHINY

7. MITIGATE is to lessen the SEVERITY

8. FLAG is to droop in SPIRITS

9. UBIQUITOUS means in all PLACES

10. ERUDITE means having great LEARNING

Final Exam Drill #33

1. TENUOUS means lacking STRENGTH

2. ASSUAGE is to cause to LESSEN

3. SEINE is a type of NET

4. AMENABLE means open to SUGGESTION

5. INIMICAL means causing HARM

6. PUNDIT is someone who expresses OPINION

7. ATTENUATE is to lessen in THICKNESS

8. PUNCTILIOUS means attentive to DETAILS

9. SATIATE is to satisfy to EXCESS

10. ABSCISSION is the act of making a CUT

Final Exam Drill #34

1. IMPERTURBABLE means characterized by great CALM

2. HIRSUTE means having a lot of HAIR

3. ADULTERATE is to reduce the PURITY

4. MISOGYNIST hates WOMEN

5. MARTIAL means having to deal with WAR

6. RENEGE is to go back on a PROMISE

7. WAFT is to float on the AIR

8. AVER is to state as a FACT

9. PETROUS means like a ROCK

10. BOLSTER is to provide SUPPORT

Final Exam Drill #35

1. i
2. c
3. b
4. h
5. d
6. g
7. a
8. f
9. e
10. j

Final Exam Drill #36

1. e
2. g
3. a
4. d
5. f
6. h
7. c
8. i
9. b
10. j

Final Exam Drill #37

1. b
2. d
3. a
4. g

5. e
6. c
7. h
8. i
9. f

Final Exam Drill #38

1. g
2. a
3. d
4. c
5. e
6. i
7. b
8. h
9. f
10. j

Final Exam Drill #39

1. c
2. b
3. f
4. i
5. e
6. d
7. a
8. g
9. h
10. j

Final Exam Drill #40

1. d
2. e
3. a
4. j
5. i
6. b
7. c
8. f
9. g
10. h

Final Exam Drill #41

1. e
2. b
3. d
4. a
5. h
6. f
7. i
8. c
9. g
10. j

Final Exam Drill #42

1. d
2. b
3. f
4. e

5. a
6. c
7. h
8. i
9. g
10. j

Final Exam Drill #43

1. i
2. f
3. c
4. a
5. d
6. g
7. h
8. b
9. j
10. e

Final Exam Drill #44

1. h
2. e
3. d
4. g
5. a
6. c
7. i
8. f
9. b
10. j

Final Exam Drill #45

1. b
2. d
3. b
4. b
5. a
6. c
7. d
8. a
9. d
10. b

Final Exam Drill #46

1. d
2. h
3. g
4. a
5. f
6. b
7. e
8. i
9. c
10. j

Final Exam Drill #47

1. b
2. f
3. i
4. a

5. j
6. c
7. g
8. h
9. e
10. d

Final Exam Drill #48

1. b
2. f
3. d
4. c
5. i
6. g
7. a
8. j
9. e
10. h

Final Exam Drill #49

1. f
2. e
3. g
4. i
5. a
6. c
7. d
8. b
9. j
10. h

Final Exam Drill #50

1. b
2. e
3. d
4. a
5. g
6. f
7. c
8. i
9. h
10. j

Final Exam Drill #51

1. c
2. h
3. a
4. d
5. j
6. b
7. e
8. i
9. f
10. g

Final Exam Drill #52

1. FALLACY is a false BELIEF
2. TIMOROUS means lacking CONFIDENCE
3. TIRADE is a harshly critical SPEECH
4. ACUMEN means having keen INSIGHT

5. EXIGENT means requiring immediate ACTION
6. USURY is charging exorbitant INTEREST
7. AUGUST means having great DIGNITY
8. PROSCRIBE is to place RESTRICTIONS
9. SUBPOENA is used to make someone TESTIFY
10. PROVIDENT means looking to the FUTURE

Final Exam Drill #53

1. APOSTATE betrays his or her FAITH
2. UNTENABLE incapable of being DEFENDED
3. RECANT is to retract a BELIEF
4. AXIOM is a universally recognized PRINCIPLE
5. RUE is to feel great REMORSE
6. PROLIX means using many WORDS
7. TAWDRY means lacking good TASTE
8. BOMBASTIC is pompous SPEECH
9. NATTY means stylish in DRESS
10. PUSILLANIMOUS means lacking COURAGE

Final Exam Drill #54

1. b
2. h
3. f
4. e
5. i
6. c
7. d
8. g
9. a
10. j

Final Exam Drill #55

1. intransigent and recalcitrant
2. fallacy and tautology
3. inimical and deleterious
4. erratic and mercurial
5. impassive and imperturbable
6. arrest and forestall
7. slake and satiate
8. fetter and table
9. abrogate and renege

Final Exam Drill #56

1. d
2. f
3. b
4. a
5. e
6. h
7. c
8. j
9. g
10. i

Final Exam Drill #57

1. REVERENT means feeling profound AWE
2. BELIE is to inaccurately REPRESENT
3. HACKNEYED is a phrase that is WORN
4. AVARICE is greed for WEALTH
5. REPINE is to feel DISCONTENT
6. LIST is to lean to the SIDE
7. BANE is a source of HARM
8. IMPASSIVE means revealing no EMOTION
9. INDEFATIGABLE means tending not to TIRE
10. SALUBRIOUS means promoting HEALTH

NOTES

NOTES

NOTES

NOTES

NOTES

NOTES